The Drowned and the Saved

Les Wilson is a writer and an award-winning television documentary maker who has specialised in Scottish historical subjects. His work includes films about the 'Lighthouse' Stevenson family; engineer Thomas Telford; writer, adventurer and political activist Robert Cunninghame Graham; the principal chief of the Cherokee nation, John Ross; and the artist who created the monumental Kelpies sculptures, Andy Scott. He has made documentary series about Scotland during World War Two, and the history of the Scottish regiments. He lives on the island of Islay

D0529182

Also by Les Wilson:

Scotland's War (with Seona Robertson), Mainstream, 1995

Fire in the Head, Vagabond Voices, 2010

Islay Voices (with Jenni Minto), Birlinn, 2016

THE DROWNED AND THE SAVED

When War Came to the Hebrides

Les Wilson

BIRLINN

First published in 2018 by Birlinn Ltd
West Newington House
10 Newington Road
Edinburgh
EH9 1QS
www.birlinn.co.uk

ISBN: 978 1 78027 543 7

British Library Cataloguing in Publication Data
A catalogue record for this book is available from the British
Library

Printed and bound in Great Britain by
MBM Print SCS Limited, Glasgow

MIX
Paper from
responsible sources
FSC® C117931
FSC
www.fsc.org

For Jenni

Contents

Illustrations

Port nan Gallan on the Oa.

The *Tuscania* funeral procession passes through Port Charlotte.

The US flag and the Union Jack flying at Port Mor.

The salute is fired at Kilnaughton Cemetery.

The first *Tuscania* mass funeral at Kilnaughton.

American survivors of the *Tuscania* after the first funeral.

The Stars and Stripes carried at the *Tuscania* funerals.

David Roberts, survivor of the sinking of the *Otranto*.

Captain Davidson in his cabin on the *Otranto*.

Bodies of *Otranto* victims at Kilchoman churchyard.

The victims of the *Otranto* are re-buried in a second funeral.

American Red Cross workers deliver emergency supplies.

Lieutenant James Jeffers of the American Red Cross.

Survivors of the *Otranto* treat their rescuers to afternoon tea.

The American Monument on the Mull of Oa.

Maps

Foreword

Lord George Robertson of Port Ellen

Even for a Hebridean island used to some foul weather and occasional wrecked ships, the events of 1918 in Islay must have been especially grim. To experience one major troopship disaster that February was traumatic enough for a small island community already hit severely by casualties on the distant Western Front. But to face another disaster only a few months later was unprecedently awful.

Islay was not rich, it was agricultural and it was quiet. The great boom in Scotch whisky drinking had not yet stimulated the small island distilleries and tourism was in its infancy. To this peaceful rural community was to come a visitation of brutal violence and profound sadness.

The torpedoing of the liner *Tuscania*, carrying 2,000 troops, in February 1918 brought to the island both dead victims and survivors in huge numbers. It happened in the night, it happened on the remote and inhospitable cliffs and rocks of the Mull of Oa and it brought forth bravery, service, humanity and the resources of the islanders to a quite remarkable degree.

Two hundred soldiers and sailors died. It was the biggest loss of American military lives in a single day since their Civil War. When news hit the US, the shock was considerable.

When the troopship *Otranto* fell victim to a collision off the western rocky shores of Kilchoman in October of the same miserable year, the last of the so-called Great War, the previous experience was useful. But the double shock was to leave lasting legacies of pain and mourning. Another four hundred perished.

My maternal grandfather, Malcolm MacNeill, was the police sergeant on the island in 1918. With his three constables, he was in effect the public authority on Islay. Yet nothing in his training or experience could have prepared this son of a shepherd from Inverlussa on the neighbouring island of Jura for the challenges he faced on these grim days in the last months of the First World War.

Just a few years earlier, another police constable serving in Port Ellen, Norman Morrison, wrote in his autobiography:

> The duties of a country constable on the whole are gener-
> ally speaking, interesting and pleasant, particularly when
> one is stationed in a district which is free from crime.
> Routine work is easy and sometimes even fascinating.
> To the lover of the beautiful in nature, the life is really
> an ideal one.

Before patrol cars and an air service and the telecommunications we now take for granted, the scale of the difficulties Sergeant MacNeill faced was simply immense. He had to travel by bike in hellish weather to the remote extremities of the island. He had to organise the rescues, the handling of survivors, the recovery and cataloguing of the dead, the recording of events and the communications from and to the legion of top brass who eventually descended on the scenes of these disasters.

He was not alone in his endeavours, for the scale of the tragedy and its aftermath brought out the very best in a hardy, resilient and resourceful Islay population.

The American Red Cross, on the scene in the weeks after each event, was unsparing in its praise:

> It is quite impossible to say too much of the humanity
> of these peasant people, of their readiness to accept any
> hardship in the name of mercy, of the gently, steadfast
> nursing they gave the soldiers, virtually bringing them
> back to life.

One might quibble with the word 'peasant', but the sentiment expressed speaks of what these American professionals found when they arrived on the scene.

My grandfather, known to me by the Gaelic word *Seanair*, bearing the enormous responsibilities of the day, was systematic and diligent in his efforts. His notebook, in copperplate handwriting, accounting for all the bodies, was found in a cupboard of his son Dr Hector MacNeill. It is now in the Museum of Islay Life, and is a remarkable chronicle of profound sadness; his descriptions of often unidentifiable battered corpses cannot leave any reader unaffected.

The reports he had to write each night after his travels (written twice so as to keep a copy) were to be followed by the painstaking follow-up letters to bereaved families. The interment of bodies, the organising of survivors, the identification of the islanders who had opened their homes and shared their food and clothing, the recording of the bravery and sacrifice that were shown – all fell to these few local members of Argyllshire Constabulary whose lives were changed forever.

He himself was – exceptionally for a country police officer – to be honoured after the war with one of the first medals from the newly created Order of the British Empire. That MBE, the property now of his great-grandson – another Malcolm MacNeill – is also on display in Islay's Museum.

I was born in the Police Station in the Islay village of Port Ellen, my father having returned from Second World War service to take up duties as a policeman on the island where his father-in-law had been a police sergeant before him. I went from there, via a life in politics, to become Britain's Secretary of State for Defence and then Secretary General of NATO, the world's most successful military alliance. I saw conflict and witnessed how humanity deals with mass casualties. I am consequently filled with admiration at what my fellow islanders did at that time.

The stories in this book, collected brilliantly by Les Wilson, articulate the dramas of both disasters and show how a rural community rose to the immense challenges of tackling them. We see the kindness of islanders with so little, who gave so much. How they produced clothes and food for the survivors and tenderness and compassion for the dead. How coffins were made, graves dug, a Stars and Stripes made and sewed overnight by local women to ensure the fallen lay under their own flag.

When I made a BBC Scotland radio programme a few years ago about the two disasters, local Port Ellen fisherman and my friend, Jim McFarlane, related how he was told of people openly weeping in the streets as the carts with bodies passed. I also stood in the home in Kilchoman of Duncan McPhee, the grandson of one of the two teenage McPhees who waded into the surf when the *Otranto* went down, armed with a walking stick, to reach and save two men from certain drowning. As we remembered that act of heroism I recalled what my grandfather had recorded of that night: 'The oldest inhabitants in the neighbourhood of the wreck say that they never saw a heavier sea on the Machrie Sands and very seldom a higher tide.'

But the *Tuscania* and *Otranto* and the lasting effect of their sinking are not forgotten on Islay. Rising tall above the sheer cliffs and rocks of the Mull of Oa and at the closest point to the sunken *Tuscania* is the mighty monument to those who died a century ago. The cemeteries at Kilchoman and Kilnaughton may have lost the American graves, almost all the bodies being solemnly repatriated to the US and to Brookwoods Cemetery near London, but British sailors still lie there. In Kilnaughton Cemetery, by Port Ellen, there remains the only American grave left on Islay. Roy Muncaster's mother wanted him to stay where he died.

So many lives lost. So many lives saved. So many survivors looked after. A community rising to the tragic occasion, everyone pulling together to counter what fate had thrown at them.

In many ways this is the story of a special island and its strong, resilient, resourceful people. Out of tragedy came inspiration, and out of misery and death came kindness, generosity and enduring humanity.

A century has passed but the memories live on.

Lord Robertson of Port Ellen, a native of Islay, was UK Defence Secretary and NATO Secretary General. A member of the House of Commons for twenty-one years, he was elevated to the House of Lords in 1999. He is one of the sixteen Knights of the Thistle, Scotland's oldest and highest honour, and is Chancellor and Knight Grand Cross of the Order of St Michael and St George. He is one of only four UK citizens to hold the US Presidential Medal of Freedom, America's highest decoration and only rarely given to foreigners.

I hear those voices that will not be drowned.
Charles Montagu Slater,
Libretto for *Peter Grimes* by Benjamin Britten, 1945

Introduction

Driven against a rocky coast in a savage winter storm, David Roberts fought for his life. The deep-rooted human instinct for survival was on the side of this rookie American soldier, but nothing else was. He recalled: 'A wave about as high as a house came over me and whirled me around like paper in a whirlwind.'

Roberts was exhausted, frozen and in danger that – at just seventeen – he could never have imagined, far less been trained for. If hypothermia didn't kill him, the mountainous waves could plunge him underwater and hold him there until his lungs flooded with freezing brine. And there was the wreckage. Flung around by the wind and waves, an angry mass of shattered timber was pounding shipwrecked men against the rocks of the Hebridean island of Islay's gnarled west coast. The experience has been likened, by the current coxswain of Islay's lifeboat, to being thrust into a meat grinder. By some fluke, or miracle, young Roberts kept his head above water, without being crushed or knocked unconscious, and the crashing waves hurled him onto a rock, frozen, battered, half-drowned, but alive. Hands reached out to him. A boy, hardly older than Roberts himself, was hauling him to safety. Donald McPhee was risking his life. His younger brother, John, had to hold on to Donald's belt to prevent him being swept out to sea as he dragged the young American ashore.

Roberts was one of nearly five hundred men who had been thrown into the water when a British ship, carrying American soldiers to the trenches of the Western Front, foundered off Islay after a catastrophic collision in a storm. Only twenty-one made it ashore alive, and two of them died shortly afterwards. In the days that followed, hundreds of drowned and battered bodies were washed ashore. The wreck of HMS *Otranto* was the greatest tragedy in the history of the convoys that took more than a million young American soldiers – doughboys – to the Great War in Europe.

Eight months earlier, Islay had seen another naval disaster off its coast, when the troop transport SS *Tuscania* – with more than 2,000 US soldiers and nearly 400 British crew aboard – had been torpedoed by a German U-boat. On a pitch-black February night, a relentless swell drove overcrowded lifeboats onto the island. Boats were smashed against the rugged shore, tumbling men into the sea. Many were rescued, but 126 bodies were washed ashore for the islanders to gather, attempt to identify, and bury with dignity amid an outpouring of grief.

The sinking of the *Tuscania* was a symbolically significant milestone in twentieth-century world history – the point when the isolationist USA began to shed blood in Old Europe's wars. As the official history of the American Red Cross during World War One says: 'The *Tuscania*'s dead represented, in a way, the first American casualties in the war . . . the sinking of the *Tuscania* was, as one might say, a special occasion, like a particular battle.'

In telling the story of the loss of the *Tuscania* and the *Otranto*, and of the Hebridean islanders who buried the drowned and tended the saved, I have, whenever possible, based the narrative on the words of people who were directly involved. These accounts come from letters, diaries, memoirs, speeches and interviews in newspapers, as well as from the records of official inquiries. Inevitably, inconsistencies occur. Even the number of men lost is not certain. It seems likely that 470 men died on the *Otranto*, 358 of them American soldiers, while the estimated losses of soldiers and crew on the *Tuscania* varies from 166 to 'over 200', 222, 245 and, according the National *Tuscania* Survivors' Association, 266. There are also inconsistencies in the reported timescale of events. This is likely to be at least partly due to witnesses having their watches set to three different time zones – American, British and German.

For me, the meeting of David Roberts and the McPhee brothers on a storm-lashed shore – one tiny scene in a huge tragedy, acted out on the stage of Islay and the seas that surround her – is a profoundly moving symbol of humanity amid the terrible Great War. The people of Islay took total strangers into their midst and treated them as their own, tending the wounded, and burying the dead with honour and respect. In America, grieving families responded to that kindness. Beneath the stormclouds of war and tragedy, a sense of shared humanity was felt across the wide and stormy Atlantic Ocean.

Today, these century-old tragedies remain part of the warp and weft of Islay's lore, tradition and life. Graves are tended. Relatives of the lost American soldiers and British sailors visit the island. Records are requested and examined in the Museum of Islay Life. Pilgrimages are made to the great monument to the American dead, which stands on the Islay peninsula called the Mull of Oa. Stories of the two ships are told, and passed on. Points on the landscape are recognised as being imbued with significance. The men and women who pulled exhausted, frozen survivors from the sea, and fed and comforted them, still have descendants living on the island. Islay's volunteer Coastguards and Lifeboat crew of today are the spiritual and sometimes the blood-descendants of those whose bravery and kindness saved lives nearly a century ago.

The shockwaves from the *Tuscania* and *Otranto* disasters struck many an American community harshly, as men who had enlisted together died together. Of the 60 war dead commemorated on Berrien County's World War One memorial in Nashville, Georgia, 25 were lost when the *Otranto* went down. The impact of World War One on Islay was also immense. The island – a community of then just over 6,000 people, scattered among small villages and isolated farms – lost more than 200 of its young men on foreign fields. But with the wreck of the *Tuscania* and *Otranto*, the devastation of war came, literally, to Islay's shores.

If I had been living in my house in Port Charlotte ninety-nine years ago, I could have looked out of my kitchen window to watch the pipers lead the first *Tuscania* funeral cortège up Main Street to the freshly dug graves at the edge of the village. The land had been donated by the local Laird, the coffins made by carpenters at an Islay distillery, the carts that carried them were lent by farmers and tradesmen, and the procession of mourners was made up of local folk who did not know the victims, but cared for them nonetheless. They had been unable to bury Islay's own war dead, who lay in France and beyond, but were determined to honour these fallen strangers and allies.

〰️

Earlier today I walked the fatal coast where *Tuscania* survivors fought for their lives as their lifeboats were driven against the rocky shores of Islay in the early hours of 6 February 1918. After more than a year of researching and writing, I needed to bring back into focus my motivation for writing this book. When I began it, I expected to confront tragedy aplenty, but what I had not been prepared for was to discover instances of incompetence and accusations of dereliction of duty on the part of British crewmen. They made hard reading, and so, before I wrote this introduction, I needed to remind myself of the countless instances of courage, endurance and humanity that appear in these pages.

I hiked out to the clifftop on the southern coast of Islay's Oa peninsula and the massive monument that commemorates the American soldiers lost on both ships. I didn't linger long. A south-south-easterly wind was blowing up and it had reached gale force and was gusting up to nearly 60 mph by the time I returned to the car. It was a reminder – if such was needed – of how wild and dangerous the coast of Islay can be. I had stood in the lee of the monument and watched the ferocious seascape. More than four hundred feet beneath me lay the rocks where – in the pre-dawn morning, 99 years ago to the day – *Tuscania* men died as their lifeboats were dashed ashore. Close by were the farmhouses where survivors were given sanctuary by kindly islanders. About fifteen miles to the northwest lay Kilchoman Bay, where nearly 500 *Otranto* men were thrown into the sea and where 19 lived because local people were kind and brave. Three thousand miles to the west of where I stood lay America.

The great and powerful Republic of America . . . and the little island of Islay. Two very different communities forever linked by events that were tragic, but which were shot through with heroism, fortitude, kindness and respect.

Les Wilson, Port Charlotte, Isle of Islay, 6 February, 2017

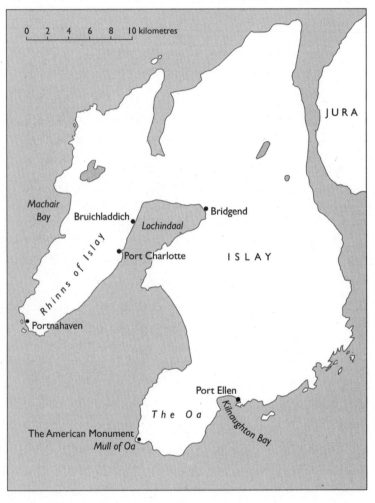

Islay

1

A Stroke in the Dark

It came on them like a strange plague, taking their sons away
and then killing them, meaninglessly, randomly.

From Iain Crichton Smith, *The Telegram*

Islay lies on a bed of ancient rock, set amid often angry waters at the edge of the Atlantic Ocean. Ireland is to the south,
mainland Scotland to the east, and Newfoundland nearly 3,000
miles due west. Islay isn't the biggest of the Hebrides, or the
most populous, but its strategic position on the western seaboard
of Scotland makes it stand out in the histories of immigration,
emigration and war.

The islanders had already drunk deeply from the well of grief
when tragedy washed up on their shores in February 1918. By
the time the troopship *Tuscania* was torpedoed, 125 Islay men
had already been killed in the war, and many hundreds more
were still fighting on land and at sea. On an island of small
and closely knit communities, not a family would have been
untouched.

The pain of parting when men are called to war was captured
by Islay bard Duncan Johnston, who served in the Argyll &
Sutherland Highlanders until he was gassed in 1916. His song
about leaving a girl to go to war, *Sine Bhàn* (*Fair Sheena*), is still
sung on Islay today. Such a theme could have moved a soldier
to write in English, French, German or Russian, but Johnston
wrote in his native Scots Gaelic. Here are just two stanzas:

> *Feumaidh mise triall gun dàil*
> *Chi mi 'm bàrr a croinne sròl.*

M' 'eudail bhàn, o soraidh slàn!
Na caoin a luaidh, na sil na deòir!
Cha ghaoir-cath' no toirm a' chàs'
Dh' fhàg mi'n dràsd' fo gheilt is bròn
'S e na dh'fhàg mi air an tràigh,
Sìne Bhàn a rinn mo leòn.

Parting time is drawing nigh,
Flags are waving at masthead,
Darling child, O do not sigh!
Do not cry, my lovely maid!
It isn't war or cannon's roar
Unmans me now and makes me mourn,
My heart is left on yonder shore,
My lonesome lass; my sweet, forlorn.

Hebridean islanders were used to partings. Since the mid-eighteenth century there had been mass emigration from Highland Scotland, and names like New York, Philadelphia, Buffalo and Chicago tripped easily off the tongues of Islay folk who had kin there. By the outbreak of war in 1914, Islay's history was already deeply entwined with that of the brave new republic across the ocean. But within four years the islanders had learned a fearful new geography – Mons, Ypres, Neuve Chapelle, Loos, the Somme, Gallipoli. Islay people had blood relations in these places – fighting in the trenches, or already in their graves.

Most of the fallen had worn the uniforms of famous Scottish regiments, including that of the Argyll & Sutherland Highlanders, which has a long tradition of recruiting on Islay. Some islanders, who in peaceful times had sought to make new lives far from home, fell alongside Canadian and Australian comrades. Islay men also died simply following the peacetime calling of merchant seaman. Others, many of them fishermen, were killed while serving in the Royal Naval Reserve and the RNR Trawler Section – a fleet of commandeered fishing boats that had been converted to serve as minesweepers. Minesweeping was a dangerous job, and cost the lives of at least two Islay men.

Some of the bodies of Islay's dead were never found, but most lie under plain, uniform headstones in foreign fields now maintained by the Commonwealth War Graves Commission. At home on Islay, friends and loved ones had been denied the farewell rites of funerals, or graves to visit and tend. But Islay was soon to be overwhelmed with funerals and graves. The losses of the *Tuscania* and the *Otranto* gave the war-weary islanders a purpose and a cause to unite behind. Soldiers and sailors who had survived the shipwrecks found safety, sustenance and kindness among the islanders. The dead found hearts that would grieve for them and willing hands to lay them to rest.

~

Islay is the southernmost island of the Inner Hebrides, lying between the Scottish mainland and Northern Ireland. At 240 square miles it is Scotland's fifth biggest island. The mild climate favours agriculture and tourism, but winter gales are common. Even today Islay's lifeline ferries to the mainland, with all their sophisticated navigation and stabilising equipment, cancel sailings in extreme weather.

Islay was, and remains, an island of scattered villages and farmhouses. Today it is home to just over 3,000 people, but the 1911 census shows that the pre-war population was twice that. About 80% of the islanders spoke Gaelic. The great majority of the people lived by farming, fishing and distilling whisky (for which the island is justifiably famous). Native islanders are called Ileachs, and their surnames appear again and again in Islay's history, on its war memorials and on today's electoral roll – Anderson, Campbell, Currie, Darroch, Ferguson, Gilchrist, Johnstone, MacArthur, MacDonald, MacDougall, McIndeor,

MacLellan, MacMillan, McPhail, McPhee, MacTaggart . . . and many more.

Islay was remote. The first motor car didn't arrive until 1914, there were no telephones, the first aeroplane didn't land on Islay until 1928, and the island wasn't connected to mainland electricity until 1965. But when war broke out in 1914 Islay enjoyed strong family and community ties that gave islanders a pride of place and a vigorous local culture.

Four years of conflict took its toll. By the dawn of 1918 Islay, like the rest of Britain, was sick of war. As well as the carnage inflicted on soldiers and sailors, civilians were suffering from shortages, rationing, rising prices and taxes, and were in constant dread of the 'deepest sympathy' telegram. A letter from the spring of that year, now in the Museum of Islay Life, reveals something of how the island was being affected. In it, Robert Smith of Laggan Farm brings his friend, Andrew Barr, an artillery corporal serving on the Salonica front, up to date with the news.

> You would hear that young Walter MacKay is reported killed, but I understand that they have not got word from the War Office. It is a pity if it is true. Two of the McCuaigs who used to be at Laggan are 'missing', Neil and John, nice boys they were. John Bland is here just now. He was in Italy and had only been three days in the trenches when he was hit in the eye by some shell splinters and has been in hospital since until recently. He is nearly better but has to wear glasses. He is a 2nd Lieut in the 5th Cheshires. Last night Laggan Bay was livened by the presence of 6 mine sweepers which spent the night there, anchored near the Big Strand. This is the season for Gulls eggs and the Bowmore boys are on the hunt for them Sundays and Saturdays. Farmers are going to be hit hard under the latest Budget, they have to pay

taxes on double the rents. Laggan will have to tootle up to the tune of about £31-10/-. If Kaiser Bill has called the tune somebody has to 'pay the piper' but folk are well off that have only got to pay instead of fighting. I am going to be hit this time not paying income tax, alas, but through the increased rates for postage, 1½d a go after 1st June. I must 'huff' some of my "best girls" to save writing. With regard to writing oftener I would like to do so but I am not so keen on writing letters as I used to be and since the War began one has not so much pleasure in writing, everything being overshadowed by the 'Great Adventure'. Yet I would gladly do so, when you are so keen to hear news of the old country and of that particular 'tight little island' out in the Atlantic. Yes, I wish you were back home again and may the day not be far distant.

Charles MacNiven, an Islay bard with a talent for pawky humour, lamented that the war with Germany was cramping his social life by taking Islay's young men out of the marriage market.

Tha 'm pòsadh dhìth san rìoghachd seo, se sin aon nì tha
dearbhte,
Tha feum air tuille shaighdearan chum oillt chur air a' Ghear-
mailt.

This country's short of marriages, that's one thing that's
shown for certain,
For more soldiers are essential now for frightening the
Germans.

The Kilchoman bard would be writing in a much more serious tone before the war was over.

In April 1917 the might of America – expressed through its dynamic industrial economy and the youth and vigour of its people – came to the aid of the Old World and entered the war that had been bleeding Europe dry. Once at the front, America's men and machines would decisively tip the balance and doom the Kaiser's Germany to defeat. But before the American 'doughboys' – the equivalent of Scottish 'Jocks' or English 'Tommies' – could get to the trenches, they had to cross the Atlantic Ocean. The Atlantic would exact a heavy toll for that crossing, paid for in young lives. Tides, currents, geology and weather conspire to make these seas hazardous, but when you add the most deadly machines of war that mankind could invent, tragedy beckons.

Throughout the war Germany attempted to lay siege to Britain, starving her of food, men and munitions. Although the Atlantic is wide, the paths of the sea narrow as they approach the great ports of Liverpool and the Clyde. It was in these waters that ships – British, allied and neutral – were most likely to face the wrath of the U-boats of the *Kaiserliche Marine*, the Imperial German Navy. By the end of the conflict, nearly 15,000 British merchant mariners had lost their lives. Much of the carnage had been wrought by U-boats. One such victim was the *Tuscania*, a luxury liner converted into a troopship. Today she lies 80 metres below the waves between the Islay peninsula called the Mull of Oa, and Rathlin Island, off Northern Ireland.

A more ancient foe than U-boats is the wild Atlantic that unrelentingly pounds Islay's rugged western shore. These waters are a constant battleground where the forces of nature are in eternal conflict. One evening in Port Charlotte's Coastguard station, as the barometer fell and the ferries to and from the mainland went on 'amber alert', I quizzed one the men dedicated to cheating the sea of even more lives about the extremes of Islay's weather. Donald Jones has been a volunteer Islay Coastguard for about 40 years. This, and being a farmer at Coull, on the exposed west coast of the island, has made him an expert on the ferocity of Islay weather. He told me: 'Down south, if they get a breeze they call it a "gale", and if they get a gale, they call it a "hurricane". We *really* get hurricanes – we get extremes of wind on Islay. And if you have tide and wind coming in opposite directions, that increases the size of the waves. The last place I'd ever want to be is on a ship that's foundering off the west coast of Islay in a storm.'

The prevailing westerly winds have the uninterrupted breadth of the Atlantic to gather force, and winter storms can bring gusts of more than 100 miles an hour screaming over the island. It was a storm of this power that sank the armed merchant cruiser, HMS *Otranto*. Today she lies less than half a mile off Islay's Kilchoman Bay, which is overlooked by the last resting place of many of her crew.

~

Long ago, Islay's location – lying between mainland Scotland, Ireland and the islands of the Outer Hebrides – allowed her to become the centre of a great medieval sea power, the Lordship of the Isles. But while the waters surrounding Islay have long been a highway, they are also cruel and treacherous, even in times of peace. Despite the dangers, sailors have navigated these waters since Mesolithic peoples first hunted and gathered in this land and seascape, just after the passing of the last Ice Age twelve thousand years ago. The Celtic tribes of Scotland and Ireland were connected by the sea, rather than divided by it. The Vikings arrived in the Hebrides by sea, and ruled them by sea. Trade with the New World – emigrants one way and tobacco the other – flowed in and out of Scotland though Islay's waters.

Untold numbers of ships have perished off Islay, and its people became used to a grim harvest being cast up on their shores. In light of what happened to the *Otranto*, the story of one such wreck is worth retelling. In April 1847, the *Exmouth of Newcastle*, an old brig crammed with 240 Irish emigrants bound for Canada, was wrecked off Sanaig on Islay's northwest coast. She'd set sail from Londonderry, but had turned back in the face of a storm. It may be that her captain mistook the Rhinns of Islay lighthouse for the one on Tory Island, off Ireland. In such conditions it was an understandable, but calamitous, blunder. The vessel was dashed against the jagged coast of Islay and, according to a witness, 'reduced to atoms'. Captain Isaac Booth went down with his ship, and only three of the ten crewmen made it ashore alive. The emigrants were battened down in the hull, and had no chance of escape. Every one perished. It is believed that about 180 of them were women and children. They had been exiled by the poverty and starvation caused by the Irish potato famine, but instead of new lives in the New World, they met a terrifying end on the storm-lashed coast of Islay. A hundred and eight bodies were recovered and buried. It is a hard hike to get to where the unmarked mass grave probably lies, but a monument to the victims, with an inscription both in English and in Irish Gaelic, stands by the road end at Sanaigmore. The tragedy has lingered long in the collective memory and tradition of Islay, and the late Peggy Earl recorded a poignant tale of the disaster. 'There was living at the time a little girl called Eleanora McIntyre. She found a doll on the shore and took it home with her. The owner of the doll, so the story goes, was buried nearby. That night Eleanora dreamed of a sad and tearful little girl crying for her doll, so the next day she buried the doll with its owner.'

Storms and shipwrecks were once attributed to 'God's will', and whatever was washed upon the shores of Islay was seen by islanders as manna from heaven and theirs for the taking. Even the survivors of wrecks were sometimes plundered. At the close of the eighteenth century, the island's Stent Committee – a local 'parliament' of gentlemen and landowners – condemned the robbery and ill treatment of those washed ashore. 'This Meeting not only collectively, but individually pledge themselves to use their utmost exertions, not only for the preservation of the property of the individuals, who may have the misfortune to be wrecked on these coasts, but also for bringing to condign punishment all and every such person as may be found plundering from wrecks.'

The islanders seemed to have taken this to heart, for Islay now has a distinguished history of emergency organisations staffed by volunteers. Britain's Coastguard Service began operations on Islay in 1928, but, according to Donald Jones, a Coast Watch has been operating on Islay for about 150 years. 'I think it was probably first started to catch smugglers, before it got into rescuing people. Then they built a number of look-out posts, including one at Portnahaven and one at Coull. I imagine the lifesaving apparatus would have been at Kilchiaran farmhouse on the coast where the *Otranto* foundered. Not that I remember it!' Donald has been a Coastguard for 40 years and is one of the 16 volunteers currently serving on the island. His son, Andrew, is one of the team, and their colleague, Neillan McLellan, is one of four generations to serve, or have served.

Britons had been brought up to believe that they ruled the waves, not to fear that their great nation could be starved into surrender. But, by 1914, the United Kingdom could no longer feed itself. The nineteenth-century Industrial Revolution had transformed the country as the peasantry left their fields in their hundreds of thousands to work in factories and make Britain the workshop of the world. The British now dined on the fruits of their empire and trading networks, but these imports – which by the outbreak of war made up nearly two-thirds of the UK's diet – were vulnerable to naval blockade. The blockade was a military tactic that had its origins in the medieval siege; the enemy was surrounded, and then starved into submission. The Kaiser's Imperial Navy came close to achieving this. By 1916 food was in short supply and prices high. Sugar had gone up by 166%, and eggs and fish cost double what they had in peacetime. There was even a shortage of potatoes. At one point, Britain was just three months from starvation.

Germany had been quick to understand Britain's vulnerability. It had never been one of history's great maritime nations, like Britain, France, the Netherlands and Spain, but Germany had now overtaken Britain as an industrial nation and ranked second only to America. Its production of steel had increased by 800% in the three decades up to 1910, and it was a world leader in the production of chemicals and electrical goods. Although economic and technological prowess had allowed Germany to build an effective navy, it knew that it was unlikely to win a Trafalgar-scale battle. Britain's fleet of Dreadnoughts – each with their ten 12-inch guns mounted in revolving towers protected by 11-inch steel armour – remained the most powerful naval force in the world. But the Germans had been quick to develop new weapons that the Nelsonian Royal Navy was sceptical of – mines and submarines. These, Berlin calculated, could be used to lay siege to Britain and force her into seeking terms. A starved Britain, short of the materials of war, would be no match for the German Army on the Western Front.

In John Buchan's 1915 novel, *The Thirty-Nine Steps*, Richard Hannay, the expatriate Scots mining engineer recently returned from South Africa and heading for a host of adventures, neatly outlined German strategy: '. . . Berlin would play the peacemaker, and pour oil on the waters, till suddenly she would find a good cause for a quarrel, pick it up, and in five hours let fly at us. That was the idea, and a pretty good one too. Honey and fair speeches, and then a stroke in the dark. While we were talking about the goodwill and good intentions of Germany our coast would be silently ringed with mines, and submarines would be waiting for every battleship.'

Buchan was right. Britain's long extended coastline offered a multitude of opportunities for a war of attrition against the Royal Navy. German submarines began the war with David and Goliath effectiveness. On 3 September 1914, *U-21* sank the British cruiser HMS *Pathfinder* with a single torpedo. The 'tinfish' struck the *Pathfinder* close to her magazine, blowing her apart and giving her the dubious distinction of being the first modern warship sunk by a torpedo. Less than three weeks later, Kapitänleutnant Otto Weddigen's storm-battered submarine, *U-9*, surfaced to re-charge its batteries after a night lying on the seabed. Sighting three British warships ploughing towards him, Weddigen dived again and fired a torpedo at a range of about 500 yards. The cruiser, HMS *Aboukir*, suffered a direct hit and sank almost immediately. Believing that the *Aboukir* had hit a mine, rather than having been torpedoed by an enemy submarine, the other cruisers, HMS *Hogue* and HMS *Cressy* steamed to pick up survivors – and were sunk in rapid succession by the *U-9*. The 500-ton submarine had destroyed 36,000 tons of British warships in just a few minutes.

The *Kaiserliche Marine* was triumphant, and the Kaiser awarded every *U-9* crewman the Iron Cross. The British Admiralty had a collective nervous breakdown. The Commander of the British High Fleet, Admiral Sir John Jellicoe – described by historian Hew Strachan as a worrier, a centraliser and a hypochondriac – pessimistically told the Admiralty: 'It is quite within the bounds of possibility that half our battle-fleet might be disabled by under-water attack before the guns opened fire at all.' The ensuing war between British Royal and Merchant Navy seamen and the German U-boat crews was described by Winston Churchill as 'among the most heart-shaking episodes of history'.

The prize scalp of Germany's mine and submarine strategy was Lord Kitchener's. He was Britain's Secretary of State for War, the nation's most famous living soldier, and the 'poster boy' of the 'Your Country Needs You' recruiting image. Kitchener was on a diplomatic mission to Russia – to encourage the beleaguered Tsar to stay in the war – when his ship, HMS *Hampshire*, struck a mine that had been laid by submarine *U-75* off Marwick Head on Orkney. It was *U-75*'s first mission. She would end up sinking, damaging or capturing 15 British, allied or neutral vessels during the war.

The Royal Navy, with its traditions of Trafalgar and broadsides on the high seas, was slow to understand the danger of the lone wolf U-boat prowling undetected beneath the waves. A suggested early British tactic to defeat submarines was for patrol vessels or fishing boats to smash U-boat periscope lenses with a hammer, or put a bag over them. The Admiralty also failed to adopt the convoy system for merchant ships, which were struggling to feed and arm Britain, until well into 1917. It was a mistake that the military theorist and historian, Basil Liddell Hart, called its 'blindest blunder'. Britain had a lot to learn.

German's *U-bootwaffe* were formidable warships. There were only 20 of them in operation at the outbreak of war, but their early successes, and a growing belief that they alone could bring victory to Germany, sparked a building frenzy that saw 309 more launched. Even after heavy losses, Germany still had more than 170 submarines in service at the end of the war.

The fall of Belgium in 1914 gave Germany the use of the Channel ports Zeebrugge and Ostend, thereby extending the amount of time the smaller inshore classes of submarines could spend harrying enemy shipping. The Germans believed that this war of attrition – *materialschlacht* – could bring Britain to its knees. The Battle of the Atlantic and the wrath of the U-boats reached their height in the spring of 1917. Month on month that year the tonnage of lost shipping rose – 298,000 tons in January, 468,000 in February, 500,000 in March and an unsustainable 849,000 tons in April. That month alone, 413 vessels were sunk. Winston Churchill recalled: 'The U-boat was rapidly undermining not only the life of the British islands, but the foundation of the Allies' strength, and the danger of their collapse in 1918 began to look black and imminent.'

U-boats were a triumph of German engineering. The first keel of a German Navy submarine, the *U-1*, had been laid in 1905. It had serious limitations – but within a decade, ambitious development by engineers, prompted by ruthless military strategy, had created several classes of deadly effective underwater war machines. The *UB-77* – which would sink the *Tuscania* – was of a successful coastal submarine class, the UB type 111. Built in Hamburg, she was commissioned in 1917 and was captained from the beginning by Kapitänleutnant Wilhelm Meyer. The *UB-77* carried ten torpedoes that could be fired from four tubes at the bow and one at the stern. Under Meyer served two officers and 31 men. Although submarines were feared by the British, the lives of their crews were precarious. The amount of time submarines could spend under water without surfacing to recharge their batteries was limited. Their hulls were thin and, if surprised on the surface, they were sitting ducks. Being a submariner was not a job for the nervous or claustrophobic. Kapitän Meyer described the life of his crew: 'The submarine service was arduous and dangerous work. The U-boat that left its home port had to reckon with the 50% probability of never returning . . . mines and nets under water, destroyers, motorboats and armed steamer "sub-chasers" on the water's surface, flying machines and airships above us, all combine to exterminate us. It was serious and novel duty the Fatherland required. For us it was a life of struggle and self-denial.' The *UB-77*'s twin diesel engines could drive her along at more than 13 knots on the surface, while her electric motors gave her an underwater speed of less than 8 knots. The description of her as a 'coastal submarine' is confusing. It means that she was small, manoeuvrable and with shallow draft that allowed her to hunt in coastal waters – but her range was nearly 9,000 nautical miles.

U-boats roved the coasts of Britain preying on whatever they encountered. The Hebrides and western seaboard of Scotland were a happy hunting ground, as it was here transatlantic shipping began to funnel in around Ireland toward Liverpool and the Clyde. One U-boat even surfaced in the bay at Hirta, one of the St Kilda islands, 45 miles west of the Outer Hebrides, and shelled the radio station there. On Islay, a story still circulates of an audacious German U-boat that would slip into lonely *Glas Uig* on the east coast of the island, and land a party of ration-weary sailors to 'requisition' a sheep for the pot. I was sceptical of this story until I visited *Glas Uig*, a narrow but deep inlet with an ancient landing stage where cattle were once loaded onto boats for the mainland. If ever an enemy submarine wants to make a surreptitious landing in the Hebrides, this is the place to do it.

❦

Although the British Admiralty had been slow to develop tactics to overcome the submarine threat, it had been quick to understand the need to wage total war. For four years from 1914, the shipyards of the River Clyde dedicated themselves to the greatest and most mechanised war humanity had ever known. The demand for new warships and replacements for merchant vessels, culled by pitiless submarine warfare, made the Clyde yards a paramount part of the war economy, directly regulated by the UK government. Most of the ships which feature in these pages were Clyde-built. The *Lusitania* was launched at John Brown's yard at Clydebank. The *Tuscania* was the product of Alexander Stephen & Sons Ltd of Linthouse in Govan. The troopship *Kashmir*, which fatally collided with the *Otranto*, was built by Caird's of Greenock, and HMS *Mounsey*, the destroyer which rescued hundreds of men from the stricken *Otranto*, was built by Yarrow's yard in the west of Glasgow. The destroyers HMS *Mosquito* and HMS *Grasshopper*, which saved men from the torpedoed *Tuscania*, were built at Fairfield's in Govan.

～

The scene is now set. At the centre of the stage stands the storm-harried and war-weary little island of Islay, with its trans-atlantic ties of blood and culture. Now its young men serve in Britain's Army and Royal and Merchant Navies. Both sides in this European conflict seem evenly matched, and there is no end in sight to the war. Enter, now, the other great player in this tragedy – America.

2

The Grand Miscalculation

I hear a mighty thunder . . .
Stuart K. Hine, *How Great Thou Art*

By the time America declared war on Germany, on 6 April 1917, jingoism had worn thin in Britain. More and more young men marched to war, and longer and longer casualty lists returned from the front. It would be many months before America became an effective ally and, in the meantime, 1917 went badly. The British Army was severely bloodied at Arras and at Gaza in Palestine, and in the Battle of the Atlantic German U-boats came close to strangling Britain. Things went badly for Britain's allies too. Sections of the French army had mutinied and many of the 'poilus' (hairy ones) – the French equivalent of 'Jocks', 'Tommies' and 'doughboys' – had simply deserted their trenches. On the Russian front, following the Bolshevik overthrow of the Tsar's regime, the fighting had almost ceased and Russian soldiers were actually fraternising with their German foes.

On the home front civilians were worn down by grief, uncertainty, lack of manpower, rationing and the sheer joyless-ness of waging total war. But the entrance of America into the conflict had at least rekindled the hope of victory. When war broke out in 1914, Americans had been anxious to keep out of Old Europe's conflicts. They had supplied Britain and France with arms and munitions (at commercial rates) but in the end it was German strategy, not British diplomacy, which brought America into what could now be truly called a World War.

Germany's Admiral Alfred von Tirpitz has been described by historians as 'ruthless,' 'rasping and energetic' and as having 'dangerous genius'. These descriptions all fit him perfectly. Von Tirpitz was also the man who embodied the strategy that did more than anything else to drag America reluctantly into the war. It was his pitiless policy of 'sink on sight' that aroused the sleeping giant across the Atlantic, and ensured the defeat of the Germany he served.

One can only speculate how different the outcome of World War One would have been without America's intervention in 1917. But different it would have been. That year, Germany and its Austrian allies were dealt a massive stroke of good fortune. They had been fighting on two fronts – against Britain and France in the West, and against Tsarist Russia in the east. But the Russian army had been virtually paralysed as the old regime imploded in the face of Red revolution. When Lenin and the Bolsheviks came to power in October, they pulled Russia out of the war – allowing Germany to release 44 divisions to the Western Front.

But in the meantime, the Fatherland had provoked a hitherto peaceful-minded United States of America to side with its enemies. It had managed to replace one enemy with an even more powerful one. American was the dominant industrial nation, with 35% of the world's manufacturing capacity – easily more than twice that of Germany or Britain. In his history of World War One, *The World Crisis*, Winston Churchill commented: 'Of all the grand miscalculations of the German High Command none is more remarkable than their inability to comprehend the meaning of war with the American Union.' The political and military blunder made the final defeat of Germany inevitable. It profoundly shaped world history, and it would even bring the grim reality of total war to the shores of a small Inner Hebridean island on the very fringes of Western Europe.

Britain and Germany tried to throttle the lifelines that brought each other the food and munitions that they desperately needed. Britain started it. Even before war was declared, the British Grand Fleet steamed out of Portland Harbour, off Dorset, to Scapa Flow, the natural deep-water harbour in the midst of the Orkney archipelago. From there, it would dominate the northern waters, keeping the German fleet mainly confined to port, and halting all merchant ships – even from neutral countries – bound for Germany. All of the Reich's saltpetre came from Chile, and although less important to the explosives industry since the introduction of cordite, it played a vital part in the manufacture of fertilisers and Germany's ability to feed itself.

In July 1915, while the Germans went hungry, beef, lard, ship's biscuits, and coffee and cocoa beans that had been bound for Germany, but captured by the Royal Navy, were auctioned off at the Trades Hall in Glasgow. In an attempt to beat the blockade Germany even built U-Cruisers – huge cargo-carrying submarines. The *Deutschland* sailed from Bremen in June 1916, with a cargo of dyes, and returned crammed with rubber, nickel and tin. But the feat was more a propaganda victory than a reliable and efficient supply chain in a time of total war. German civilians in urban areas existed on 1000 calories a day, less than half what is required to preserve health and strength. A British report – written in 1921 but suppressed for forty years – revealed that German scientists estimated that more than three-quarters of a million of their countrymen died as a direct result of the British blockade. If the British fleet couldn't inflict a Trafalgar-scale defeat on Germany, it would starve her of food and the materials of war. Historian Basil Liddell Hart called the British blockade 'perhaps the most decisive act of the war'.

Germany agonised over its response. Gaining favour was a ruthless 'sink on sight' strategy that would make every merchant ship bound for Britain – even those from neutral nations – a legitimate military target. The strategy created a rift between

Germany's politicians and its military leadership. The politicians were fearful that such action could drive neutral America into their enemies' camp. The generals and admirals were desperate to use every weapon available to them. The military won the argument. On 4 February 1915, the Kaiser declared unrestricted war on every merchant ship found in the North Sea. Even the vessels of neutral nations would be sunk on sight. America and other non-combatant nations were outraged.

Until then, the gentlemanly custom of Prize Regulations had prevailed. A warship would challenge a merchantman to reveal its name, cargo and destination. If this were deemed to breach a blockade, the warship would order the merchant seamen to abandon their ship before blowing her out of the water or capturing her. The crew in their lifeboats would then be told their position, pointed in the direction of the nearest port, and wished good luck.

Germany did not hide its 'sink on sight' policy from the world. Its embassy in America published advertisements in US newspapers warning potential passengers against making a particular scheduled liner crossing of the Atlantic.

NOTICE!

TRAVELLERS intending to embark on the Atlantic voyage are reminded that a state of war exists between Germany and her allies and Great Britain and her allies; that the zone of war includes the waters adjacent to the British Isles; that, in accordance with formal notice given by the Imperial German Government, vessels flying the flag of Great Britain, or any of her allies, are liable to destruction in those waters and that travellers sailing in the war zone on the ships of Great Britain or her allies do so at their own risk.

IMPERIAL GERMAN EMBASSY
Washington, DC, 22 April 1915.

That liner was the *Lusitania*. On 1 May, with 1,962 passengers and crew aboard, she sailed from New York's famous Pier 54. Three years earlier, the *Carpathia* had docked there to disembark more than 700 *Titanic* passengers it had saved from drowning. Six days after leaving New York, the *Lusitania* was off Kinsale on the southern coast of Ireland, and only hours from docking at Liverpool, when its course fatally intersected with that of German submarine *U-20*. The U-boat's 30-year-old captain was Walther Schwieger, who would prove to be one of the *Kaiserliche Marine*'s most effective U-boat commanders. Schwieger fired a single torpedo, which struck the *Lusitania* on her starboard side, beneath the wheelhouse. The explosion that followed ripped a hole in the vessel's hull and she lurched heavily into a starboard list. The crew frantically strove to launch lifeboats, but the severe angle of the list made it almost impossible. Some of the boats were smashed or overturned when they hit the water, and only six out of 48 were usable. Six boats for nearly 2,000 souls. About twenty minutes after being torpedoed, the *Lusitania* plunged beneath the waves.

The German newspaper, *Kolniscle Volkszeitung*, hailed the sinking: 'A success of our submarines which must be placed beside the greatest achievements of this naval war.' Nearly twelve hundred passengers and crew died as the ship went down, mostly by drowning or hypothermia. On board were 139 Americans, of whom 128 perished. America – which was not at war – was outraged by the ruthless slaughter and, slowly but steadily, the tide of US public opinion began to turn from neutrality to thoughts of war.

Britain's hands weren't exactly clean in this ghastly affair. The 1914 edition of *Jane*'s *Fighting Ships* described the *Lusitania* as an 'Armed Merchant Cruiser', and it is now known that as well as passengers she also carried ammunition and other materials of war. Germany had a strong case that the ship was a legitimate target, but the sinking horrified America. The

USA had been deeply opposed to any involvement in the European conflict. The young democratic republic could see no natural allies in a war between despotic Tsarist Russia and the British Empire on one side, and the Kaiser's Germany and the Austro-Hungarian Empire on the other. In any case, America's Civil War was still within living memory – just half a century away – and the loss of perhaps as many as 900,000 lives was seared into the national consciousness. Americans wanted peace and prosperity.

Although President Woodrow Wilson was quick to condemn the *Lusitania* atrocity, he was reluctant to rise to even serious provocation. Wilson was a highly principled Presbyterian son-of-the-manse with Scottish grandparents on his mother's side, and a Scots-Irish grandfather on his father's. He hated war, believed in the powers of international diplomacy, and was determined to keep America neutral. He had even fought and won the 1916 Presidential election with the slogan 'He kept us out the war'. Just days after the *Lusitania* had foundered, President Wilson told a Philadelphia audience: 'There is such a thing as a man being too proud to fight. There is such a thing as a nation being so right that it does not need to convince others by force that it is right.' While there were influential American 'hawks' and Anglophiles, who urged military support for Britain and France, there were thousands of recent German immigrants who would have happily seen America fight on Germany's side. Although long-established German families were well integrated into US society, many newcomers attempted to return to their fatherland and enlist in the German forces. Irish-American Catholics were also often hostile to Britain – especially after the suppression of the Easter Rising in 1916.

The explosion that sent the *Lusitania* to the bottom of the sea reverberated around America for nearly two years. Many of those who heard it believed it was a call to war. A 'Preparedness' movement sprang up – demanding that America arm itself for a conflict that many believed was inevitable. Ex-President Theodore Roosevelt was a supporter of 'Preparedness' and an outspoken critic of neutrality. As for the Irish-Americans and German-Americans who opposed the war, Roosevelt denounced them as 'hyphenated-Americans' with divided loyalties.

Today, it is hard to think of American power in terms other than that of 'the industrial military complex,' and of being the most powerful military nation in the world. But in 1915 the US Army and Navy were tiny. If America had a potential enemy on the horizon it was Mexico. That year the revolutionary general, Pancho Villa, crossed the US border to raid the New Mexico town of Columbus. American cavalry had been successful in breaking up Villa's forces, but US generals had developed no tactics for European trench warfare, or the use of aircraft, submarines, tanks and poisoned gas. One explanation for 'doughboy' being the American slang for a common soldier, is that it was coined by cavalrymen during the Mexican war as a derogatory term for the sweaty, dusty infantry who soon resembled adobe, the mud and straw building material of the American South-west.

The sinking of the *Lusitania* prompted only a modest increase in the size of the US Army and Navy. Germany watched carefully, and calculated. America had manpower and industrial might, but it did not have a great army and war machine. America wanted peace and prosperity at home, not battles on a distant continent. Under pressure from America, Germany had abandoned its sink-on-sight strategy. But now, concluded the Reich, America's threats were hollow. As the war in Europe dragged on – with both sides facing economic disaster as well as military defeat – Germany confronted a momentous strategic and political question. Should it once again declare unrestricted submarine warfare? In theory, the decision lay in the hands of the Kaiser, and two factions fought to influence him. But Kaiser Bill ran wartime Germany in name only. The power behind the throne was exercised by Paul von Hindenburg, Germany's Chief of General Staff, and Erich Ludendorff, the German Army's Quartermaster General. Although von Tirpitz had been removed from office the previous year, his 'sink on sight' strategy had its champions in von Hindenburg and Ludendorff, Germany's *de facto* military dictators and warlords. Meanwhile Germany's civilian leader, Chancellor Theobald von Bethmann-Hollweg, strongly opposed the strategy.

By now, the land war in Europe had stagnated. Both sides hammered away at each other from formidable defensive positions. The prospect of either side mounting a crushing assault that brought swift victory was nigh impossible. In the meantime, Germany was slowly starving. On 8 January 1917, at an audience with the Kaiser, the military made the case for a resumption of unrestricted submarine warfare. The Kaiser agreed. It was a blow for Chancellor Bethmann-Hollweg, who finally capitulated, and according to Ludendorff, said: 'The U-boat campaign is the "last card." A very serious decision! But if the military authorities regard the U-boat campaign as necessary I am not in a position to oppose them.' The Chancellor had the grim duty of announcing the strategy he had so strongly opposed to the *Reichstag* and the world. It was a desperate final throw of the dice. Germany knew such draconian action might bring America into the war on Britain and France's side – but it counted on dealing Britain a knockout blow before Uncle Sam unfurled his banner. The wrath of the U-boats was let loose on military and merchant, allied and neutral ships alike. Month on month the losses mounted – peaking, as already mentioned, in April 1917 when 849,000 tons of shipping was sunk. In that time German only lost nine U-boats.

Seven American merchant ships went to the bottom before President Woodrow Wilson had had enough. He and his country had finally woken up to the mighty thunder from Europe. In April 1917, America declared war on Germany. The wording of America's declaration painstakingly makes clear that the United States had been sorely provoked.

> Whereas the Imperial German Government have committed repeated acts of war against the Government and people of the United States of America: Therefore be it resolved by the Senate and the House of Representatives of the United States of America in Congress assembled: That a state of war between the United States and the Imperial German Government which has been thrust upon the United States is hereby formally declared . . .
>
> Congressional Resolution, April 6th, 1917

The message was clear – and directed as much to the American public as the German government – the state of war had been 'thrust upon the United States' by Germany's 'repeated acts of war'. But while America went to war reluctantly, it would fight that war with all its might. The Congressional Resolution goes on:

> . . . that the President be, and is hereby authorized and directed to employ the entire naval and military forces of the United States and the resources of the Government to carry on war against the Imperial German Government; and to bring the conflict to a successful termination all the resources of the country are hereby pledged by the Congress of the United States.

As the American government cranked up the machines of war, it was bloody business as usual in Europe. The island of Islay earned more than its share of heart-breaking telegrams. Just ten days before the US declaration, Corporal Ronald McLugash from Tighvulin in the parish of Kilchoman fell in the fighting that followed the strategic German withdrawal behind a carefully prepared defensive position, the Hindenburg Line. The 22-year-old Argyll & Sutherland Highlander was the 86th man from Islay, and its sparsely populated neighbouring island of Jura, to be killed since the war began. On 9 April, three days after America entered the war, the battle of Arras began. The strategy was to smash through the German defences and force their smaller army to fight an unequal campaign on open ground, without the advantage of entrenched positions. Scottish divisions were to the fore in the mainly British and Canadian assault. For nearly 40 days the battle raged on. One officer reported that: 'the place might have been mistaken for Hades instead of Arras'. The average daily casualty rate was 4,076 – higher than it had been at the Somme. About a third of the estimated 159,000 British casualties were Scots. On the very first day alone, four Islay men and one from Jura were killed.

Winston Churchill would later muse on President Wilson's reluctance to go to war, and how the conflict would have been shortened by an earlier intervention: 'What he did in April, 1917, could have been done in May, 1915. And if done then what abridgment of the slaughter; what sparing of the agony; what ruin, what catastrophes would have been prevented; in how many million homes would an empty chair be occupied today; how different would be the shattered world in which victors and vanquished alike are condemned to live?'

But, better late than never. Britain and France now had a new and powerful ally – if a hopelessly unprepared one. The United States peacetime army, including the part-time National Guard, was about a twentieth the size of Germany's, with many of its soldiers trained only as cavalrymen or coastal defence gunners. But America was a young and vigorous nation, with gifted technocrats, efficient industries and a population of 120 million. Once stirred, it would be unstoppable. America went to work.

Industry, food production and manpower were mobilised for the war effort. The skills and efficiency that had been building America into a great economic power – it had overtaken Britain in 1910 – would swiftly make her into a great military one. Within weeks of declaring war the US government passed the Selective Service Act. By the end of the conflict it would have drafted nearly three million men, and turned an Army trained for skirmishes on the Mexican border into a world-class military power. By the summer of 1918 more than a million American doughboys would be serving in France – having arrived there at a rate of up to 10,000 a day.

Sergeant Harry Richards of the 107th Sanitary Squad had served in the 1915 punitive expedition against Mexico, but when he stepped aboard the *Tuscania* on his way to Europe he was one of very few men on board with experience of war. The doughboys were keen, but mostly untested.

America insisted that its doughboys weren't used to fill the ranks of the depleted French and British units, but fought in American armies under American command. Their strength and vitality would prove decisive against weary, malnourished and dwindling German forces. Even just the psychological effect of their presence must have been demoralising for war-weary German soldiers. The arrival of the doughboys had the opposite effect on the French and British. In April 1918, the writer and feminist, Vera Brittain, who had volunteered to serve as a nurse in France, was struck by how the tall, vigorous and smartly dressed newly arrived Americans contrasted to 'the under-sized armies of pale recruits to which we had grown accustomed. At first I thought their spruce clean uniforms were those of officers, yet obviously they could not be officers, for there were too many of them; they seemed, as it were, Tommies in heaven.'

But this was a full year in the future. In April 1917, this army of doughboys still had to be recruited, equipped and trained. And then it had to cross the Atlantic and get to the trenches of

France. This would be a massive logistical challenge. A 1921 official American history of the war concluded: 'This was a military supply situation of unprecedented difficulty. No nation has ever attempted to maintain a great army over such a distance, nor was a line of supply ever so beset with peril.' In the path of the young Americans who would cross the Atlantic were skilled, dedicated and ruthlessly efficient German patriots sworn to stopping them from getting there – men like *Kaiserliche Marine* U-boat commanders Walther Schwieger and Wilhelm Meyer. Could such heroes throttle the flow of American men and munitions and bring Britain to her knees?

❧

In October 1917, America set in motion a plan to ship thirty Army divisions – 1,200,000 men – to Europe. More than half would travel in British ships, the majority of them liners that had been designed and built for times of peace. The *Tuscania* was a pride of the Clyde. Launched from Alexander Stephen & Sons' yard at Linthouse in Govan, she was built as a luxury liner for Cunard's subsidiary, the Anchor Line, to ply the Glasgow–New York route. At more than 14,000 gross tons she could accommodate 271 people in the lap of luxury, 246 in second-class cabins, and nearly 2,000 more 'steerage'-class passengers. In 1916, while berthed at New York, the *Tuscania* was used as a location for a silent movie, starring and written by actress Valentine Grant. *The Daughter of MacGregor* tells of a Scots lass escaping with her dog from a wicked stepmother and going on to foil timber thieves in Florida. But the *Tuscania* was destined to take part in a greater drama. She was launched the month after war was declared and it wasn't long before she had a rapid-fire 4-inch naval gun fitted near her stern, and was drafted into a new role – that of troopship. Her newly designed 'dazzle' camouflage – slabs of jagged geometric shapes in white and olive-drab – weren't designed to hide her when at sea, but to confuse enemy gunners as to her distance, as the stripes of a herd of galloping zebras are said to confuse predators. One US journalist would describe the *Tuscania* as 'a painted Jezebel of the sea'.

The troops who would sail on the *Tuscania*'s fatal voyage were mostly an advance party for the 32nd US Infantry Division. The 32nd was first formed at Camp MacArthur at Waco in Texas in July 1917, although some of its units had origins in the Civil War. The soldiers were raised from the National Guards of Wisconsin and Michigan states. The National Guard – recruited and organised along state, not federal, lines – was America's reserve military force, made up of (mostly) part-time volunteers. It provided about 40% of the US units that fought in France.

Before the 27,000-strong new division left for Europe, a handful of British and French officers and NCOs joined it as instructors in trench warfare, and the 32nd built its own trench system at Waco for combat training. When the division was reviewed by generals from Washington, D.C., its commander, Major General William G. Haan, was commended for the capacity, energy and tact with which he'd trained his men for overseas service. Private Edward Lauer, who had joined the Wisconsin National Guard as soon as America declared war, recalled: 'The final parade is something I shall never forget – all regiments with bands and Color Guards followed by the usual company formations – marching past the grandstand – where General William G. Haan, our beloved Commanding General and his Staff and other Generals from Washington DC, returned the salute.'

By crowded train and ferry the men travelled to the embarkation piers on New York's Hudson River. US Army efficiency in getting men to war didn't factor in comfort, but at Hoboken the Red Cross built the biggest coffee machine in the world – and then built a bigger one on the Chelsea Pier side of the Hudson. In a single day, New York Harbour could dole out ten tons of hot coffee, three tons of rolls, about a ton of cigarettes and several hundredweight of ice cream and cookies.

The Americans travelled light. They took with them their short, but accurate, American-made .30-calibre rifles, but once in France were issued with their heavy equipment – British and French tanks, field guns and aircraft. This allowed the troopships to cram more men beneath their decks. The day before the *Tuscania* sailed, 2,000 soldiers clattered up her gangplanks in their heavy boots and winter greatcoats and made their way to the crowded accommodation below. A report into the fate of the *Tuscania* later described most of the men as 'landlubbers', but a few had crossed the Atlantic when they had emigrated to America. Thomas Evans and Frank Sharpe were both corporals in C Company of the 107th Supply Train. They had been friends from boyhood, having been born in the same town in North Wales. Privates John Sloss, from Lochwinnoch, and fellow Scot, Alexander McAlister of a successful farming family from Meikle Kilmory on the island of Bute, were also crossing the Atlantic for the second time. Sergeant Everett Harpham and Private Roy Muncaster were more typical – American-born and with no experience of the sea. They were true 'landsmen' and had worked for the National Forest Service before enlisting. Privates – and brothers – Stephen and James Gurney, of Glide, Oregon, were also foresters with the 20th Engineers. Arthur Siplon, of the 100th Aero Squadron, was from Michigan, Private Wilbur Nutt was from Ohio, and Private Leo Zimmermann was from Wisconsin. They would have been familiar with the Great Lakes, but they'd never seen anything like the Atlantic Ocean before.

On 24 January 1918, the *Tuscania* left New York Harbour. Later in the war the 32nd Division would adopt a shoulder patch featuring a red arrow – symbolic of it being the first Allied division to pierce the Hindenburg Line. But before it could win honours, it had to get to the battlefields of Europe that lay across the winter Atlantic. Ignorant of the dangers of the sea and the reality of trench warfare, most of the 2,000 doughboys who sailed on the *Tuscania* thought they would soon be heading home with the war over, echoing their leader, General 'Black Jack' Pershing's words, 'Heaven, Hell or Hoboken . . . by Christmas.'

Wisconsin doughboy, Private Leo Zimmermann, described how the soldiers were ordered below decks to hide their numbers and the identity of their units from potential spies. Only when they were at sea were the men allowed a last look at their homeland. Edward Lauer too remembered that the authorities feared espionage. 'The ship's whistle blew, and orders were given to go below deck to hide the cargo of American soldiers from the prying eyes of spies.' Writer and journalist Irvin S. Cobb – on his way to cover the war for the influential magazine, the *Saturday Evening Post* – also sailed with the convoy, and reported: 'Transatlantic journeys these days aren't what they used to be before America went into the war. Ours began to be different even before our ship pulled out from port. It is forbidden me to tell her name, and anyhow hers doesn't in the least matter, but she was a big ship with a famous skipper, and in peacetimes her sailing would make some small stir ... Instead we slipped away as if we had done something wrong. There were no waving of hands and handkerchiefs, no goodbyes on the gangplanks, no rush to get back on land when the shore bell sounded . . .' Arthur Siplon, who served with the Aviation Section of the Army's Signal Corps, recalled getting on deck just in time to 'wave good-bye' to the Statue of Liberty.

For two days the *Tuscania* headed north along the New England coast to the great harbour at Halifax, Nova Scotia, Canada, where Convoy HX-20 was assembling. There the men got a grim foretaste of what the war in Europe was like. Much of Halifax was a bombed-out ruin. Less than two months before, munitions ship *Mont Blanc* had collided with another vessel as it entered the harbour. Her crew abandoned her, and the *Mont Blanc* – now heavily ablaze – drifted into the pier. Local fire crews had fought the blaze from the shore, but the ship erupted into the greatest pre-nuclear man-made explosion ever – gauged by number of casualties, force of blast, radius of devastation, quantity of explosives material and value of property lost. Its TNT equivalent might have been 2.9 kilotons. It is believed that 1,900 people died, with 9,000 injured. The entire north end of Halifax – 325 acres – was destroyed. Snow had fallen and the temperature fell to 20 degrees below zero. For the men on board the *Tuscania*, it was a sobering introduction to the realities of modern war.

On the morning of 27 January twelve ships manoeuvred into five columns. In the vanguard was HMS *Cochrane,* a heavily armed British cruiser. In its wake sailed troop transport ship, *Baltic*, followed by the *Tuscania*. At the rear sailed the USS *Kanawha*, a former collier that Leo Zimmermann says was 'bristling with guns as a rear protection against sub attacks'. To the *Tuscania*'s port and starboard were columns of troopships and cargo boats. The ships sailed six cable lengths (just over half a nautical mile) from those in front and three from the vessels on either side. Writer Irvin S. Cobb was travelling on board – it can now be told – the *Baltic*, a requisitioned White Star ocean liner that, until 1905, had been the biggest ship in the world. The huge vessel steamed directly ahead of the *Tuscania*, and Cobb watched the *Tuscania* trail in the *Baltic*'s wake: 'Hugged up close to our ship, splashing through the foam of our wake as though craving the comfort of our company.'

It was hard sailing. The entire convoy followed a carefully planned and coordinated zig-zag course to confuse enemy U-boats. Accurate navigation and skilled seamanship were needed to keep the convoy together and avoid collisions in darkness and foul weather. Every skipper was well-versed in the 'Convoy Bible' – an instruction manual officially called *War Instructions for British Merchant Ships* – that spelled out 200 rules for survival. In essence they boiled down to four main principles: sailing in carefully coordinated zig-zags; maintaining silence and a night-time blackout; posting alert lookouts; and the strict closure of watertight doors. Troopship captains were also under strict orders not to stop to rescue survivors from any ship that was torpedoed. No troop transport was to be allowed to become a sitting duck.

Britain had been slow to adopt the convoy system to protect its ships, but, by May 1917, younger and wiser heads had begun to prevail at the British Admiralty. As an experiment, a flotilla of merchant ships, travelling together in formation and protected by U-boat hunting warships, sailed from Gibraltar to Britain. The tactic was a success, and was quickly adopted for transatlantic crossings. The first American troops had crossed the Atlantic in May the previous year. In the intervening eight months, not a single troopship had been lost on the voyage to Europe. Convoys gave ships protection and security, but at night Leo Zimmermann found the ocean a lonely place. 'In the evening the ships faded away in the enveloping gloom, like phantoms on the horizon. The blue stern light of the *Baltic* alone discernible at night beckoned us on. Above deck it was quiet, except for the whistle of the wind through the rigging and the incessant pounding and lashing of the salt-sea waves along the sides of the liner.'

On board the *Tuscania* were 2,336 American soldiers, with 51 of them 'casual' (replacement) officers. Then there was a variety of different units, including the 20th Engineers, and the 100th, 158th and 213th Aero Squadrons. New Yorker Thomas Conway had enlisted in the 213th, but hadn't learned to fly yet. Once in Europe he would be trained to fly the French SPAD, the effective fighter biplane that was the weapon of choice for American World War One air ace, Eddie Rickenbacker. The USA didn't establish a separate Air Force until 1947, and the Aero units were squadrons of Army flyers and ground support technicians.

The 32nd Division troops on board comprised the 107th Engineer Train; the 197th Military Police; the 107th Supply Train; and the 7th and 8th Sanitary Squads. The US Army's 'Sanitary Squads' were first formed in June 1917. The government realised that germs were as deadly as bombs and bullets, and enrolled officers and men with 'special skills in sanitation, sanitary engineering, in bacteriology, or other sciences related to sanitation and preventive medicine, or who possess other knowledge of special advantage to the Medical Department'. These units of the 32nd Division were an advance guard, sent to prepare a camp in France where final battle training would happen.

The *Tuscania*'s British crew comprised 239 officers and men, and two stewardesses. Its captain was experienced 59-year-old, Perth-born Peter McLean, and his crew were mostly Scottish merchant sailors employed by the Anchor Line, and not military personnel, although the ship had been fitted with a 4-inch naval gun that sailors had been trained to use. The *Tuscania*'s days as a luxury liner were far behind her. Living conditions were cramped and uncomfortable. Many of the men had never been to sea before, and when the weather got rough seasickness was rife. The stench must have been terrible. The ship had been built with accommodation for animals, and there were 30 mules on board, but most of the stable space was occupied by soldiers. Leo Zimmermann's bunk was a coffin-shaped box in a converted horse stall. The dining rooms were inadequate, and men were assigned table places and strict times when to eat. The food was basic, mostly unsalted potatoes served with fish, cheese or 'slum' – slumgullion, a stew made from whatever the cooks had to hand.

The winter crossing was a stormy one, and Edward Lauer tells that it was not without incident. 'On February 3rd – Sunday night around 1.00 am – there was an awful crash, and the men rushed up on deck with their lifebelts on. We must have passed over the wreck of a sunken ship – others thought it was a tidal wave as some water rushed down the main stairway into our quarters. We finally returned to our bunks and slept through the night.' The ship's captain, Peter McLean, added lifeboat drills to the usual physical exercises practiced by the troops. The men would don their lifejackets and muster beside their assigned lifeboats, along with the *Tuscania* crewmen who were detailed to lower them if the order ever came to abandon ship. At night, the soldiers slept in their clothes, with their lifebelts hanging at the head of their bunks. One evening the men saw, on the horizon, a frigate on fire, the smoke from it wreathing a rising red moon.

Cramped conditions below deck helped spread illness. Private James Gurney, of the 20th Engineers, contracted scarlet fever, and was confined to the sickbay. The diary of fellow forester, Harry A. Kelley, who enlisted in California, tells of rough seas, poor food, being sprayed with evil-smelling disinfectant by the *Tuscania* crew and being ill. His entry for 4 February reads: 'I remain sick; have been moved to state room. I volunteered for submarine guard duty, but too sick to do it.' The dangers of the crossing and the vigilance of the ships' officers are neatly summed up in Irvin Cobb's description of the *Baltic*'s captain.

> Our Captain no longer came to the Saloon for his meals. He lived upon the bridge, ate there and, I think, slept there – what sleeping he did. Standing there all muffled in his oilskins, he looked even more of a squatty and unheroic figure than he had in his naval blue, presiding at the head of the table; but by repute we knew him for a man who had been through one torpedoing with great credit to himself and through numbers of narrow escapes, and

we valued him accordingly and put our faith in him. It was faith well placed, as shall presently transpire. I should not say that there was much fear aboard; at least if there was it did not manifest itself in the manner or the voice or the behaviour of a single passenger seen by me; but there was a sort of nagging, persistent sense of uneasiness betraying itself in various small ways. For one thing, all of us made more jokes about submarines, mines and other perils of the deep than was natural. There was something a little forced, artificial, about this gaiety – laughs came from the lips, but not from points further south.

On the morning of 4 February, the convoy was joined by eight British destroyers that had steamed out of Lough Swilly, on the north coast of Ireland, to escort it on the dangerous final stage of the voyage. Nervous passengers, like Edward Lauer, were pleased to see them. 'I went up on deck and saw eight destroyers all around us, so we felt a bit safer, as we were going into the submarine zone.' The 'submarine zone', or 'danger zone', was where the wide ocean narrowed into the channels that led to Britain's west coast ports. That night the weather was rough. The soldiers were nervous. When the *Tuscania* dropped with a crash into a deep trough in the sea, men woke believing they'd been torpedoed.

Close buddies Sergeant Everett Harpham and Private Roy Muncaster served with the 20th Engineers, a forestry regiment that would manage French forests and turn trees into the timber necessary for barracks, bridges and duck-boards for trenches. They'd both graduated in forestry from the University of Washington. Twenty-five-year-old Muncaster had left his job as a ranger in Washington State's Olympic National Forest to join up. On the evening of 4 February, they and the rest of the *Tuscania*'s passengers were treated to an on-board entertainment, at which Sergeant Ben Chindgren of Oregon sang the popular song, 'Asleep in the Deep'. It was an uncannily prophetic choice.

> Loudly the bell in the old tower rings,
> Bidding us list to the warning it brings. Sailor, take care!
>   Sailor, take care!
> Danger is near thee. Beware! Beware! Beware! Beware!
> Many brave hearts are asleep in the deep, So beware!
>   beware!
> Many brave hearts are asleep in the deep, So beware!
>   beware!

3

A Terrible Detonation

~

Bheir an cuan a chuid fhèin a-mach
(The sea will claim its own)
Gaelic proverb collected on Islay by Gilbert Clark

On the night of 4 February 1918, as the doughboys enjoyed
their homespun entertainment on board the *Tuscania*, the
German submarine, *UB-77*, was cruising off the north coast of
Ireland. Its commander, 29-year-old Kapitän Wilhelm Meyer,
remembered: 'Having given up hope of sighting prey in that
area, I decided to head for the entrance to the North Channel,
intending to enter the Irish Sea.' Well before sunrise the following morning, the U-boat was on the surface, watching and
listening. Meyer believed that British cruisers 'were as thick as
fish in that region'. When enemy destroyers loomed out of the
darkness, Meyer gave the order to dive. Seawater gushed into
her ballast tanks and *UB-77* slid beneath the surface.

The day dawned. Tuesday, 5 February. The sea was choppy,
with a strong breeze from the south. Convoy HX-20 was off
the north of Ireland, preparing to turn south and steam down
the North Channel toward Liverpool. The *UB-77*'s logbook
tells of a cat-and-mouse hunt in which the U-boat was both cat
and mouse: 'Cruising in North Channel, 10 miles from Scotland, 7 from Ireland. 8.07 am. Quick dive owing to destroyers
appearing out of the darkness.'

Lurking just below the turbulent surface of the sea, the
crew of *UB-77* listened in tense silence to the thrumming of
destroyer propellers. And then, another sound – the engines
of a much bigger ship. A convoy was close. Kapitän Meyer

scanned the horizon with his periscope. '9.20 am, a 2000-ton steamer sighted. Range 2000 metres. Attempt to reach positon ahead of her fails. The submarine constantly breaks the surface owing to the swell, and destroyers are sighted in the vicinity. The attack is therefore abandoned.'

At 11.30 am Meyer surfaced to let his diesel engine recharge the batteries that powered his vessel underwater, but quickly dived to avoid enemy patrol boats. At 3.05 pm *UB-77* resurfaced and continued down the North Channel. That afternoon, around 4.00 pm, the Americans on board the *Tuscania* caught their first glimpse of the Scottish coast. Wisconsin private Clarence Krueger recalled: 'The upper deck was thronged with an eager bunch of boys glad once more to see land.' Corporal Russell Brunette was sitting on his bunk, about to go for supper, and was slipping his knife and fork into his puttees, as he liked to keep his hands free to keep his balance on the rolling ship. He would tell his parents: 'The trip had been lovely all the way, and we had given up all thoughts of seeing a submarine.' First Lieutenant George Newton Thall of Los Angeles had also forgotten about submarines and was preparing himself for France, by reading a book on 'No Man's Land'. Patrick Cox, one of the *Tuscania*'s crew, was asked by a soldier, 'Well, are we past all the danger yet?'

'No,' replied Cox, 'We are still in the danger zone and may get a torpedo amidships at any moment.' Despite Cox's pessimism (or dry Glasgow humour), the soldiers were likely to be in Liverpool by morning. Their excitement and hopes must have been high – but so were those of *UB-77*'s commander. Fifteen years later Meyer recalled: 'At 5:50 pm I decided to scan the horizon for one last look at the Atlantic. With surprise and trembling I spotted an enormous cloud of black smoke on the western horizon, heading directly towards us. I immediately ordered the *UB-77* swung around, and headed directly towards the smoke cloud, which was advancing south-easterly toward the channel, evidently having taken the extreme north route across the Atlantic. Soon I was able to detect a huge sea-going caravan, headed by a medium-sized vessel, followed by a larger white vessel with two smokestacks, a large cruiser with four smokestacks and from six to eight smaller vessels. The whole caravan was flanked with what looked to us like myriads of destroyers. I cruised above water back and forth and in front of the advancing transports, trying to ascertain the chances of attack. I resolved to attack. I steered north-east. Dusk made visibility poor. There was constant danger we might underestimate the speed of the transports and be run down in their path.'

The 'larger white vessel with two smokestacks' was the *Tuscania* – camouflaged in the 'dazzle' style with 'cubist' slabs of white and olive-drab paint. Meyer clambered up from the control room into the cramped commander's attack position situated high in the conning tower, and squinted into the eyepiece of the attack periscope, trying to get a fix on a target. Meanwhile, his navigation warrant officer scanned the sea through the main periscope, on the lookout for enemy destroyers.

Convoy HX-20 was now deep in the danger zone. Vigilance was intense, and on the *Tuscania* the eyes of fifteen lookouts kept watch. On every vessel in the convoy lookouts were permanently posted to give warning of a U-boat on the surface, a periscope or the wash of a torpedo. Destroyers prowled the waters, guns and depth charges at the ready. The North Passage was a danger zone for U-boats as well as troopships. The winter sun had set around 5.10 pm, and the sleek low profile of a submarine would have been difficult to spot in the dark and the heavy seas. Kapitän Meyer weighed the risks to his ship and 34-strong crew against the possibility of dealing their nation's enemies a deadly blow. Two devastating G-7 torpedoes lay primed and ready in *UB*-77's Number 1 and 2 bow tubes.

Meyer later revealed: 'I had decided to attack without submerging. Suddenly, however, the destroyers pulled up all along the line, so that the leading destroyer was abreast of the leading transport. I thought we had been detected, because we were directly ahead of an advancing triple line consisting of a destroyer, a transport and another destroyer. When there was no further sign that we had been detected I decided to submerge.' Beneath the surface, Meyer struggled to relocate his prey in the dark through the *UB-77*'s periscope. 'My hands trembled as I moved the sighting apparatus, because I knew that if I stayed much longer where we were, the submarine would be rammed and sunk. Suddenly a vague ghostly shadow crept across the sighting mirror. Then atop this shadow appeared the outline of a smokestack. I recognized this shadow as the largest transport. I immediately ordered two torpedoes fired.'

Meyer's logbook records the time of attack as 7.40 pm. The fateful meeting of *UB-77* and the *Tuscania* happened at latitude 55 degrees 22 minutes north, longitude 6 degrees 13 minutes west – in layman's terms, between the Scottish island of Islay and Ireland's Rathlin Island. It was a black night. Not one of the *Tuscania*'s fifteen lookouts saw the U-boat or the trail of foam left in the wake of the two torpedoes. Meyer recalled: 'The crew and I listened in suspense for many minutes. Then a terrific detonation told us that we had hit our target.'

≈≈

On board the *Tuscania*, men were shuffling in and out of the dining hall as the cooks doled out the second sitting of supper. Among them was Arthur Siplon. 'Then it came – a tremendous crash on the starboard side. The cry went up quickly, "We've been hit. We've been torpedoed!"' Clarence Krueger of the 107th Supply Train recalled: 'One of the boys had just looked at his watch and it was fifteen minutes to six. The words were no more than uttered when a terrible explosion occurred. The force of the shock threw us all in a heap.' John Loftis, of the same unit, wasn't sure if the ship had been torpedoed, or had struck a mine, but remembered being plunged into darkness for eight minutes before emergency lights were turned on. Private Edward Lauer, of Milwaukee, who was on his way to supper when the torpedo struck, had to grope his way up two stairways in the dark to find his assigned lifeboat station. John McMahon, a seventeen-year-old mess-room steward from Glasgow, reported that the ship was filled with smoke and took a strong list to starboard.

One of Meyer's two torpedoes had struck the *Tuscania* amidships, near the boiler room. It was of the new G7 type – Germany's most advanced – seven metres long and packing a devastating 195-kilo warhead. When Thomas Smith, a boatswain's mate from Glasgow, heard the explosion he turned to a friend, saying, 'They've got her now.' Smith's laconic observation was chillingly, but not surprisingly, fatalistic. Merchant seamen like him had no illusions about the peril they faced on every voyage, and knew that several ships were sunk every day by German U-boats. In the same 24-hour period that the *Tuscania* was torpedoed, submarines also sank the British ship *Mexico City*, the American *Almanace* and the Spanish vessel, *Sebastian*, all in the Atlantic; the British cargo ship *Cresswell*, in the Bristol Channel; and the Italian passenger ship *Caprera*, in the Mediterranean.

The 2,573 souls aboard the *Tuscania* were soon in no doubt that they had been struck by a torpedo. 'The word was immediately passed that the ship had been torpedoed,' one of the two women on board later told a newspaper. The women, Mary Carson and Flora Collins, were experienced Anchor Line stewardesses that war had failed to deter from carrying on their peacetime jobs. In an interview one said: 'I was on the saloon deck, and immediately proceeded to my berth to get my lifebelt. In the darkness this was not an easy matter, as the alleys were crowded with soldiers, but there was less excitement than might have been expected under the circumstances.'

US Army doctor, Captain William MacKintosh, was already exhausted when the torpedo struck. There was an outbreak of mumps aboard the ship, and some cases of scarlet fever. MacKintosh had spent the afternoon examining patients and supervising the routine disinfection of the former luxury liner's third-class Smoking Room, which had been requisitioned as an isolation ward. He was just dozing off on his bunk when he was thrown to the floor by a 'very sudden and voluminous mixture of crash and jolt', and found himself in total darkness. The porthole of his cabin had been blown in by the impact of the torpedo, and icy salt water was streaming into his cabin, soaking him as he blundered around. 'I immediately realised what had occurred. My first efforts to reach my flashlight were unsuccessful as I was momentarily disorientated by fright.' Recognising his own signs of fear and panic helped MacKintosh to quickly conquer them. His first thought was to grab his lifejacket. His second was for his patients. He ran to a cabin across the corridor to check on a second lieutenant who had been confined to his bunk ever since the *Tuscania* left Halifax. The explosion had done wonders for the patient, who had now recovered sufficiently to have fled his sickbed for a lifeboat. 'He had gone, and I ran on to the main saloon stairway where men were racing to the boat deck in the dark. The only persons speaking were the ship's officers who were trying to keep things steady and saying that there was no danger immediately. I therefore ran back down to the forward hold to give light to 94 men with mumps I had placed there. I had lost my light after a little and returned to C Deck where I went to room 98 to see if two scarlatina cases had got out. One needed help, and after turning him over to a bunch of men on the next deck I went for my boat crew.' Private James Gurney was one of the seriously ill scarlet fever patients in the ship's isolation ward. Somehow that evening, willing hands got him into a lifeboat.

Within seconds of the explosion, Captain McLean had rattled out commands – all the time fearing that the U-boat might finish off his sitting-duck ship with another torpedo. The emergency generator was fired up, an SOS was transmitted, watertight doors were slammed shut and red submarine-warning rockets fired from the bridge into the night sky. Leo Zimmermann thought they looked 'like spurts of blood'. As soon as the extent of damage to the *Tuscania* was understood, the order came from the bridge, 'Troops to the boat stations. Lifeboats out.' In the darkness the Americans fumbled their way to their assigned lifeboats. On some decks, flares were lit to guide them, illuminating the ship in an unearthly light. Leo Zimmermann says that, at first, speech was 'muffled for a time in fright'. Then the men began to crowd onto the deck where the heavy list to starboard caused many of them to stagger and fall. Some struggled to pull on lifejackets over heavy greatcoats. Mess Steward, John McMahon, reported: 'There was no real panic. I heard soldiers, in the first few moments of the darkness, shouting, "Keep cool. No crushing. You'll get there." The list became gradually worse.' Thirty-six-year-old crewman Thomas Smith rushed to the deck and began lowering the starboard-side lifeboats. He found the soldiers lining up, waiting to get into the boats to which they had been assigned. John McCance, an engine-room storekeeper from Glasgow, had been 17 years at sea and had a clear idea of what to do in such circumstances – he hurried to his locker to collect £16 and six sticks of tobacco he had stashed there.

So far, the casualties had been limited to the section of the ship where the torpedo had struck, but the impact there had been devastating. Yorkshireman J. S. Peters, who served as a 'spare man' in the engine room, reported carnage among the stokers. 'Only two or three got clear out of the 22 on that watch. One chap had a miraculous escape. After the boat was struck – whether it was the force of the explosion or the inrush of water I don't think he right knows himself – he found himself lifted right on top of the boilers, where there was a gangway leading to the deck. That saved him. Another fireman had gone to the engine room for a drink of water, and was on his road back when a watertight door slipped down in front of him just grazing his nose; but that got him off with his life.'

Meanwhile, the rest of convoy HX-20 forged ahead at full speed. On board the *Baltic*, journalist Irvin Cobb had been in a stateroom playing the 'American sport of trying to better two pairs', when an officer entered and said: 'Better come along, you fellows, but come quietly so as not to give alarm or frighten any of the women. Something has happened. The *Tuscania* – she's in trouble.' By the time Cobb reached the deck, the *Tuscania*'s lights – her emergency lights and flares – 'seemed especially brilliant'.

I should say she was not more than a mile from us, almost due aft and a trifle to the left. But in the winter evening the distance increased each passing moment, for we were running away from her as fast as our engines could drive us. We could feel our ship throb under our feet as she picked up speed. It made us feel like cowards. Near at hand a ship was in distress, a ship laden with a precious freightage of American soldier boys, and here we were legging it like a frightened bird, weaving in and out on sharp tacks. We knew, of course, that we were under orders to get safely away if we could in case one of those sea adders, the submarines should attack our convoy. We knew that guardian destroyers would even now be hurrying to the rescue; and we knew land was not many miles away; but all the same, I think I never felt such an object of shame as I felt that first moment when the realization dawned on me that we were fleeing from a stricken vessel instead of hastening back to give what succour we could.

The convoy's eight destroyers quartered the sea, seeking out the enemy U-boat before it could attack the now-fleeing convoy. Beneath the waves Meyer and the crew of *UB-77* 'waited breathlessly' for the shock of depth charges. When nothing came, the U-boat resurfaced to see the stricken *Tuscania* listing heavily to starboard. As HX-20 disappeared into the night a radio operator at the British Admiralty base at Buncrana in the north of Ireland tapped out the order in Morse Code: '*Pigeon, Mosquito* and *Grasshopper* – return to assistance of *Tuscania*.' Swiftly, the three destroyers homed in on the stricken troopship.

His last view of the *Tuscania* was a sight that would haunt Irvin Cobb for the rest of his life. 'Never again will a red rocket fired at night be to me anything except a reminder of the most pitiable, the most heart-racking thing I have ever seen – that poor appeal for help from the sinking *Tuscania* flaming against that foreign sky.'

One *Tuscania* crewman reported that a lifeboat had been lowered from above where the torpedo had pierced the *Tuscania*'s hull, and was driven into the hole by the inrush of water, forming a plug that helped slow down the sinking. But nobody knew how long the *Tuscania* could stay afloat, and even if it did, the emergency masthead lights made it an easy target for a second attack. There was also the danger that panic would overthrow all the experience of the crew and the discipline, but – at first – the emergency drill went as planned. The soldiers knew their assigned stations, quickly assembled at them and waited in line for their allotted boats to be launched. Veteran British officers on board, who had already been torpedoed several times, were reported to have, 'marvelled at the coolness of the men'. Arthur Siplon, of 100th Aero Squadron, was so unfazed by the situation that, when he realised that he wasn't wearing his lifejacket, he decided to go 'some decks below' to fetch it. 'The trip down was made without mishap, for faint lights were still burning. However as I was about to return they went out leaving me in total darkness. I felt my way about and reached the upper companionway. My fingers were feeling along the walls when the lights again came on dim and flickering. As I looked about I saw I was near an office with a grilled window that stood open. It appeared someone left in a hurry, for lying on the desk in the office were stacks of money as though prepared for payday. Glancing quickly at the money, I left in a hurry to regain my place with my boat crew. When I arrived several asked me where I had been. I told them, and also related the information about the money. Two members of my squadron, both Irish and rugged, wanted definite information about the location of the money. I gave them exact directions, and then we were shortly separated.'

Newspaper accounts, based on interviews with survivors, tell of doughboys singing a comic song *Where Do We Go From Here Boys?* as they were waiting in line to get into lifeboats.

> Where do we go from here boys,
> Where do we go from here?
> Slip a pill to Kaiser Bill
> And make him shed a tear.
> And when we see the enemy
> We'll shoot him in the rear.
> Oh, joy, Oh, boy, where do we
> Go from here?

The doughboys were silenced when it was pointed out to them that – as the *Daily Record* puts it – 'the occasion was not one for the indulgence of singing'. But other accounts have the soldiers singing *The Star-Spangled Banner* and *My Country 'Tis of Thee*. Survivors were widely quoted in newspapers as saying that there was 'no panic', but Everett Harpham, of the 20th Engineers, told his brother in a letter home that he 'had not the slightest idea of getting out of the mess alive.' Private David

Rickerd, of A Company, 170th Supply Train, recalls meeting a defeated man from his company: 'He expressed conviction that it was all over with us, and that he did not care much what happened. He went to his station and I to mine. I did not see him again.' Few men were as cool as Private Clarence Bradshaw of the 20th Engineers. While standing on deck, waiting for a lifeboat or the chance to board a destroyer, he pleaded with his officer to be allowed to go back below deck to pick up his rifle. Eventually, he was given permission, and Bradshaw won the distinction of being the only American soldier to survive the sinking of the *Tuscania* who rescued his rifle.

The *Tuscania*'s doughboys had practiced mustering at their allocated lifeboats while crossing the Atlantic – but none of the American officers or men had ever lowered a lifeboat or abandoned ship before. This was the real thing – in the dark, in February, and in the cross-hairs of an enemy periscope. Arthur Siplon recalled: 'All was not well. The ship's crew had evidently little training in the handling of the lifeboats. In addition the ship almost immediately listed badly to the starboard, thus making it difficult to release lifeboats on the opposite side. Some men attempting to take the boats down were spilled into the chilling water like dice from a box. This was caused by lines getting fouled, and then some excited person would cut loose one end with disastrous results. One lifeboat was chopped loose on both ends, and dropped down on a loaded one already in the water.'

The Anchor Line stewardesses made it into a lifeboat mostly filled with soldiers. A *Tuscania* crewman took the tiller. 'There was great difficulty in getting the lifeboat away from the side. The soldiers, somewhat inexperienced in the use of oars, were instructed how to use them and after many efforts we got clear of the *Tuscania*, and avoided the risk of being drawn under should she disappear suddenly.'

First Lieutenant Herbert Bartholf, of the 158th Aero Squadron, found that his men's boat station was directly above where the torpedo had struck, and that the boats or the davits that lowered them were damaged. One that they managed to lower into the sea immediately filled with water. Bartholf abandoned the lifeboat station and finally got his men aboard life rafts that he found in the waist of the ship.

With the *Tuscania* listing steeply to starboard, the lifeboats on the port side rasped their way down the hull into the water, only to be battered into the steel hull by the waves. Oars were broken as the men tried to fend off their little vessels from the ship. Descending lifeboats crashed down on ones already in the water, killing men or throwing them into the sea. First Lieutenant Donald Smith said: 'I saw another boat dropped so that it hung perpendicular, spilling the 25 or more occupants into the water like sacks of beans, then went down stern first among them. At least half our loss must have been due to men being crushed by falling lifeboats, by getting to the water and being crushed between boats and the side of the liner.'

Edward Lauer had groped his way through the dark to reach his assigned lifeboat station, only to find that the lowering of the boats had descended into chaos. 'The first lifeboat let down went wrong, ropes tore and plunged into the water, with men catapulting into the sea. Our second lifeboat was let down correctly, but when the crew reached the bottom, they unhooked the boat and left us. I waited for the next lifeboat and when it reached our deck, found it filled with exception of four seats. When I tried jumping over the rail, one of the officers held us back with a menacing pistol. As soon as the boat reached water's edge, I noted the empty seat, jumped over the rail and slid down the rope as they were leaving the side of the *Tuscania*. The lifeboat was about ten feet from the ship when I reached the water, so I braced my foot against the steel plate and swung into the lifeboat with one foot. Whitey Hansen, who followed me down the rope, also swung into the lifeboat, as I was still holding onto the rope. Stanley Kujawa, who went down into the water with the torn rope was yelling between the ship and lifeboat, so Whitey and I pulled him into the lifeboat.' The ship's heavy list meant that the surviving boats on the starboard side had swung outwards from the gunwale, and were too far out to jump into. Men plunged into the sea. Any lifeboat that drifted aft, and into the still churning propeller, was doomed.

Corporal Thomas Evans was relieved to see Frank Sharpe, his boyhood friend from North Wales, pulling away from the *Tuscania* in a lifeboat. Evans was still stuck on the sinking ship, but it was Frank Sharpe, not Evans, who would die that night. The lifeboat that James Purington climbed into with 40 others capsized, and they were all thrown into the water. Purington grabbed hold of two oars that he found lashed together and floating in the sea. He hung onto them for three hours in the freezing February water before he was picked up. Privates Clarence Norgren and Roy Muncaster, of the 20th Engineers, were helping launch a lifeboat when Ondis Powell, an acquaintance of Norgren's, attempted to slide down a rope. Norgren recalled: 'Just after he went over the side I heard a cry and I believe he fell into the water. Did not see him again.' Norgren and Muncaster both made it safely into lifeboats. Interviewed more than a decade later, Harry Schostak of Chicago remembered: 'I could see men in the water trying to swim to lifeboats that stayed afloat. It was an awful thing to hear the men screaming for help and I was tempted to leap in myself because the ship was listing more to the starboard every minute. I kept my head, however, and it was a lucky thing that I did.' From their lifeboat, the two Anchor Line stewardesses, Mary Carson and Flora Collins, saw men plunge from a badly lowered lifeboat into the sea. The men on the stewardesses' boat pulled some aboard, but many of those in the water had been killed by lifeboats falling on them.

First Lieutenant Warren T. Smith had led his men of the 6th Battalion, 20th Engineers, to Lifeboat Station 12 on B Deck.

Their 74-capacity lifeboat was hanging at a dangerous pitch, but men kept sliding down ropes to get to it until it was dangerously overcrowded. 'Suddenly the rope at the upper end gave way and we fell to the water bodily. That rope was probably cut but I am not certain of this. We struck the *Tuscania* violently several times before being able to push off as it was difficult to extricate the oars on account of the crowded condition. In time we rowed about 200 yards away where we were picked up by the British destroyer *Grasshopper*, after about 40 minutes or about 6.50 pm.' Clarence Krueger's squad waited an hour for their turn to get into a lifeboat. But when their time came, the lowering ropes were hopelessly tangled. 'Several of the boys were in the boat trying to lower it evenly. Then without any warning the rope of one end gave way and the occupants of the boat were precipitated into the cold, icy water. The second shared the same fate, thus leaving our company without means of escape.' Once he'd lowered three boats for American soldiers, boatswain's mate Thomas Smith ran to his own designated lifeboat to find that it had been blown away. He eventually launched a life raft and was able to pull from the water fourteen soldiers and two of the *Tuscania*'s crew.

❦

The effect of a warm body being suddenly plunged into cold water can be fatal. Any temperature below 15 degrees centigrade pumps up the heart rate of anyone thrown into the sea, causing them to hyperventilate and panic. Islay Coastguard, Duncan Jones, reckons the temperature of the sea in these waters in February to have been just eight degrees. 'The first thing that happens when you hit cold water is to take a sharp intake of breath as cold water shock hits you. You can't help it but you gasp for air, and you don't have to take in much water into your lungs to drown you. I'm not a medical man, but I think it can be as little as half a pint. Then there's the cold. The body takes all the blood from the extremities to the core to try and preserve the core. That just takes about five minutes in the water at that temperature, and from then on your arms and your legs just stop working properly. After half an hour in the water with nothing to keep you afloat you'd be lucky to be alive.'

❧

Army doctor, Lieutenant Joseph C. Kimball, had seen lifeboat 14A successfully launched with one soldier in it – and watched it begin to drift away as the man was unable to control it. Kimball threw the man a rope and together they managed to pull the lifeboat back alongside the liner's hull, but found his anxious men reluctant to slide down the rope into it. He led the way, but a wave pulled the lifeboat from beneath him and he slid into the sea. He grabbed hold of the lifeboat's lifelines and hung on. Kimball's watch was in his trouser pocket. Immersed in salt water, it stopped immediately. Men began to descend after him and pulled him into the boat. Soon there were about 60 men on board, and they pushed off from the slowly sinking *Tuscania*. One of the men on board was the ship's 3rd Engineer, who put out a sea anchor to stop them being blown by the stiff southerly breeze far from where the SOS had been sent out. Lieutenant George Newton Thall, who had been assiduously reading a book about fighting in No Man's Land when the torpedo struck, now found himself in a very different danger – dangling on a rope over a rough and chilly sea. Much to Thall's surprise he fell into a lifeboat which was loaded perilously deep in the waterline with 65 men on board. After three hours they were picked up by a trawler.

John McMahon, the 17-year-old mess steward, had made it into one of the first lifeboats to be launched. 'The sea was pretty rough, and it was bitterly cold. There were 53 in my boat, including two stewardesses. We rowed off quickly. We saw one or two men struggling in the sea – I suppose they must have jumped into the water – but we could not take them aboard; we could not have held another one in our boat. We were four and a half hours before we were picked up by a British armed patrol.' One of the stewardesses aboard that lifeboat told of being rescued. 'The darkness, which was quickly falling and the heavy sea running, made it quite awesome. After being afloat some forty minutes a destroyer appeared, and we were taken aboard. The transference of the boat's company to the warship was carried through with great difficulties but, thanks to the conduct of the man-of-war's men, it was carried through and with the greatest care.' The destroyer soon had 350 survivors on board, several of whom were injured. And then, another soul was rescued. The stewardess related: 'In the darkness we discovered a man clinging to an upturned boat, and owing to the heavy seas running, his rescue was not readily effected. However, the man-of-war's men eventually succeeded in throwing a lifeline and pulling him aboard.'

By about 7.00 pm all the lifeboats that could be launched were in the water, but the majority of crew and soldiers were still on board the foundering *Tuscania*. Their only hope was that the destroyers could rescue them. Then out of the darkness, one appeared. The men on the *Tuscania* began to cheer. According to Harry Schostak, the *Mosquito* circled the liner three or four times, dropping depth charges against any lurking U-boat before coming alongside to take men off. The *Mosquito* was skippered by Commander Thomas Balfour Fellowes. His first act on reaching the stricken transport was to pick up survivors clinging to an upturned lifeboat.

❧

Seconds after firing her torpedoes, the *UB-77* had found a destroyer bearing down on her and had dived to 30 metres. Twenty minutes, and a few underwater nautical miles later, at 7.58 pm, she surfaced to watch the death throes of her prey, which now had a severe list to starboard with her stern deep in the water. Meyer recalled: 'It looked like a spectre of a horse rearing its hind legs. The doomed ship was visible to us only because of the searchlights of the destroyers. It was like sitting in a motion picture theatre, viewing a silent film drama, except that we could not see a single human soul. This was probably due to the fact that we were too far away and because the *Tuscania*'s lifeboats were lowered on the port side, while we were on the starboard side. Even stranger, we did not know the identity of our victim. The minutes seemed like days before we found out, when the *Tuscania* gave out frantic signals – its name, gross tonnage and owner, Anchor Line, Glasgow. We suddenly realised that we had hit a much bigger vessel than we had first surmised.'

※

As *Mosquito* picked up men from the water, a torpedo passed under her stern. Fellowes ordered his vessel full speed ahead to where he believed the U-boat to be, and dropped a depth charge. 'I thought that this might at least frighten off the submarine and I believe that it may have done so as she gave no further trouble, but I fear that the explosion of the depth charge caused some further alarm on-board the *Tuscania* as it was thought she had been struck by another torpedo.' The commanders of the three destroyers now prepared to come alongside the *Tuscania*. It would make them sitting ducks for the U-boat and was an enormous risk. Before coming alongside, the *Grasshopper* encountered the lifeboat that Edward Lauer had scrambled into. Lauer and his comrades had previously attempted to hail another destroyer, but it had failed to see them in the dark. The *Grasshopper*, captained by Glasgow-born John Morrison Smith, now approached the *Tuscania* on her port side, and men on the troopship's deck slithered down ropes onto her. The small destroyer was soon overloaded, and turned for Londonderry with between 500 and 600 survivors aboard.

The *Mosquito* and *Pigeon* carried on in the desperate attempt to evacuate the *Tuscania*. The *Mosquito* pulled alongside the troopship's port side around 6.50 pm, according to Captain Otis K. Sadtler of the US Signal Corps. She took off about 300 officers and men. The 567-foot-long, 14,348-gross-ton *Tuscania* dwarfed the Royal Navy's destroyers that had rushed to her aid. They were less than half the troopship's length, low in the water and displaced less than 1,000 tons. For a frightened doughboy who had never been to sea before, it was a long way down from his muster station high on the *Tuscania* to the plunging and rolling deck of a little destroyer.

Men slithered down ropes onto decks and into the arms of sailors who stowed them away in every available space of the crowded destroyers. William Robertson of Coos Bay, Oregon, was sliding down a rescue rope onto a destroyer when it began to steam away. When he could hang on no more, he expected to fall to his death in the water, but landed on an overturned lifeboat from where he was rescued. Hundreds were saved that night, but for many men already in the water the arrival of the destroyers was a death sentence. One of the *Tuscania*'s engine-room crew witnessed how the rescuing ships crushed men in the water to death. 'Flashlights were playing all around, and scores of men were in the water. A destroyer coming close in to pick them up cracked a lifeboat against the side of the ship, and it wasn't a pleasing sight.' Arthur Siplon witnessed the horror from a lifeboat that he'd clambered into. In an account written years later for his five children, he recalled men thrown from badly lowered lifeboats being drawn into destroyer propellers, or being crushed between the two ships. Harold Robinson, of the 20th Engineers, recalled an agonising two-hour wait to be rescued. He said the soldiers were quiet and orderly but that the wait 'gave me time for lots of thought' and made him 'realize how sweet life really is.' Robinson and about 700 others got aboard one of the destroyers.

Soldiers had despaired when the first destroyer had pulled away. Since his squad had failed to launch their lifeboats, Clarence F. Krueger, of 107th Supply Train, had experienced three hours of 'terrible agony, waiting for death', and was now plunged into deeper gloom. 'It was awful watching the destroyer pulling away leaving the rest of us to our fate. Not a word was spoken. Every man was too busy with his own thoughts. All that could be heard was the splashing of water below us. Then out of the darkness, to our surprise and joy, another British destroyer, which I learned after was named the *Pigeon*, came up along the starboard side. It was about 7.45 when the *Pigeon* came alongside the troopship's starboard side, and the evacuation of the now badly listing *Tuscania* continued. Lieutenant Eddis, the *Pigeon*'s commander, had ropes thrown up onto the decks of the *Tuscania*. Many men slid down them to safety but, as Clarence Krueger recalled, it was a hazardous business, 'on account of the sudden storm that was raging at sea. Several of the boys lost their lives trying to reach the destroyer.'

Captain Charles E. Hetrick, who commanded a company of the 20th Engineers, had found all but two of his assigned lifeboats useless. Although he got some men away, most of his company was still stranded on the *Tuscania*. He watched the arrival of the *Pigeon* with relief, while his men stood at ease in ranks singing popular songs, led by his sergeant, Archie Moore. The *Pigeon* made fast on the *Tuscania*'s starboard side and Captain Hetrick marched his men to the stricken ship's B Deck where they clambered along lines to the destroyer and safety. Also saved by the *Pigeon* – the last destroyer to come alongside the *Tuscania* – was Worth L. Bushey, a 20-year-old serving with a medical unit of the 32nd Division. There was no rest for Bushey on board the *Pigeon*, as he and two colleagues helped a doctor on board the *Pigeon* 'fix up four men who were smashed up in a lifeboat'.

The men who had fallen into the water between the hulls

of the *Tuscania* and the *Pigeon* were in simultaneous danger of being drowned, frozen or crushed to death, but the Adjutant of the 20th Engineers, Captain James Farrin, helped fish the lucky ones from the water onto the *Pigeon* with ropes. Farrin reported that there were now so many men crammed on the *Pigeon* that Lt Commander Eddis pumped out 40 tons of oil to compensate for the weight of the extra passengers. In just 30 minutes about 750 men and 14 officers had slid down ropes to what they believed was safety.

An hour after torpedoing the *Tuscania*, Meyer resolved to attack again, 'In order to hasten the steamer's sinking', he would later tell a survivor. His U-boat dived to 11 metres and closed in on the *Tuscania*'s port side. He surfaced, and fired a torpedo from his number four tube. At that moment a destroyer made full steam in the *UB-77*'s direction and, believing that he had been sighted, Meyer ordered a crash dive. He had wrongly calculated that the *Tuscania* was still moving at a rate of two knots and aimed slightly ahead of her, therefore missing his now helpless and wallowing target. But the torpedo was now plunging towards a destroyer.

Captain Sadtler of the Signal Corps, who had watched 300 men being evacuated from the *Tuscania* by the *Mosquito*, was now amongst the nearly 800 survivors who thronged the decks of the overloaded *Pigeon*. Sadtler caught sight of the wake of Meyer's torpedo as it hurtled towards him, and believed it only missed by about four yards. 'It was due entirely to the foresight of the Commander of the *Pigeon* in signalling greater speed rather than half speed ahead that the torpedo missed her mark, and prevented thereby many casualties.' Engineer Adjutant, Captain Farrin, put the *UB-77*'s near-miss at just two yards.

Meyer resurfaced a considerable distance away. Through his binoculars he could see the destroyers and smaller craft steaming about looking for survivors. His radio operator reported that the air waves were crowded with messages in Morse code, but that there were no longer distress calls coming from the *Tuscania*. 'I assume that she had foundered. During the night we cruised backwards and forwards to the southward of the Rhinns of Islay.'

If the Royal Navy let Kapitän Meyer and the crew of *UB*-77 off the hook, British newspapers were less forgiving. The news agency, *Associated Press*, opined that: 'The fact that no other attack was made on any other ships suggests that the U-Boat had been sunk.' And Glasgow's *Evening Times* reported: 'An interview with one of the crew of the rescuing vessels strengthens the conviction that, after the submarine tried to torpedo the first rescuing destroyer, she was sunk shortly afterwards by another destroyer which located her position and dashed up and settled her with a heavy bomb.' There is a maxim that journalists are advised to follow: 'Wishing does not make it so.' Meyer and the *UB*-77 not only survived to fight another day, but survived the war.

※

Many men, like Private Arthur Siplon, were left stranded by the destroyers on the decks of the foundering *Tuscania*. 'About nine o'clock a cry went around the ship. It was, "Every man for himself." It appeared no more destroyers were coming. A pal of mine known as "Ragfoot" Smith, and some other boys wanted to go to the deck above and try and lower a boat.'

Fearing being flung into the sea, Siplon and his comrades managed to lower a boat on the starboard side, which because of the list was now close to the surface of the sea. Siplon and 'Ragfoot' volunteered to slide down to it first. 'We reached the water without mishap. As we hit the water, the whole side seemed to release men who wanted to go with us. The lifeboat according to our information was designed to carry 48 persons. We were certain we had at least sixty anxious passengers aboard. It appeared this was the last boat to get away, and we were the last men to leave the ship.' The practical foresters, Sergeant Harpham, from Oregon, and his old buddy, Colorado-born Roy Muncaster, had spent more than an hour struggling with the ropes and pulleys to launch lifeboats for other men. Eventually they slid down a rope into what they believed to be the last boat to leave the foundering liner. They pulled away as fast as they could for fear of being sucked into the whirlpool that the *Tuscania* would create as she plunged to the bottom of the sea.

The crewmen and soldiers who had made it into still-serviceable lifeboats were now bobbing about on a rough sea, in the dark at the mercy of wave, wind and tide. The *Tuscania*'s Second Officer, G. K. Lynas, was in a lifeboat with about 40 others when the little craft lurched into something hard on the surface. 'When I looked round, here's the submarine lying awash – up to see what dirty work he had done. What did we do? What could we do? We simply carried on, and soon got picked up. Everybody behaved splendidly.' That strange meeting is not recorded in Kapitän Meyer's accounts of the sinking.

The British, American and German time-zones the survivors operated under confuse the actual time the *Tuscania* finally went down, but it is likely to have been about 9.00 pm, a little more than three hours after she was torpedoed. It was just three years and two days since she had embarked on her maiden voyage. Many of the men in the lifeboats witnessed the *Tuscania*'s final moments. For Arthur Siplon the sight was unforgettable. 'We got free from the ship, by a couple of hundred yards, when a cry went up, from those who still had their eyes on the *Tuscania*. They screamed, "She's going down", and we watched her die. Our mighty ship was leaving us. Just a few short hours ago she was moving majestically towards Liverpool, England. Now the bow was lowered, throwing its monstrous stern into the air.

There it briefly paused, its stark silhouette against the stormy sky – then with a muffled explosion slid ignominiously below darkened waters. It left us with an eerie and lonesome feeling.' Sergeant Everett Harpham recalled: 'I saw the big ship go down and one could have heard the roar and rush of water upon her upper deck for miles. I do not believe that there was a living soul aboard when she plunged as all had previously taken to the lifeboats or were rescued by the destroyers.'

Fourteen-year-old crewman Patrick Cox was in a lifeboat with another seaman, a US Army captain and about 50 enlisted men. They were drifting in the direction of a light when they heard a voice cry 'Help' in the darkness. With difficulty they located another crewman, Thomas Campbell, who'd been in the water for two-and-a-half hours. He was wearing a lifejacket and was clutching an oar under his chin to keep his head out of the waves. Cox and the Americans pulled the frozen sailor aboard.

After an hour of wallowing around in the dark, Edward Lauer's lifeboat was picked up by HMS *Grasshopper*. 'The crew gave us hot soup, tea, bread and whiskey – they even took their upper clothing off and gave them to the survivors who were wet. They rescued about 300 from lifeboats, also some who had jumped into the sea.' Lauer and the other survivors were landed in Londonderry in Ireland later that night.

On hearing of the disaster the British Admiralty office in Larne had been quick to send five or six armed trawlers to the scene, among them *Cardiff Castle*, *Corrie Roy*, *Gloria* and *Elf King*. Requisitioned early in the war, these boats with their ex-fishermen skippers and crews were under direct Royal Navy command. Low in the water, they were well suited to picking up survivors.

Private Richard Poteet, of the 6th Battalion, 20th Engineers, had made it into a lifeboat with others including his F Company comrades, Privates Alpha Rice and Charles Wayne. But only yards from the *Tuscania* their lifeboat capsized and they were

all thrown into the water. Poteet never saw Rice again, but he
and Charles Wayne were able to swim back to the lifeboat and
cling on to its sides. Somehow, although he lost consciousness,
Poteet was still clinging on three hours later and was hauled
aboard the *Cardiff Castle*. Charles Wayne had vanished from
the lifeboat. Among others rescued by the *Cardiff Castle* were
Lieutenant Herbert Bartholf and a dozen men of the 158th
Aero Squadron who had taken to a life-raft when they had been
unable to launch their assigned lifeboat. They had been tossed
around helplessly on the sea for two hours before being rescued.

Captain MacKintosh, the US Army doctor, who had been
treating patients right up to the moment he had finally scrambled aboard a lifeboat, had also been soaked and buffeted by a
choppy sea before being – with some difficulty – dragged aboard
the *Cardiff Castle*. MacKintosh found that there were now 120
survivors packed aboard the trawler, and was appointed 'ship's
doctor' until the vessel reached Larne Harbour at about 5.00
am. He reported that some of the men were 'nearly gone' and
others 'beyond help'. 'I was taken care of by Miss Thompson,
Royal Terrace, Larne Harbour, and have never been treated
with such fine delicacy and sincere hospitality before in my life.'

Lieutenant Kimball and the sixty reluctant soldiers that he
had led down to lifeboat 14A were picked up as they drifted
around helplessly by trawler *Corrie Roy*. Kimball looked at his
sodden watch. It had stopped at 6.30 pm. He asked the time;
it was now 11.35. Private James Purington was one of about
forty men who were thrown out of their lifeboat when it was
swamped by the heavy seas. At first he grabbed a couple of
oars and clung onto them until he found a hefty plank that offered more buoyancy. After what he believed was three hours,
tortured by terrible cramps and thinking himself 'all in', he was
hauled out the water semi-conscious by the crew of a trawler.
As the former New Hampshire University student was wrapped
in blankets and plied with hot drinks, the sailors told him that

there were many dead bodies floating around. Purington had no idea what had happened to the 40 men who went into the water with him.

The lifeboat that Lieutenant Franklin Foltz was in had become so overcrowded that men could only stand up in it. Waves constantly broke over it and only continual bailing for many hours kept the boat afloat. Flares twice failed to attract passing destroyers and the little craft was being swept dangerously close to the cliffs of the Oa when Foltz spotted a trawler. 'We had no more flares, but I had my flashlight and believe me, it sure winked S.O.S. He finally saw us and pulled alongside, and we got our sick men on board and then went up ourselves. The trawler was the finest ship I ever saw in my life. I don't believe I was ever happier than I was right then.'

Those in the lifeboats picked up by destroyers and naval trawlers were the lucky ones. A destroyer slid past the lifeboat that Everett Harpham and Roy Muncaster shared with as many as 60 others. A Royal Navy officer shouted to them: 'Float around a while boys. We'll pick you up later.' But the destroyer never came back. It was pitch-black, the sea was rough and, as that bitterly cold February night wore on, the hopes of survivors who had not been picked up by destroyers or trawlers were fading. Arthur Siplon recalled: 'It was a cold and stormy night into which we were cast. The bottom of the lifeboat quickly filled with water. We found but three oars with which to control the unwieldy craft. There was a collapsible top, about a foot high, which could be forced up. This helped some with the buffeting waves. None of the men were dressed to withstand the cold, or the perishing waves that broke over them. We had no idea where we were headed. While we could see lights in various places we had none to direct would-be rescuers in our direction. We learned later that many were saved by searchers from the British destroyers but our boat was not seen by them.'

New York Aero Squadron corporal, Thomas Conway, was in a bad way. He had seriously ripped his hands and arms sliding down a rope into a lifeboat, and had inhaled fuel oil. Today, members of his family maintain that he spent three days in the hostile sea before his lifeboat was picked up by a trawler. His hands and arms were scarred for life, but he would tell his future wife that two survivors died on his lifeboat. Despite the desperate search by the destroyers and trawlers, not all the lifeboats were found. Wind and tides fated these boats – crammed with nearly 400 exhausted and frozen men – to be driven inexorably towards the sea cliffs of the Mull of Oa, the rugged peninsula that forms the southwest tip of Islay. One of the places they would come ashore was the tiny bay of Port nan Gallon. Ileachs of a fanciful nature claim that it is called that because a Spanish Armada galleon was wrecked there. The more likely origin of the name is that early map-makers wrote the Gaelic word 'Gaillionn' phonetically – and *Port nan Gaillionn* means 'Bay of the Tempests'. But whatever the origin of the name – storm-wrecked galleon or bay of tempests – they were heading for disaster.

4

The Boiling Angry Sea

Friends, who set forth at our side,
Falter, are lost in the storm.
We, we only, are left!

Matthew Arnold, *Rugby Chapel*

Adrift on the bitterly cold and stormy sea, doughboys and sailors fought to survive. Sixty men were crammed into that last lifeboat that Arthur Siplon and 'Ragfoot' Smith had managed to launch. No engine, no sail, and only three oars between them to steer the overladen craft – not that they knew where they were or where to go. Siplon and his companions were entirely at the mercy of the sea, and they were heading for Islay's most dangerous coast. The intensity of the storm increased and, with no steerage, the boat was pitched from crest to crest. 'Midnight came without relief, and one of many who was ailing died of exposure.' In the early hours of the morning Siplon and his companions could see land ahead and hear the roar of surf. 'The sound of it increased as we moved closer, like a dire warning of imminent disaster.'

Inexperienced and untrained, there was nothing Siplon, Smith and the others could do but wait to be driven to disaster on the coast. But on another lifeboat, the proximity of such a fatal shore spurred the frozen and exhausted Lieutenant Donald Smith into furious activity. When the first destroyer had left the *Tuscania*, Smith had shimmied down a rope and swum to a collapsible lifeboat that was floating off the troopship's stern. Neither he nor the two enlisted men in the boat with him had a faintest clue about sea survival. 'We shivered in that boat for five hours because I didn't know how to light the flares. I found them right away, although they were under water, and wasted a dozen trying to light one. It was only when we were fast approaching the rocks of Islay island that I made a thorough search for the matches that I knew were there somewhere (the boat was full over the seats but her air tanks kept her afloat) finding them in a lantern in a tin box, which took me twenty minutes to cut open because I didn't know the secret of opening them and couldn't find it in the dark and cold. With a match I read the flare directions (they are scratched, not lighted, but several operations are necessary) and in a short time was picked up by a trawler at exactly 12 midnight.' Failure to light that match, set off that flare, and attract a trawler that plucked them from the sea would almost certainly have condemned Smith and his companions to being dashed to their deaths beneath the cliffs of the Oa, or drowned in its freezing waters. That was the fate of the majority of men on the other lifeboats.

The Oa is the peninsula that forms the most southerly point of Islay. Today you are more like to encounter a golden eagle or a feral goat on the Oa than a farmer, but atop precipitous cliffs that have their rocky feet in the sea, people have raised crops and families since Neolithic times. For centuries it was a stronghold of the Gaelic language, and the name, Oa, is an Anglicisation of the Gaelic word for 'headland' – *Obha*. Once among the most densely populated districts of Islay, by 1918 clearance by landlords had reduced it to a lonely landscape of isolated farms. The Oa's hardy farmers were the first Ileachs to learn of the *Tuscania*'s fate, as the lifeboats were dashed into the merciless skerries, crags and stacks where the sea meets the land. But earlier that night, in Port Ellen, schoolgirl Isabelle Macgilvary had looked up at the sky and felt a sense of foreboding. 'We saw red flashes or flares off the coast of the Oa and wondered about them at the time.'

By about 1.00 am – nearly six hours after the *Tuscania* was torpedoed – Everett Harpham and Roy Muncaster of the 20th

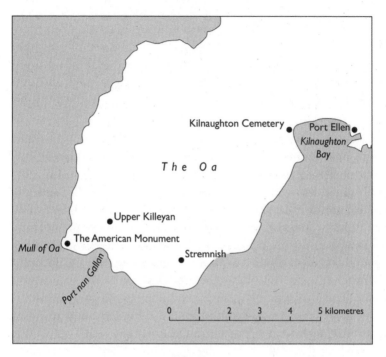

The Oa

Engineers were desperately trying to row their frail lifeboat away from the seething waves that were smashing into the rocks of the Oa. When they first glimpsed the land through the darkness they thought they were heading for a wooded island, before realising what they were seeing were cliffs. An officer hurled his flashlight ashore, and the men on board could see white foam dashing high on the rocks.

Harpham described the fight with the sea. 'We tried to row away, but we had drifted so near that the breakers were taking us in faster than we would row in the overcrowded boat. Muncaster was handling the oars when the boat struck the rocks and was very cool and courageous all through the terrible experience. I was very sick in the lifeboat myself and could do nothing but dip water to keep us from foundering. Just before we struck Roy slapped me on the back and said, "Cheer up Harp, we will get the Kaiser yet." That was the last I heard him say. Finally our boat struck a rock with a terrific crash and broke in a dozen pieces and after that it was every man for himself.'

Roy Muncaster, born to parents who had emigrated to Colorado from England, was a tall, fit, blue-eyed, cheerful American doughboy. His friend, Sergeant Harpham, remembered that he hadn't been wearing a lifejacket. Later that day, Muncaster was found drowned. Arthur Siplon, of the100th Aero Squadron, was also on a lifeboat that was hurled onto the coast. 'We were suddenly caught up by a heave and sent crashing into an immense rock. The lifeboat turned upside down throwing everyone into the boiling, angry sea. As I reached the surface the boat was in front . . . bottom side up. I could hear men screaming and praying all about me. With a great effort I scrambled up on the bottom of the boat. My pal, Wilbur Clark, also of Michigan came up near me. He too reached a place on the boat, we were the only ones to make it. But just in a brief moment a huge wave drove us both off, and into the raging sea again. It was then a matter of being buffeted about against bruising rocks, washed in with the waves and out with the undertow.'

Siplon had no idea of how long he spent being battered, bruised and half-drowned by the sea. Fortunately, he got no blow to the head and remained conscious. 'When it seemed my last breath was reached, when the next one would be my final one, I was struck forcibly in the chest. I grabbed with both hands. As the big wave went out I found I was on a point of rock near shore. I gripped it with all my waning strength, and tried to recover my breath. As the next wave went out a dark object was thrown up near me. It was another survivor; he was alive, for in the brief quiet of the receding wave I could faintly hear him offering up a prayer. He could hardly move, but I got him up on the rock with me. Though I was badly battered, two big cuts on my head, and my body bleeding in many places, my mind remained alert. Thinking that the tide might rise, I placed the arms of the boy over the rock to hold him on, and then scrambled on my hands and knees to the solid wall of rock that appeared to be the shore line. Crawling about I found a crevice in the rock. Working up into the crevice I found a small cave well above the waterline, it appeared somewhat like a shelf with a three foot opening. Upon returning to the boy we managed slowly, and painfully, to reach the cave together. Here we tried to protect ourselves against the bitter cold. We snuggled up into each other's arms like a couple of cub bears, to keep from freezing to death.'

Fourteen-year-old crewman Patrick Cox and Thomas Campbell, the *Tuscania* fireman whom Cox had earlier pulled from the sea, were thrown into the breakers when their lifeboat smashed against the Oa. Campbell found himself in the water again, close to another exhausted seaman. 'I'm finished, Tom,' the man said, and despite Campbell's encouragement, died in the water. Cox and Campbell both made it ashore alive, and later had the melancholy task of identifying the dead sailor's body.

Private Boyd Hancock of the 20th Engineers had two lucky escapes. He had been in the water an hour when George Volz reached from a lifeboat and dragged him in. Volz, a 23-year-old who had been an agricultural student at the University of Minnesota before joining the 107th Engineers, jumped into the water to help at least one other man into the lifeboat, and was later decorated for his actions. Although the only *Tuscania* crewman in the boat was washed overboard, the American soldiers managed to land on the Oa in the middle of the night, and Hancock, Volz and the others struggled ashore and huddled down until daybreak.

Leo Terzia, of the 20th Engineers, had been the first in his Company down the rope into his assigned lifeboat. He hadn't seen his brother, Fris, standing in line behind him and thought he must have been in the boat when it was lowered into the water. As the lifeboat pulled away from the *Tuscania*, Leo was devastated not to find Fris on board.

For Leo the struggle for survival had just begun. 'We were torpedoed at 6.10 pm and landed at just about 5 am after fighting the rocks for about eight hours. Out of some seven or eight lifeboats our raft was the only one that made a landing without being smashed to pieces against the rocks, but we sure had to do some fighting. We had 32 men on our boat when we left the *Tuscania* and we landed the whole bunch safely. The other boats that left alongside our boat with men aboard would show up with less than half living after being smashed against the rocks. I saw more horrible sights than I expect to ever see again. I believe that nearly all the missing were accounted for as dead near the spot where I landed and, of course, this fact made me think that nearly all the rest met the same fate. I did not close my eyes for five long nights.'

In February the water temperature is almost at its coldest in the seas around Islay – a fraction over eight degrees centigrade. That's cold enough to kill a man by hypothermia in about an hour. But before that happens, as we have seen, the body becomes increasing incapacitated as the brain shuts down the muscles of the limbs in order to protect the body's inner core temperature. Above all, the brain's mission is to keep the body's core temperature at 36.9 degrees centigrade. As it does so, a freezing man loses full use of his hands, arms and legs – and the ability to clasp onto a float, grab hold of a rock, or stagger ashore. A man's heavy, exhausted limbs can cause him to drown before the hypothermia kills him.

The desperate shivering men lucky enough to cast up alive on the shore of the Oa were saved by a hard-wired human survival instinct. Receptors on their freezing skin prompted their brains to cause muscles throughout their bodies to vigorously expand and contract, causing the survivors to shudder uncontrollably and their teeth to chatter. It was the heat created by this shivering that was keeping Arthur Siplon and Everett Harpham alive. Harpham was one of nine from his lifeboat who had been washed ashore, 'some badly injured and all nearly drowned'. He wrote to a friend in America telling him: 'We laid together by a large rock, in the wind, and had to listen to the moans and groans of our dying comrades till daylight. About twenty corpses had washed ashore beside us when daylight came and we were rescued by a Highlander.'

Later in life, Arthur Siplon described the scene in an account he wrote for his five children. 'When the first streaks of daylight appeared we saw a light moving in the distance. We called out as loudly as we could, and the light started moving in our direction. It finally arrived, and proved to be a friendly Scotch farmer, who lived close by. He told us we were on the island of Islay, off the coast of Scotland, and had landed on the most rocky, and dangerous part of the whole coastline. When daylight arrived a terrible sight met our eyes. Many dead bodies were washing about by the sea. A number of men were badly injured with broken arms or legs, or other injuries. My close pal, Wilbur Clark, who shared a brief moment with me on the upturned boat was among the lifeless forms, and "Ragfoot" Smith too, was numbered among them.' The farmer guided Siplon and the others to his home, the fittest helping the most badly injured. Once there, his family fed the exhausted men. 'His wife made scones on an ancient fireplace, fired with peat. With the scones she served hot invigorating tea, until her supply was completely exhausted.'

Sometime on that terrible night Robert Morrison, the farmer of Upper Killeyan, had waded out into the surf 'up to his neck' to throw a rope to two men clinging to a storm-lashed rock, and hauled them ashore. He then climbed halfway up a 250-foot cliff to rescue a soldier who had clambered there to get away from the sea, but was almost too exhausted to hold on. Robert Morrison carried him down on his back as he would have a stranded sheep. An American Red Cross officer later described Morrison as 'one of the greatest heroes I have ever heard of'. That night, Robert's sisters, Annie and Betsy, spent six hours baking scones to feed the exhausted and starving survivors. Meanwhile, Duncan Campbell, of Stremnish on the southeast of the Oa, pulled a half-drowned American from a cliff-face he had been cast up upon, dragged him to safety and helped him to his house, where thirteen other survivors sheltered that night.

❧

At 6 am on the morning that followed the sinking of the *Tuscania*, Isabelle Macgilvary, who had seen the red distress flares in the sky the previous night, was woken by her mother to a horror story. Bodies were being washed ashore and her father had joined other local men in the search for survivors. 'That was a very distressful day for everybody. I don't think any survivors came in at Port Ellen but bodies did. My father with his small cart conveyed some of these to the Drill Hall in the back road. He found a small black man up at the top of the Ard and was able to carry him unaided to the cart he was so slight. That affected my father very deeply, he had to come home for a while.' Isabelle Macgilvary's account gives a detailed description of the courage and fortitude of the Morrisons of Upper Killeyan. 'That night they earned the gratitude of the American people by feeding the survivors. As more came in the women went on baking all night. At that time flour was bought in bags of 10 stones. The brothers set out, one to look for men on the beach and help them up and the other to rouse neighbours. There were no telephones in Islay in 1918. Robert Morrison, with his lantern, was able to rescue a party from a very dangerous situation – they had clambered up a rock face that was apart from the cliff. He got them before they reached the top of it. His experience of rescuing sheep and cattle taught him the only safe way down. For what they did that night the men were awarded gold medals and Betsy and Annie got gold wristwatches.'

Robert Morrison was undoubtedly the 'kind farmer' who rescued Arthur Siplon from the shore. There may have been as many as 90 survivors crammed into his farmhouse that night, of whom two died, despite the care of Robert's brother and sisters. In the morning, Siplon and the other survivors were shepherded from the Morrisons' Killeyan farm to Port Ellen, the nearest village. Those who could walked, while the badly injured were dragged along in two-wheeled carts, but at least one soldier, Private Fred Benefiel of the 20th Engineers, was too ill to be moved. Of the 'at least 60' men who had been on his lifeboat, Arthur Siplon believed that only six survived. 'We suffered the greatest loss of life, as far as known, from any boat that reached the shore.'

The two small hotels in Port Ellen were quickly filled and many men were billeted with local families. Siplon recalled: 'The kindly folks of the village of Port Ellen proved to be angels of mercy. Many of the mothers gave up the best clothes of husbands and sons, most of them away to war.'

About 130 Americans had reached the shore of Islay alive that night. The *Oban Times* noted that the lifeboats 'fared very unequally on touching land', and reported that two had beached unscathed, at Killeyan and at Port Ellen. The boat that landed at Port Ellen is said on Islay to have been piloted in there by local man Duncan MacDonald, the son of a Portnahaven fisherman. The *Tuscania*'s crew-list confirms that a 24-year-old 'Scotch' man of that name served on the vessel as an electrician. One story even has it that MacDonald threatened the American soldiers on the lifeboat with a pistol to stop them attempting to land earlier, on the rocky coast of the Oa.

Dougie MacDougall, 95 at the time of writing this book, tells that his grandfather (also Dougie MacDougall) was the deckhand on watch aboard the paddle-steamer *Pioneer* which was tied up at Port Ellen on the night the *Tuscania* was lost. He heard the sound of men shouting out at sea as they tried to navigate their way into the harbour and raised the paddle-steamer's captain. 'A lot of the crew were Islay men and they knew that a boat could hit the Ard [headland] in the dark, so they started putting up lights to guide the boat in, and were shouting out to it. The young Americans were in a state, and they were packed into that boat.' As a boy, Dougie heard the *Tuscania* stories from his grandfather and other old men when he hung around a smiddy in Port Ellen, and also from Jetty Shanks, his teacher. Jetty Shanks took seven of the men who landed in the lifeboat at Port Ellen into her seafront home on Frederick Crescent. One of the survivors, Ed Brownell, told Jetty he'd ripped the sleeves off his shirt and used them to lash himself to the lifeboat to stop him being swept overboard by the pounding seas. Sergeant Harpham was billeted in a hotel where he was 'treated royally by the Scotch people' and treated for the injuries received when his lifeboat disintegrated.

Private Wilbur Nutt of Ohio was another soldier thrown into the sea when his lifeboat struck what he described as 'the fearful breakers' of the Oa. Wilbur survived, and described his experience in a letter to his parents.

On seeing we were to be cast into the sea, we bid one another good-bye, wished each other luck, and asked God to help us. We had given up all hope of living but a few minutes at the most. We could see the wave coming which every man knew would have us at its mercy. In a second our boat was upset. On coming to the surface I was quite near the upturned boat. In fact, the boat was surrounded with struggling men. I reached its side, then the rope, then the boat. Just then someone grabbed me round the neck with clasped arms and a death-like grip. With one loose arm, I grabbed the cleat at the bottom of the boat, then with one mighty leap broke myself loose and scrambled up on top, only to be dashed off again by the second wave to pass. I was then whirled about like a stick in the water with feet and arms dangling as though they were nailed on. In the meantime, I came in contact with a board lengthwise with my body, as nice as though placed there. This I clasped tightly as possible with both arms, but it was soon thrown away from me, then a wave came in, driving me close to the shore, and as it receded I felt a rock under me, clasped it with my hands, managing to hold myself until the next wave came, lifting me onto its top. It was then I was able to scramble ashore and drag myself to safety. It was impossible for me to walk, so crawling on hands and knees, I came to a post where I pulled up to a standing position and moved my arms and limbs until I became limbered up a little. It was probably between 1 and 2 o'clock am. I walked back and forth until about 8 o'clock am. At 2.30 pm I was able to get off my cold, wet clothes and have had the best of care ever since.

I have completely recovered from an acute attack of pneumonia in the left lung. I forgot to tell you I helped to lower the lifeboats, so was wringing wet with perspiration on getting into the lifeboat, and it was the sudden change and exposure that caused my illness. And to think my life was one of the few to be saved of forty or fifty in this lifeboat! It was only a miracle. One hundred and seventy nine bodies were buried on the island, in fact all the bodies found are buried there. I am very glad to think that the most the Germans can do is destroy one's life. This is the critical time and I sincerely believe that we should make the effort to make a world peace, and even if I should be called to make the great sacrifice, I thank God for being able to do even so little.

Love to all. Wilbur S. Nutt.

There was good news too for the Terzia family. Six days after the sinking, Leo, who had spent five sleepless nights worrying about his brother, Fris, wrote home: 'When our raft landed on an island off the Scottish coast we were in the most beautiful little town I ever saw, and I will never forget the treatment received from those honest-to-God people. Fris was picked up from his raft by a trawler and landed in Ireland. We are certainly strong for the English navy. They certainly did their share, and that is the only reason that we are alive today. All of the people threw open their arms to us and we have been treated royally everywhere we went.'

Leo Terzia later served as a Louisiana State Senator.

❧

Wilbur Nutt's inability to walk when he got ashore was the first sign of what is now recognised as Post Recovery Collapse. It's a syndrome that causes men who have managed to drag themselves to safety, or be dragged to safety, to have cardiac arrests and die. The phenomenon is familiar to Islay Coast Guard, Donald Jones: 'If you are in extreme danger the adrenalin will be flowing through your veins and survival is the main thing on your mind. But once you think you've made it – once someone pulls you out the water or if you just get to the beach after you've been struggling for a long time to get there, that high survival mode shuts down. Once you've been rescued, anything from fainting to death can happen afterwards, just because of the way the body reacts.'

David MacLellan, coxswain of the Islay Lifeboat explains: 'If you've been in the water a long time, your limbs are getting squeezed by the water. All the warm blood's gone to the core. The limbs are not working. As soon as they pull you out the water the pressure comes off your lower limbs and the nice warm blood runs into them and once it's cool runs back into your heart – it causes a shock, and there you go!'

The efforts of the people of Islay saved the lives of many who would have died that fateful night and in the days to follow. The *San Francisco Chronicle* paid tribute:

> Heroes also appeared among the fisher folk here. A British Colonel who came fifty miles and worked indefatigably with the survivors, mentions in his report to the War Office, Robert Morrison, coast watcher, and Duncan Campbell, for bravery. Morrison heard cries in the middle of the night, and, running down from his home on the top of the cliff, saved many men by dragging them to the higher rocks. He took care of eighty survivors at his tiny home, and still has some of the sick there. Campbell, at a point about ten miles further away, did much the same thing. He helped fourteen men to reach land, and took them to his farmhouse.

Some of the *Tuscania*'s lifeboats, driven north and west by the storm and tides, missed the perilous Mull of Oa and were driven into Lochindaal, where the coast is mostly rocky, but less rugged than the Oa. Exhausted, frozen men managed to struggle ashore, and make their way to dimly lit farms and cottages at Easter Ellister, Craigfad and Port Charlotte (Islay did not have mains electricity until 1949). The boat that beached at Port Charlotte had ten survivors on board, but more than twice that number of bodies were washed up there, dragged ashore and laid out on the pier. Fifteen bodies were found near the farm of Easter Ellister and ten more at Craigfad. Two bodies were washed up at Bowmore at the head of the loch. It was clear that there would be a massive job to do in identifying and hygienically disposing of the dead, but in the first few hours of 6 February the living took precedence.

It is sometimes flippantly said Britain and America are 'divided by a common language', but there genuinely were difficulties in communication between the islanders and some of the soldiers. About a quarter of America's World War One soldiers were foreign-born, and many of the men who had emigrated to America as adults still had little or no English by the time they joined the American army. For Port Ellen schoolgirl, Isabelle Macgilvary, there was no school for several days as her multi-lingual teacher, Mr McLachlan, interpreted for doughboys who didn't speak English. Isabelle visited many of the cold, exhausted and very often sick survivors in the billets that had been found for them. 'At night we visited the houses where they were billeted to sing to them and help them get over their state of shock. I remember being upstairs in the house, now the Trout Fly, where the MacGibbons stayed. Mrs MacGibbon had a shop there and she had two grand-daughters, whose mother had died, staying with her, Mary and Anna. The Schoolhouse had four staying and everyone who could took someone in. I know that all the houses at the Distillery had two each. They all went off next morning and many of them wrote to their kind benefactors afterwards. Indeed Anna MacGibbon later went to America and married one of them.'

Despite the care and attention given to the survivors, Arthur Siplon recalled that, 'some men did not survive the first night, because of the terrible exposure they suffered'. James Gurney, one of the forestry engineers, had made it from the *Tuscania*'s sickbay into a lifeboat and safely to Islay, but died on the island of scarlet fever and exposure. His brother, Stephen, survived. It was ten days before Stephen found out about the fate of James and could write to their mother with the news.

Sergeant Harry A. Kelley had spent 11 hours in a lifeboat before successfully landing on Islay. His terse diary reveals how the fittest survivors were quickly moved on to American bases on the mainland.

> Feb. 6. At 5:30 a.m. our lifeboat with 32 men landed on Islay, an Island off the coast of Scotland. Ireland can be seen in the distance. The people of Port Ellen are very, very kind to us.
>
> Feb. 7. We are resting up after our exposure. My ankles and legs are very painful. In good spirits, these people are so hospitable.
>
> Feb. 8. Left Port Ellen this morning, we saw more of Bonnie Scotland, great scenes that I'll never forget. The town of Tarbert welcomes us.
>
> Feb. 9. After traveling all night we passed Glasgow and London, we arrive at an English rest camp near Winchester. I am hospitalized with the Mumps. Scanty rations.

The arrival of the wretched survivors on Islay was dramatic, but nothing compared to the magnitude of the influx into Ireland.

Colonel G. D. Chamier, the British Boer War veteran who commanded the Lough Swilly garrison, reported that the *Pigeon* and *Mosquito* had landed approximately 65 officers and 980 other ranks, and about 80 of the *Tuscania*'s crew. Meanwhile, the *Grasshopper* had taken 11 officers and about 300 men. Some were suffering from injuries or exposure, but many had been ill before the *Tuscania* had been torpedoed, and had been rushed onto the decks from the sick-bay when it became clear she was sinking. Eighty men were immediately hospitalised at Londonderry. Of 550 men landed at Larne, 30 needed immediate medical attention while the others were quartered around the town. To preserve good order, Larne's 24 pubs unanimously decided to remain closed for three days until the *Tuscania*'s crewmen went home and soldiers left the town for the US training camp at Winchester in England.

The Naval trawlers had also landed men at Larne and at Carrickfergus, County Antrim. Four days after the sinking, the US newspaper, *The Morning Oregonian*, carried a 'once-bitten, twice-shy' story about an American Army captain who refused to take any more risks with submarines.

An Irish Port: A small fishing vessel returned to this port this morning without the 142 Americans it set out from here to take off from the barren northerly shore, which the Americans had reached in three lifeboats 14 hours after the *Tuscania* was sunk. The skipper of the trawler told the British Commodore here that the American Captain in charge of the party refused to embark his men on the trawler because the little vessel did not carry sufficient lifeboats to hold all of the troops in case the trawler was torpedoed.

But despite that Army captain's nervousness about boarding another British vessel, the Americans were deeply appreciative of the efforts the Royal Navy had made to rescue so many of its young soldiers. American Major-General, George T. Bartlett, the commander of the US Army's base in Britain, reported: 'I believe that the splendid seamanship and courageous action of these destroyers saved the lives of many hundreds of our forces.'

Official word of the disaster had been received at the American Army Headquarters in London at noon on 6 February, from Captain K. E. Rockey, of the US Marine Corps. Captain Rockey was the US's Acting Disembarkation Officer for the port of Glasgow. He was immediately ordered to proceed to Larne to report on the situation and do whatever he could for the survivors. He found that the Americans had been initially billeted with local people before being moved to a British Army camp. Rockey was struck by the kindness shown to the doughboys. 'Too much cannot be said of the hospitality shown to the survivors by the British troops and by the civilian population of Ireland. Instances are too numerous to mention. Clothing was provided by the Military authorities as soon as it could be done, but meanwhile the people fitted out the survivors with civilian coats, caps, sweaters, mufflers and everything needed, and individual officers and soldiers turned over their personal clothing. Concerts were arranged for the entertainment of the survivors, and Canteens and the YMCA distributed their stocks of cigarettes and candy gratuitously. Whenever the troops were moved they were sent off with parades and music, and received with the same courtesy and hot meal.'

One American corporal wrote home to his parents to tell them that at the camp he was billeted at, after hot food and drinks were served, British soldiers had surrendered their own beds to let the survivors rest. A tantalising 39-second silent film of a long line of *Tuscania* survivors walking through a town or city, preceded by a brass band, exists in the British Pathé News archive. The men are dressed in an assortment of donated clothes. Some are in their own US-issue wide-brim 'Montana' hats, others wear woollen beanies, while many sport civilian flat caps or 'bunnets'.

Attempts to quickly compile a list of survivors proved difficult and frustrating. The men were, initially, scattered. Many were in hospital. Some units had no officers, and the officers who had survived hadn't carried rosters of their units when they abandoned the *Tuscania*. The fact that America was a nation of immigrants was brought home to Rockey when he realised that: 'Many men did not speak English or know to what company they belonged'. The US National Records office in Kansas holds screeds of telegrams listing survivors – complete with corrections and revisions as the authorities struggled to draw up a definitive list of those who had been saved, those who were known to have died, and the men who were missing. The American newspapers were screaming for news, but the lists were strictly withheld from the press to spare relatives from receiving the news of the death of loved ones in their morning paper. With an absence of official sources, newspapers, like Wisconsin's *Green Bay Press Gazette*, printed news from relieved families.

A telegram received by Mr and Mrs Eugene Damaulin, Route 8, Box 32, Shawane Road, yesterday morning at 9.00 o'clock from Washington, brought the happy tidings that Frank Demaulin was reported among the list of survivors from the liner *Tuscania*.

Catherine McGinn, 109 North Ashland Avenue, mother of Michael McGinn, also received word yesterday that her son was safe.

Anthony J. Devroy has been landed safely according to a dispatch from Washington, received Saturday by his mother, Mrs J. Devroy.

Twelve New London men were on board the *Tuscania* when she set sail for her destination. Of that number, ten have already been reported as saved. Clifford Norris and William D. Spencer are the other two who have not yet been heard from.

More than a week after the sinking, the *Washington Post* reported that the list of the buried victims sent by cable contained confusing errors, and that some names might have been transcribed incorrectly. Was – the *Post* asked – E. F. Church really Franklin A. Church? Was J. P. Wasson really Thomas S. Wasson? There were scores of discrepancies among the lists of the lost, and scores of opportunities for both false hope and unnecessary anguish. Even today, an authoritative list of those lost doesn't exist.

❧

Many of the *Tuscania*'s crew were from, or from around, Glasgow and when the news of the sinking broke, wives and families gathered outside the Anchor Line's office in St Vincent Street, anxious for news. It was there Captain Peter McLean (who had been the last man to be evacuated by HMS *Pigeon*) and his surviving crew headed for. According to the *Evening Times,* seventy of them mustered there three days after the sinking and another 180 the following day. The *Daily Record and Mail* reported:

A jolly fellow is Mr W. E. Wheat, the chief steward who resides at 320 Maxwell Road, Pollockshields. Asked to give his impression of the affair, he smiled, and with a sort of Broadway accent replied: 'Why, this isn't the first. I took the *Transylvania* out and sank her in the Mediterranean. I got the *Tuscania* right from the builders and she's gone down; so I guess they'll have to build some more for me.

A reporter from the *Glasgow Citizen* interviewed one of the crew, Yorkshireman J. S. Peters, who had lived in America for six years. Peters served in the engine room and had been torpedoed four times previously – twice in the Mediterranean and twice in the Atlantic. The journalist asked the obvious question: 'Will you go to sea again?' Peters replied: 'I want to be an engineer; there's good money just now, and when I've made enough I'm going ashore to school. So, it's another ship for me; there's nothing else for it.' Attempts to interview Thomas Wilkinson, a young steward, failed as he could only speak in an almost inaudible whisper. His shipmate, the Yorkshireman Peters, explained that Wilkinson had been sitting in a holed lifeboat up to his neck in icy water for six hours before being rescued.

On Islay – once the survivors had been saved, nursed and comforted – the prompt burial of the dead became the priority. The sentiments, culture and traditions of the islanders dictated that this must be done with dignity and reverence. Almost every islander by this time was related to, or at least knew, Islay men who had fallen in the war, but very few of them had had the opportunity of a funeral to say farewell to these loved ones. Confronted with the bodies of strangers, there was an outpouring of grief, love and respect from the Ileachs. James McFarlane, one of today's old-time Port Ellen fishermen, recalls being told by Isabelle Macgilvary that groups of women huddled together in the streets and wept as cartloads of corpses, 'as stiff as statues', were carried past on their way to the Drill Hall which served as a temporary morgue. The bodies of these young American allies were treated as if they were the sons, brothers and husbands of Islay. Jetty Shanks told Dougie MacDougall that the village 'seemed unreal with the soldiers, all young boys, lying there', and Dougie recalls that the scene played on the minds of the people of Port Ellen for many years.

Arthur Siplon drew up a grim accounting of those who had washed up on the Oa: 'It was found that 132 men were alive, although many badly injured, and 87 were dead. It was an overwhelming task to ask this small village to assume funeral arrangements for such a large number of strangers among them. The heavy hand of Death had brought them problems they were ill prepared to meet. They did not hesitate however, every human effort possible was put forth by them, to take care of matters in an orderly fashion.' The Oa and Port Ellen were not the only Islay communities that the *Tuscania* tragedy touched. The *Oban Times* reported:

> A boat and crew of ten survivors landed at Port Charlotte and sought shelter in the early hours of the morning. They were kindly treated. Very soon news arrived that many dead bodies were being taken from the sea, and many being washed ashore. At Port Charlotte twenty-two bodies were landed and laid upon the pier. Near Easter Ellister fifteen bodies came ashore, and near Craigfad ten bodies were found. All were fine young men in military uniform and on Friday the bodies, to the number of 47, were collected at Port Charlotte Distillery. Coffins are being provided, and arrangements were being made for the interment to take place near Port Charlotte on Saturday. The sad proceedings have created great gloom and sorrow throughout the Rhinns district. Mr Hugh Morrison of Islay has taken a very kind interest both in the welfare of the survivors, who have been kindly treated at the Port Charlotte Hotel, and in the disposal of the dead. He personally chose a piece of ground near the village to form a burial-ground where the whole of the unfortunate young men are laid to rest.

Four cemeteries – at Kilnaughton, near Port Ellen; two on the rugged southern coast of the Oa; and one at Port Charlotte on Lochindaal – were created for the dead. But before the bodies could be buried, every attempt was made to give each lifeless body a name. Much of the responsibility fell on the shoulders of Islay's most senior policeman, Sergeant Malcolm MacNeill, whose grim job it was to attempt to identify the dead. Most of the soldiers had worn identity discs, but where these had been torn from bodies by the sea, fingerprints were taken. As the days passed, the violent action of sea on rocky coastline and the natural putrefaction of bodies made that job more difficult and ghastly.

≈

On Thursday, 7 February, news that survivors and bodies had been washed ashore on the coast of Islay reached the American Army Headquarters in London. US Army Captain, Charles M. Rotch, was ordered to the island. He arrived at 4.00 pm that day. Because the report had said that two of the survivors had pneumonia, Captain Rotch was accompanied by a US military doctor, Lieutenant Herman Chase, and two nurses. The American Red Cross too responded, shipping a detachment of US nurses from its own hospital at Mossley Hill in Liverpool directly to Islay. Their vessel made 'an almost record run to Islay'. That same day the *Los Angeles Times* received a telegram reporting that 44 bodies of a suspected death-toll of 100 had been washed up on rocks fifteen miles from the scene of the torpedoing. They published the news the following morning:

> All were Americans and their bodies were mutilated beyond recognition. A pathetic feature is that although all the victims wore tags no identification numbers had been put on them because these Americans had not yet been assigned to definite Army units. Therefore, there is no way to identify them and they will be buried in one grave.

In the stormy winter days that followed the sinking of the *Tuscania*, 126 bodies were washed ashore on Islay. New grave-yards had to be hastily prepared in often quite remote places. Plots were obtained from the island's major landowners – on the Oa from the Kildalton Estate, in the Rhinns from Islay Estate.

✑

Islay carpenter, James MacTaggart, kept a diary of his working life. From his humdrum account of daily events, the horror of the *Tuscania* disaster leaps out of the pages of the simple lined notebook he wrote in.

> Sat: Dressed wood for cart. *Half Day*. At home afternoon (killed pig).
>
> Mon. Feb.4. Dressed wood for cart & jobbing at Fore-land sheds
>
> Tues:　　　　　"　　　　"　　　　"　　　　"　　　　"　　　　"
>
> Wed: Salvaging lifeboat at Black Rock.
>
> Thurs: Making coffins for bodies of American soldiers washed ashore at Port Charlotte. Drowned of SS *Tuscania* which was torpedoed by a German Submarine off north coast of Ireland. (had to work overnight)
>
> Frid: Making crosses for soldiers' graves.
>
> Sat: At soldiers' funeral.
>
> Mon. Feb. 11. Finishing graves.

At Port Charlotte, the men were buried on the raised beach only yards from the cold salt water of Lochindaal, close to a 4,000-year-old Neolithic chambered burial cairn. On the Oa (at Kilnaughton, and at two sites beneath the cliffs on the southern coast close to Kinnabus and Killeyan farms) the same tragic ritual was played out – a religious service, a piper playing a lament, a party to fire a gun salute, and the flags of the two nations whose dead were being commemorated. Britain's Union Flag would have been easy to obtain. Every school and Territorial Army drill hall would have had one. But Islay had no Stars and Stripes, and no way of getting one in time for the burials. And so, on the eve of the first funerals, a dedicated group of local women sat up through the night sewing an American flag. Arthur Siplon recalled: 'They would make a flag, even as Betsy Ross had made the first one – with their own hands. They searched their homes, and found the necessary red, white and blue – they cut out the white stars and tenderly sewed them on the field of blue.' The sewing of the flag meant a lot to the American survivors, like Siplon, who attended the funerals. It would mean a lot to families of the deceased to know that their sacrifice had been properly honoured. And today it means a great deal to the people of Islay to know that these efforts were appreciated, and that the flag, later gifted to President Woodrow Wilson, is now the property of the Smithsonian Museum of American History in Washington DC.

Islay's *Tuscania* flag is redolent with symbolism. There is a powerful American legend that the first Stars and Stripes was sewn by Betsy Ross, from a pencil drawing given to her by George Washington. Betsy was the wife of George Ross, whose uncle had signed the American Declaration of Independence, and was of a Scottish family descended from the Earls of Ross. At the time of writing this book, a group of Islay women are sewing a reproduction of that flag, which will be used at the 100th anniversary commemoration of the *Tuscania*'s loss. A decade after the sinking of the *Tuscania*, and at the request of an official at the Smithsonian, Hugh Morrison, the Laird of Islay Estate, wrote an account of the sewing of the flag.

Dear Mr. Havenel,

I delayed answering your letter of June 11th until I returned to Islay and was able to consult our old

Housekeeper, Miss Mary Armour, with regard to the American Flag which was made in this house at the time of the disaster to the transport *Tuscania* in 1918. At four o'clock on the evening before the funeral of the victims of the *Tuscania* disaster, I asked Miss Mary Armour if it was possible to make an American Flag to carry at the funeral. Mrs Forbes, the wife of the then factor of Islay estate, had an Encyclopaedia where John MacDougall, the estate joiner, got all information as to the size of the Flag and the correct number of stars and stripes. John made a plan from which Miss Mary Armour and her helpers, Jessie MacLellan, Mary Cunningham and Catherine MacGregor, were able to cut the cloth to the right dimensions. There was no time to send for suitable material and the stars and stripes were made of white cotton calico; the blue part of figured calico turned outside in; and the red stripes of Turkey twill, all procured at the local merchant's in Bridgend. Jessie MacLellan and her Mother cut the stars and sewed them on the blue. The Flag was completed about 2 a.m. next morning. At the funeral, an American survivor carried the Flag. I should like to add that I remember how anxious everybody in Islay was to show every possible honour to the soldiers of the United States who had come over to fight for the cause of the Allies in the Great War.

Yours sincerely,
Hugh Morrison.

❧

The funeral procession left Port Charlotte, led by the crew of HM Yacht *Sea Fay*, a steam yacht, built by Lobnitz & Company of Renfrew in 1902, that had been requisitioned and armed by the Navy, and was based in Oban for most of the war. A Royal Navy officer wrote to the cousin of Captain Philip Lighthall, of the US Engineers, one of the victims buried that day. 'A funeral procession was formed headed by a firing party from HMS *Sea Fay* & a detachment of local volunteers. Two pipers gave their services. Fifteen men of the USA acted as pall bearers & the coffins were conveyed from the mortuary in lorries.' The same officer reported that the temporary cemeteries of Islay now held 182 American dead – 53 at Port Charlotte, 83 at Port Ellen and 46 on the Mull of Oa.

A photograph by Archibald Cameron, Islay's skilful and hard-working photographer of the time, reveals the grim solemnity of the funerals. The cortège makes its way through Port Charlotte from the temporary mortuary at the village's distillery to Port Mor, a field on the lochside just half a mile away. The dead travel on the backs of open lorries. Everyone else is walking. The weather is clearly terrible. The wet road shines, an umbrella is carried aloft over a surpliced clergyman, and people are hunched up against the rain and wind. Two pipers lead the way, followed by two or more ministers. A few yards behind them come four trucks bearing the dead, and behind them a throng of dark-clad mourners. Hardly a soul stands by the roadside watching the cortège pass – they are all part of it, following the dead to the hastily laid-out cemetery. Perhaps 400 people turned out to mourn that day.

In Cameron's photograph of the burial ceremony at Killeyan on the Oa, the American flag can be clearly seen. The caption Cameron attached to the photograph reads 'US Soldiers singing *The Star Spangled Banner.*' The Islay-sewn flag is captured in a photograph of the salute being fired at Kilnaughton, the cemetery that lies between Port Ellen and the Oa. Isabelle Macgilvary watched the funeral cortège leave Port Ellen for Kilnaughton. 'It was very emotional to see the bodies, stiff as statues in their splendid uniforms carried out of the Drill Hall and laid reverently on lorries. Coffins were unobtainable for such a number, almost 100.'

Survivor Arthur Siplon attended the funeral to mourn the loss of one of his close friends. 'Into the graves the bodies of these American boys were carefully lowered. Among them my close pal Wilbur Clark, 18 years old, the 1917 honor student of his class in Jackson, Michigan. When the last mournful note of "Taps" floated away the ceremony came to an end. The folds of the homemade flag whipped smartly in the winter's chilling wind. Proudly it flew on a foreign shore, an unusual flag – made by the kindly hands of Scotch mothers to honor the sons of mothers they never knew.'

The American press followed the aftermath of the tragedy closely. Wisconsin's *Green Bay Press/Gazette* reported:

A SCOTCH SEAPORT, Feb 12th: Up till Tuesday night, a week after the disaster, 171 victims of the ill-fated Tuscania had been laid to rest at different points on the Scottish coast. These were divided as follows: Americans, 131 identified and 33 unidentified; crew four identified and three unidentified. The last seventeen of these bodies recovered – all Americans – were buried this afternoon, villagers again coming many miles in a downpour of rain to pay their simple tribute to the American dead. A British Colonel who has worked day and night since the disaster helping the Americans bury their dead announced today that the people of the nearby countryside had started a public subscription to erect a permanent monument to the Americans. There are eight Americans still here too ill to leave, several of them still dazed by their experience. They are quartered in nearby farmhouse and village hotels.

America is traditionally a land of powerful regional or state newspapers, rather than coast-to-coast national ones. Up and down the land, editors responded to America's worst news of

the war so far with fulsome tributes to their own communities'
dead. In Waco, Texas, where the 32nd Division had trained,
the *Independence News* reported that 7,000 people were expected
to pay tribute to the dead at a memorial service in the city. *The
Leader*, of New Richmond, Wisconsin, published a moving
obituary of Raymond Butler, a young stenographer who had
rejected a cushy job at Army HQ in Washington to fight in
Europe with his comrades.

All the earthly remains of the young man, whom we all
knew, now lie in a trench alongside the bodies of 77 of
his shipmates, who also gave their lives in doing their bit
putting an end to the barbarous warfare now being carried on by Germany, on the sunny shore of Scotland not
far from the rocky coast where the sea gave up the dead.
For one week friends and relatives of Private Butler anxiously scanned the lists, of rescued soldiers, that appeared
in the newspapers, hoping, hoping always hoping that
his name would appear amongst the names of those alive
and well. But such was not written on the book of fate
and Wednesday evening's papers finally gave his name
as one of the nation's heroes who gave up his life that
his country might be kept 'The land of the free and the
home of the brave'. Raymond would have been twenty
years old this April and had made his home in this city
the greater part of his life . . . On January 1, he enlisted
in the Division of Forestry and was assigned to the 6th
Battalion, 20th Engineers, stationed at Camp American
University, Washington DC. The last word his folks had
from him was dated January 22. The letter stated that they
were packing and getting ready to leave for France . . .
he had a choice of a clerical position in Washington or
accompanying his regiment to France and as several of his
friends were going across, he chose to accompany them.

The burial of the bodies was a painfully drawn-out affair. Incoming tides brought a succession of bodies ashore, some right onto Port Ellen beach. Isabelle Macgilvary recalled that local boys had fun jumping on and off an upturned lifeboat that had been washed up opposite what is now St Columba's hall (then a United Free Church). 'One day one looked underneath and saw a hand. Two dead American soldiers were under it, trapped under their seats. We often wondered if these could have been saved.'

At least one lost soul, whose body never made it to land, had the dignity of a formal burial. While on mine-sweeping patrol nearly two weeks after the *Tuscania* went down, John Mair, the skipper of the Grimsby-registered steam trawler, *Bellona*, found the body of a uniformed man, kept afloat by his lifebelt long after his death. Mair remembered: 'It was necessary to bury him at sea. After sewing the body up in canvas, I read the funeral service and then quietly lowered him to his grave.'

Three weeks after the *Tuscania* was torpedoed, on 26 February, Major General George T. Bartlett, the US Army's most senior officer in Britain, summed up the events on Islay.

One hundred and forty four men put ashore at various points on Islay Island, Scotland, and it is believed that considerable loss of life occurred in making a landing on this rocky coast. Two of these men subsequently died. One hundred and seventy-seven dead bodies were washed ashore at scattered points on Islay Island, one hundred and forty-five of these have been identified and finger prints have been taken of the remaining thirty-two unidentified bodies; all bodies have been buried with military honours, graves marked with a wooden cross with grave numbers marked thereon. Many bodies were found without identification tags and a few with blank identification tags. One officer and 66 men are still carried as missing, making a total loss, identified and missing, as four officers and two hundred and eight men. Working conditions on Islay Island were found to be difficult due to lack of material, transportation, labor and inaccessibility. The Military, Naval and Civil authorities, the inhabitants of the Scottish and Irish commands gave the most sympathetic aid to the sick and casualties, assisted in every way practicable to afford the dead proper burial with military honours, and received the survivors with enthusiastic receptions, warm hospitality and generous kindness.

The writer, Irvin Cobb, who had witnessed the torpedoing of the *Tuscania* from another troopship, would write memorable accounts of the tenacity and courage of black American troops fighting in France, but his first 'scoop' was written before he even landed there. 'The memory of what happened that night off the Irish coast is going to abide with me as long as I live. It was one of these big moments in a man's life that stick in a man's brain as long as he has a brain to think with.'

About 2,000 men – American soldiers and British crew – had been rescued at sea or struggled ashore on Islay after the *Tuscania* was torpedoed. Because many had been rescued by different ships, and landed in different ports, it was several days before the final death-toll was known. At the time it was believed that 166 men died that night but it is now widely accepted that the death toll was over 200. In the days that followed 126 bodies came ashore on the island. Since time immemorial Islay men had gone to war, fighting for clan chief, king or country. Now war had come to Islay.

5

They Put Iron into Our Souls

*When you come out of the storm, you won't be the same
person who walked in. That's what this storm's all about.*
From Haruka Murakami, *Kafka on the Shore*

The German press rejoiced over the sinking of the *Tuscania*,
believing American morale had foundered along with the British
troopship. The *San Francisco Chronicle* reported:

> German newspapers are gloating over 'the psychological
> effect' which they expect the sinking of the *Tuscania* to
> produce in America. *Kolniscle Volkszeitung* says the event
> must unfailingly dampen the spirits of the Americans and
> proceeds: 'Sundry American vessels, some with muni-
> tions and perhaps a small number of soldiers have been
> sunk before. But so far as we know, this is the first case
> of a big transport with a considerable number of troops
> aboard falling victim to our U-boats. As such vessels must
> be convoyed with great care, our U-boat's achievement
> is all the more remarkable and gratifying.'

The loss of the *Tuscania* and around 200 of the enemy,
many of them young Americans, was a propaganda victory for
Germany and a blow to Britain's new ally, but far from demoralising the American public, it tempered the steel of determination. President Woodrow Wilson cabled Britain's Chamber
of Shipping to say that the 'distressing disaster to the troopship
Tuscania has strengthened our common sympathies and given
additional proof of the manhood and gallantry of our people'.

US newspaper editorials ran with the recruiting slogan, 'Close the ranks and get in!' The *San Francisco Chronicle* believed that the spirit of seven young men from the Redwood Coast town of Eureka captured the spirit of the nation.

When news of the disaster reached Eureka, Thursday night, seven husky young lumberjacks who had been figuring on going to the war said: 'That's our cue, and here we go.' An hour later they had quit their jobs and shortly after they were aboard a train bound for San Francisco to enlist in the 20th Engineers, whose 6th Battalion was aboard the transport. Tired and hungry the young men arrived at the Army Recruiting Station, 660 Market Street, late last night. But if they were tired and hungry patriotism burned strongly in their hearts. 'A lot of the boys of the 20th came from our part of the country,' said Frank Roberts. 'The Kaiser can't pull any off that sort of stuff and get away with it.'

Young Americans were now keen for a fight. Portland newspaper *The Oregonian* reported that the loss of the *Tuscania* prompted a spike in recruitment at the Marine Corps Recruitment Center in New York. Three days after the sinking more men enlisted than on any other day since America had declared war on Germany. The experience of being torpedoed hadn't even dampened the *Tuscania* survivors' enthusiasm for action. Under the headline, 'Torpedoed Foresters Anxious for Revenge,' the *Southern Lumberman* published a letter from Private Harold E. Robinson of the 20th Forestry Engineers Regiment. Robinson had been rescued by one of the British destroyers, and was now safe in a British Army base, from where he wrote: 'Of course, we lost all of our equipment, and most of us are wearing some part of the British uniform. I sure wish you could see us now though, we are feeling the best ever. I am enjoying myself as best as I ever could any place out of the USA. I am anxious now to get into it, as we boys all feel we have a personal grudge to settle with old Kaiser Bill, and they all say, "Let us at him."'

More than five weeks after the sinking, Charles Bennett, a private in the 6th Battalion, 20th Engineers, was still flat on his back in an American hospital in England, and had been told he'd be there another ten days. His traumatic experience and injuries had made him more eager for a fight. He wrote to his aunt and grandmother that he hadn't been seasick on the journey, had contemplated transferring to the Navy, but had changed his mind: 'I want to fight an enemy that I can see.' An American officer who had survived the torpedoing told *The Scotsman*: 'They succeeded in getting only a fraction of our fine fellows in addition to our boat, but they have put iron into our souls, and we will repay them when the chance offers.'

Increased belligerence wasn't confined to the young. Newton Baker, the level-headed lawyer who had become Secretary of the US War Department, said: 'It is a fresh challenge to the civilised world by an adversary who has refined but made more deadly the stealth of savage warfare. We must win the war and we will win the war. Losses like this unite the country in sympathy with the families of those who have suffered loss. They also unite us and make more determined our purpose to press on.' Baker, whose father had served with the Confederate cavalry during the American Civil War, had the reputation of being a pacifist, but is quoted as saying: 'I am so much a pacifist I'm willing to fight for it.' Evidence of America's increasing antagonism towards Germany was welcomed in Britain. *The Times* even went as far to quote at length the leader column of the *New York American*, owned by the US newspaper tycoon William Randolph Hearst.

The war is no longer three thousand miles away; it has come to the doors of every American home. The torpedo that sank the *Tuscania* will prove a fatal missile for Germany. We know our task now. We have to whip Germany. Many of us didn't want to be dragged into this hideous maelstrom of the European war, but the President said 'Fight' and the Congress said 'Fight.' The nation, however, to tell the truth, was at no time greatly stirred with enthusiasm, never greatly nerved to sacrifice and to battle. The war seemed so far off, so vague, so much a matter of parading and speech-making and knitting, so little a stern matter of suffering, wounds and death. But now the nation is aroused, and angry. We are going to beat Germany if it takes any number of years and all the blood and wealth we have to spend. The sinking of the *Tuscania* has bound up all American hearts in a firm resolve to fight to a finish against German frightfulness.

In the grim mathematics of World War One casualties, the loss of around 200 soldiers and sailors on the *Tuscania* does not compare with the great battles of the Western Front, or Gallipoli. But not since the American Civil War had so many American soldiers died in a single military action. The shock of the loss led to speculation that spies had given away the *Tuscania*'s position to the German Navy. The *New York Herald* demanded to know, 'When are the hangings to begin?'

The House of Commons was assured that the British Government was 'fully satisfied with the organisation of the convoy' and that 'every precaution was taken'. but the conspiracy theory was only finally laid to rest fifteen years after the war, when Kapitän Wilhelm Meyer revealed that his fatal encounter with the troopship in the North Channel had been 'sheer good luck'.

❧

Exactly a month after the loss of the *Tuscania* the Prince of Wales visited Glasgow for a morale-boosting tour of the vitally important shipyards, but took the time to meet 154 merchant mariners who had survived being torpedoed. The Prince spoke with many of them personally, including the Anchor Line stewardesses, Mary Carson and Flora Collins. This was just one among many instances of the outpouring of respect, sympathy and kindness toward those whose lives had been changed forever by the event. Neil Campbell, Port Charlotte's postman, received a letter from the Secretary for Scotland (the post was later renamed Secretary of State for Scotland):

Dear Sir,

I have to acquaint you that your name has been brought to my notice as Secretary for Scotland, in connection with services which you rendered at the time of the landing in Islay of American survivors from HM Transport *Tuscania*. I am glad to take this opportunity of expressing my appreciation of the humanity and public spirit which you gave evidence of on this occasion.

> Yours faithfully,
> Robert Munro.

The Governor of California wrote to Mrs Alexander Currie of Port Ellen:

Dear Madam,

I have just heard from one of our Californian soldiers, who is with the US Expeditionary Forces, and who was on the *Tuscania* when she was torpedoed, of the splendid treatment which you and your fellow towns-people accorded the survivors who were landed at Port Ellen. I am told that you personally treated the boys with the same sympathy and tenderness that their own mother would have used. I deeply appreciated what you did for these

boys under such trying circumstances. Such acts make us
realize the strength of the bond that unites the people of
this nation and Great Britain as Allies, and it is the spirit
of which you have given evidence that is going to keep
us fighting side by side until the victory is won.

Yours very truly,
William Stephens.

When all the surviving doughboys had recovered sufficiently
to leave Islay, the islanders were left with the American dead. It
may be that the burial of these strangers served as an outlet for
the grief of men and women whose friends, sons and brothers lay
far from home in the fields of France or the Gallipoli peninsula.
Across the Atlantic, American families now experienced the same
sense of loss. For many of them, their only sense of closure came
from scraps of information sent from Islay. It is a heartbreaking
experience to read the surviving letters sent to the island pleading
for information about the fate of sons. Many of these were addressed to Sergeant Malcolm MacNeill, Islay's senior policeman.

Union City, Tennessee USA, Dec 1, '18

Dear Mr MacNeill,

I have read of the rescue work you did for the victims of
the *Otranto* as well as those of the *Tuscania*. I want you
to know our hearts go out to you good people. I lost a
precious boy when the *Tuscania* was sunk. I wrote to Mr
Copeland asking a few questions, but did not receive an
answer. I would so much like to have the contents of his
water soaked pockets, such as handkerchiefs, letters etc.
Were the boys dressed in dry clothes and put in separate
coffins? Are their names kept sufficiently marked that
they may be identified when time comes to send their
bodies home? If you haven't time to answer this please

ask some woman who knows of these dear ones to write to me. I will appreciate the least scrap of information. We are rejoicing over peace, and I hope to have my second son home soon. I can hardly bear to think of the fate of my oldest son.

Sincerely,

Mrs S. Talley

Mother of Milton Talley

No. of grave 38 (I think)

The Museum of Islay Life which holds Mrs Talley's letter does not have Sergeant MacNeill's reply to Mrs Talley, but it does have evidence that he made enquiries on her behalf. From Bowmore, MacNeill wrote to Constable Alexander MacLean in Port Ellen.

Look up your notes . . . and let me know what property, if any, was found on the body of Milton C. Talley, No 35 Kilnaughton. Can you remember how many of those buried at Kilnaughton were put in coffins? I have had a most pathetic letter from this man's mother saying she had already written to Mr Copeland? (Mr Campbell probably) but received no answer.

Constable MacLean replied:

I beg to inform you that the property found on the body of Milton C. Talley, victim of *Tuscania* disaster and buried No 35 Kilnaughton is as follows:

One gold ring.

One cigarette case.

One watch.

So far as I remember only 37 of those bodies buried in Kilnaughton were coffined.

Some of the letters that crossed the Atlantic to Islay were filled with joy and gratitude. Jean Currie, who had taken two survivors into her Port Ellen home, received official thanks from the American Red Cross, and a flurry of other mail.

Dear Miss Currie,

Alva Bowman who was on the *Tuscania* when it was torpedoed has written me that he has been so kindly entertained in your home. Being his sister, I must write you to try to express my appreciation. I am sure you will understand my anxiety about the boys, my two brothers, both of whom are in the war (or perhaps Fay has not yet left the containment for France). You, being so near the theatre of war, understand even better than I, the danger even in crossing the ocean, to say nothing of the actual fighting at the front. I hope that if Fay should meet with the same misfortune that Alva did he will also be as fortunate in reaching a place of safety and his lot cast among people so hospitable. If you should find the time to write me a letter once in a while I would be more than pleased. It takes a letter so long to reach me from over there. At the best I can only hear from the boys occasionally. It seems that a letter from you would be like a letter from them almost. If you never find it convenient to write and no correspondence develops between us I shall always feel that I am your grateful friend.

Mrs Curtis Reedy
Sioux Falls, South Dakota

Corporal Fay Bowman had not yet crossed the Atlantic, but was still at Camp Mills, New York, from where he sent a cheery postcard to his brother's Good Samaritan.

Friend Miss Currie, how do you do. I'm glad to meet you. Ha!

Of course I am taking a great deal of liberty in writing, but you don't mind do you! I am coming over soon. Take good care of my Bro. until I get there.

Lovingly your friend,
Corporal Fay D. Bowman.

❧

The bravery and dedication of Islay people in the rescue of survivors, and the dignity and kindness they showed to the drowned and the saved, are beyond doubt. The Ileachs had taken the doughboys to their hearts, and America responded with gratitude to the little island on the western fringes of Europe. But there was growing disquiet within the American military about what had happened on board the *Tuscania* in the hours between its being struck by the torpedo and its sinking. Surviving American officers were interviewed about what they experienced and witnessed. Citing only minor exceptions, they are full of praise for the conduct of the doughboys.

Captain James M. Farrin, Adjutant 6th Battalion, 20th Engineers:

Conduct of men: Excellent. On account of boat drill held every day after departure every man on board knew his place. When the emergency arose it was met calmly and without panic.

Captain O. K. Sadtler. US Signal Corps:

With the exception of one company of engineers, this was the only time that the enlisted personnel was not absolutely under control and remained at their posts, quietly until ordered away by their officers. The absolute confidence in their officers and willingness to do as told is highly commendable and from undisciplined men, is most remarkable and speaks well for the prospects for the new American Army. The officers of the above mentioned Engineer Company, apparently lost control of their men and a great amount of unnecessary noise and confusion resulted.

But when they come to describing the behaviour of the *Tuscania*'s British crew, the transcripts of the interviews make uncomfortable reading. The surviving US Army officers fired a barrage of criticism at the sailors. One officer would have gladly fired a pistol at them. Like the soldiers, the *Tuscania*'s seamen had been assigned lifeboat stations to assemble at if the order came to 'abandon ship'. Once there, their duty was to lower the lifeboats into the water, unhooking them from their davits to allow further boats to be lowered. But when the *Tuscania* was being abandoned many of the ropes had been cut from their davits, not unhooked. This rendered the lowering gear useless. The crew was also supposed to help the inexperienced American soldiers into the boats. But, very often, that did not happen.

Captain James M. Farrin, Adjutant 6th Battalion, 20th Engineers:

The crew was not in evidence in any part of the ship which I visited. They were conspicuous by their absence.

1st Lieutenant Shelby M. Saunders, 20th Engineers:

Members of the ship's crew were most conspicuous by their absence, there not being a single one at my station.

Captain David Davis Hall, D Company 6th Battalion, 20th Engineers:

Conduct of ship's crew very bad, excepting Captain. Lieutenant Tholl [Thall] and myself lowered four boats at my station without any assistance from the ship's crew. I was to have five but none came up.

Lieutenant Richards Jarden, 6th Battalion, 20th Engineers:

The conduct of the *Tuscania* crew was very lax, 12 of them were assigned to my station and only one helped lower our boats and he was more worked up over it than any of my men. Had the other 11 been on the job and done their bit, I have every reason to believe that my two boats, Nos 13 & 13B, would have gone away with their full amount of men and in very good order.

Captain Charles E. Hetrick, F Company, 6th Battalion, 20th Engineers:

Without waiting for boats to be loaded entirely with men, they (the ship's crew) cut the ropes instead of unhooking the blocks. As the ship was still under way one end was cut loose first, and allowed boats to swing around and capsize.

1st Lieutenant Arthur Chamberlin, F Company, 6th Battalion, 20th Engineers:

I sent a detail to assist the crew to lower the boat, but before they got there the crew had lowered the boat, not stopping to take any of the men. A few of them succeeded in jumping into the boat as she was lowered, but they were thrown into the water by one end being lowered before the other, causing the boat to hang at an angle of 45 degrees. Upon the boat landing in the sea my men in the water begged the ship's crew to pull them in the boat, but they paid no attention to them, but asked each other for a knife to cut the davit rope. Cutting the ropes prevented us from lowering any more boats from that davit. The ship's crew started rowing away. I commanded them to return alongside and take the men. They paid no heed to me, and I cursed and threatened them but they paid no heed. If I had a pistol I would have killed them in the boat as they were leaving.

1st Lieutenant Maurus J. Uhrich, 6th Battalion, 20th Engineers:

Saw but one of ship's crew at Number 17 Boats, and he knew little or nothing about the boats; this does not refer to the ship's officers of whom I saw nothing. I would recommend that each officer be armed with loaded pistol.

Even when the Americans and British were in the same lifeboats, the *Tuscania* crew failed to impress the US officers. 2nd Lieutenant Charles Scott Patterson, 20th Engineers:

There were 12 of the ship's crew and 39 enlisted men and myself in this boat, and the conduct of the crew was not what was expected, with the exception of two men. There were to be only 6 of the ship's crew on this boat and when it pulled away I discovered it had 12. Master at Arms, John MacLean, and one other man (name unknown) were the only ones I noticed assisting in the handling of the lifeboat. MacLean rode in the stern and guided the boat and did all in his power in assisting and handling the boat.

Captain Rockey, the US Marine Corps officer sent by the American military to deal with the aftermath of the disaster, compiled a damning report:

> The conduct of the American troops, with one or two possible exceptions, was all that could be expected. The men remained cool and obeyed orders. The conduct of the ship's crew and the British Naval gun crew on the other hand was very bad. The men deserted their stations, lowered boats for themselves, and in their frantic haste cut away the lower blocks instead of releasing the tackle, which put the falls temporarily out of commission. The casualties as shewn by the data now available are 3 officers and 219 men. They may be divided into two classes – those lost in abandoning ship, and those lost making a landing at Islay Island. Considering that the ship remained afloat for three hours after being hit and the work of the Destroyers, the first class of casualties might have been prevented, and with proper knowledge of seamanship the second class greatly reduced, if not prevented entirely.

Captain Rockey concluded that the principal cause of the loss of lives was:

> Dereliction of duty on the part of the ship's crew whose duty was to lower the boats.

An even more damning report came from 1st Lieutenant Donald Smith, a *Tuscania* survivor who wrote personally to the Commander General of the US Army in London. A soldier, he described himself to the general as someone who 'has experience as a sailor once around the world and on the Great Lakes and is therefore not talking quite as a landlubber'. Smith wrote:

It is a fact that the loss of nearly 200 of our men on the SS *Tuscania* was due to causes completely within our control. The ship was afloat for three hours and five minutes after being struck, and during the first hour, the list to starboard was not so excessive so as to interfere with the launching of the lifeboats on the port side, that is to say, there was ample time to launch every boat on the vessel (except the two or three smashed boats). While there was quite a stiff breeze from the south, the sea was not so rough as to make the launching of boats even difficult. There was boat capacity for every man on board. There was time to launch them, yet approximately 1350 of our men remained on board, after the last boat had left the ship. Had the *Tuscania* sunk in 1hr 10 mins – as did her sister ship, the *Transylvania*, when torpedoed in the Mediterranean – undoubtable all these 1350 would have been lost. The first destroyer came alongside 1hr 15mins after the torpedo struck, the second 1hr 30 mins.

Smith was able to channel his traumatic experiences on board the *Tuscania* not only to level criticism, but also to make recommendations aimed at making transatlantic convoys safer. He was also astute enough to understand that – after the attrition of more than three-and-a-half years of war – Britain's Merchant Marine was not what it had been. Many experienced officers and men had already perished. The *Tuscania* had more than a dozen 14-year-olds among its crew, and many more not much older. Some surviving 'old salts' had no doubt learned from bitter experience the self-preservation code of 'every man for himself'. Lieutenant Smith concluded that American

Port nan Gallan on the Oa. The Gaelic origin of the name is probably 'Port nan Gaillionn' – 'Bay of the Tempests'. Both the living and the dead came ashore here. (Les Wilson)

In driving rain, the Tuscania *funeral procession passes through Port Charlotte on its way to the burial ground at Port Mor. (Museum of Islay Life)*

A surviving American soldier holds the US flag made by the women of Islay, and a British sailor holds the Union Jack, at the burial ground at Port Mor. (US National Archives)

The salute is fired over the graves of Tuscania *victims at Kilnaughton Cemetery. (US National Archives, College Park, Maryland)*

The first Tuscania *mass funeral at Kilnaughton. The American survivors, with the hand-made US flag, stand to the right of the clergyman. Forty-four American soldiers were buried that day. (US National Archives)*

BURIAL OF AMERICAN SOLDIERS IN ISLAY.
6A. A FEW OF THE SURVIVORS. AT KILNAUGHTON CEMETERY. 12/2/18.

A few of the American survivors of the Tuscania *pose after the first funeral with the US flag. George Volz, who had dragged comrades from the sea into his lifeboat, is on the extreme right of the back row. (US National Archives)*

Forty-eight stars had to be tacked onto each side of the blue fabric to create the Stars and Stripes carried at the Tuscania *funerals. Local women completed work at 2.00 am on the morning of the first burial. (Les Wilson)*

David Roberts, one of just 19 survivors of nearly 500 men who were thrown into the sea as the Otranto *foundered off Islay. (Museum of Islay Life)*

Captain Davidson in his cabin on the Otranto. *He had commanded the ship for two years before going down with her off Islay. On the desk is a photograph of his wife and daughter. (By kind permission of his grandson, Nick Hide)*

Bodies of Otranto *victims at Kilchoman churchyard. The church was used as a morgue but, when it was full, bodies were laid out among the graves outside. (US National Archives)*

Once enough coffins had been made on Islay, the victims of the Otranto were re-buried in a second funeral at Kilchoman. Survivors are to the fore, while islanders stand behind. (Museum of Islay Life)

American Red Cross workers deliver emergency supplies to Otranto survivors who had been given refuge in an Islay cottage. (American Red Cross)

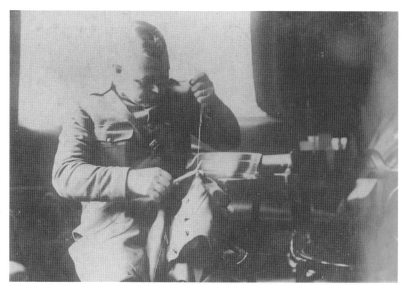

Lieutenant James Jeffers of the American Red Cross worked tirelessly for the relief of survivors and the recovery of the dead, here sewing a survivor's uniform back together. (American Red Cross)

Survivors of the Otranto treat their rescuers to afternoon tea at the Bridgend Hotel. One wears a piper's bonnet and one a tea-cosy! (American Red Cross)

The American Monument on the Mull of Oa commemorates the US dead from the Tuscania *and the* Otranto. *(Jenni Minto)*

soldiers crossing the Atlantic had to be trained to look after themselves:

> Practically all our loss would have been avoided had our men had a single opportunity to lower a boat into the water. We had 24 hours in Halifax Harbour in smooth water, where an honest lifeboat drill could have been held. It is folly to depend on the crews of British ships to do the work of lowering the boats. Practically all the old sailors are in the Navy and I understand that fully one third of every merchant crew shipped, consists of lads who have never been to sea before. The ship's officers are competent, but they are nearly all very busy for some time after an accident, and it is inevitable that on a torpedoed transport, expecting to go down every minute, the soldiers are not going to stand around and wait until someone comes and lowers a boat for them. They will lower them themselves, quite rightly, for it is an even chance no one will come at all, and in order to do so effectively, these land lubbers, as most of our soldiers are, must have at least one chance to learn how to do it. British ships have never made much of a practice of putting a boat in the water during boat drill when they are loaded with US soldiers. Certainly when there is a golden opportunity for it as there was for us at Halifax – they should have orders to stage the regular thing.

It had been Lieutenant Donald Smith who had struggled with the survival equipment on his lifeboat, and had only just in time managed to light the distress flare that had brought a trawler to the rescue of him and two others shortly before they would have been smashed against the rocks of the Mull of Oa. He wanted others to benefit from this traumatic lesson. Smith concluded:

With the possibility of our men being afloat for hours, even days, in a lifeboat, it would be highly valuable if at first the officers, then through them every man aboard were shown where matches, flares, compass, food, water, axe, etc. were kept in the lifeboats, also the way in which the flares are lighted. The exact position of the various articles should actually be pointed out. The lighting of a flare should be illustrated. This would not be a difficult proposition but would rather be a means or relieving the tedium of the passage, and it may be most valuable. The above is suggested by my own experience. I was in a smashed-in collapsible.

Major General George T. Bartlett, an old professional soldier who had entered West Point Military Academy as a cadet just the year after General Custer had made his last stand at the Little Bighorn, weighed the evidence and penned a detailed report on the disaster that made recommendations that could prevent future loss of life, and make the aftermath of any subsequent tragedy less distressing:

I emphatically recommend that the boat drill of all troops include the actual lowering and manning of lifeboats. I believe it is most advisable for all officers of organization or casual detachments to carry rosters on their person of their organization or detachment, in order that the checking or accounting for the survivors or missing, should such a disaster again occur, will be more accurate and greatly expedited to the relief of relatives and all concerned.

On Islay, Sergeant MacNeill would have heartily agreed. He had to attempt the identification of bodies – often headless, missing limbs and badly decomposing – that were still being washed up, six weeks after the tragedy. In a letter dated 21 March, that was forwarded to the US Naval Office in London, MacNeill lists 10 bodies that had come ashore since 13 February and were buried at the cemeteries at Port Charlotte, Kilnaughton and Port nan Gallan. He had only been able to identify five of them. Three of the others had been headless. MacNeil also reported that Private Fred Benefiel of the 20th Engineers had died at Killeyan Farm on 15 February and had been buried the following day.

And still they kept coming. American Statistical Officer, Lieutenant Paul Wilson, visited Islay on 26 April to find that the body of another soldier had been discovered the night before. 'We attended the funeral of this soldier and were able to identify him as – Earl Wisenberger, Company A, 107th Supply Train. No identity disks were found with the body but his underwear was marked 'Co. A 107th Supply Train'. As only one man was reported missing from this organization it was decided that Wisenberger was the man. Finger prints were taken. We found that the graves are well taken care of and that crosses have been erected over about one third of the graves, the others having been fenced in and well mounded.'

Sometimes, the families of the lost soldiers needed more than an official account of their loved ones' fates, and wrote directly to islanders. Ruth, the grieving sister of Otis Hutchins, a Quartermaster Sergeant from Wisconsin, wrote to Christina, wife of John Campbell of Shore Street, Bowmore, seeking reassurance about her brother's funeral. Mrs Campbell had previously written to the family of William Moore, another victim. Her reply to Ruth Hutchins makes it clear that her brother, Otis, and William Moore were the two soldiers washed up at Bowmore, Islay's 'capital', at the head of Lochindaal. Mrs Campbell wrote: 'Both William Moore and your brother were found in the one spot and brought in our machine to the police station, where they were laid out until the funeral day. You can rest assured that both boys had a nice burial, and were laid away in coffins without a bruise, as the spot where they came ashore was nice and sandy. But a great many of the boys had been dashed very much against the rocks.' The bodies of the two soldiers were driven the ten miles to be buried in the newly created cemetery at Port Charlotte, where Mrs Campbell planted pansies on the graves.

Christine Campbell confirmed that Otis had a wristwatch and a ring when his body was found, which had been collected by Sergeant MacNeill. She added: 'I was talking to him the other day about those matters, and he feels very much annoyed at you not having received them yet after all the trouble in Islay keeping each boy's belongings separate. The sergeant thinks the American government must have them in their possession by this time. I do hope you will get the articles all right . . . Give your mother my deepest sympathy and I hope she will feel pleased at her boy being laid carefully away. I had an inquiry from another mother in America about her boy, and when I inquired about him he had been buried with 43 other bodies in one grave without any coffin, and I felt very much hurt at having to tell her, poor lady. But how many of our own boys have been blown up in the air, never to see or hear anything about them again. But, thank God, there are signs of it coming to an end.'

As well as stiffening American resolve, the loss of the *Tuscania* taught lessons. When the *Moldavia* was sunk in the English Channel on 23 May that year, with the loss of 55 American soldiers, a full and accurate list of victims and next-of-kin was quickly issued because non-commissioned officers had been sure to save the company rosters as the ship was sinking under them. Confusion and an agonising wait for news by the families of men on the ship had been avoided. The American Red Cross in Britain had also learned a priceless lesson, as its history of the period makes clear. 'The *Tuscania* served the Red Cross as a lesson, grim, but invaluable, and it set to fortifying itself against whatever Fate, abroad in British waters, might later contrive with submarine, or mine or storm along the Kingdom's rocky shores.'

The great armada of troopships carrying Americans to Europe had only just begun when the *Tuscania* was torpedoed. The menace of the U-boats was still fearsome and the Red Cross began preparing for the worst. Five emergency stations were created along the northern coast of Ireland. Each had a well-stocked warehouse full of everything that shipwrecked soldiers might need. Plans to billet survivors were made, and for making sure that any hospitalised soldier would be visited. Motor transport would be provided by supplying owners of private vehicles, which had been mothballed for lack of petrol, with fuel to transport shipwrecked Americans. While grateful for the work of the British in the wake of the *Tuscania* sinking, the American Red Cross made the decision that, from this point on, it would look after its own.

Within two weeks, a string of well-stocked emergency stations had been set up in Belfast, Larne, Ballycastle, Londonderry and Buncrana – the five points in the Irish mainland where the survivors of U-boat attacks would most likely be landed. In store were 6,000 sets of blankets, underwear, shirts, tunics, caps, pairs of shoes and toiletries. Another store was set up in Liverpool with supplies that could quickly be dispatched by trawler or destroyer to Islay or other remote places on the Scottish coast. The American Red Cross's appetite for warm and comforting clothes prompted a touching gesture from an Islay fisherman. At the Red Cross's London headquarters a parcel arrived with an Islay postmark. It contained a case of black llama wool socks that had been washed ashore following the wreck of the *Tuscania*. The fisherman, who might well have made use of the socks himself, forwarded them to the Red Cross with his respects and good wishes.

In 1920, most of the bodies of Americans buried on Islay were exhumed and repatriated to the USA, or buried in the American Cemetery at Brookwood in Surrey. However, one American still lies buried in Islay soil. Private Roy Muncaster, the forestry graduate who volunteered for the 20th Engineers and drowned when the lifeboat he was desperately attempting to row to safety smashed against the rocks of the Oa, lies in Kilnaughton Cemetery. Private Muncaster left a mother and three sisters in Denver, Colorado. His family's wishes were that their son and brother remained where the people of Islay buried him with respect and sorrow, and to the sound of a lament played on the Highland pipes as a homemade American flag fretted in the wind. Roy Muncaster is commemorated in the Olympic National Forest in Washington State, where a mountain is named after him in the area he once served as forest ranger.

The body of John Sloss, who had joined the US Army after emigrating to America, was finally buried in his hometown of Lochwinnoch in Scotland. Seriously ill, fellow Scottish doughboy, Alexander McAlister, was transferred to a hospital in Rothesay on his home island of Bute, where he died and was buried nearly three weeks after the sinking. The bodies of British crewmen and unidentified bodies remain on Islay. Until recently, one headstone read: 'Unknown Negro/S.S. Tuscania/5th February 1918/Known Unto God'. This has now been replaced with a stone that makes no reference to the race of the victim. Progressive thinking questions whether the colour of a man's skin was ever worth mentioning, but there is also serious doubt as to whether the man was black. Racial prejudice in 1918 meant that African-Americans served in segregated regiments and there is no record of any being on the *Tuscania*. Was this unfortunate individual a dark-skinned Hispanic, or Native American, or perhaps a member of the British crew? Some people have speculated that he was a mixed-race *Tuscania* fireman from Paraguay who had settled in Liverpool. Whoever he was, his memorial is worthy of our honouring.

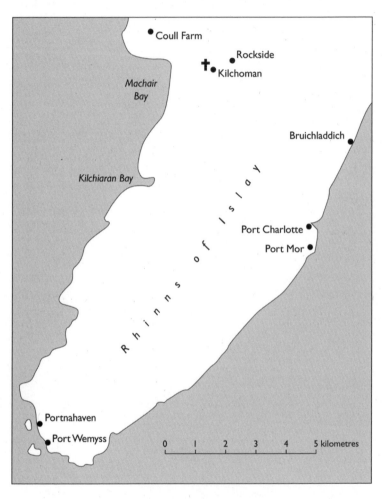

The Rhinns of Islay

6

I Heard the Siren Warning

He strack the top-mast wi' his hand,
The fore-mast wi' his knee,
And he brake the gallant ship in twain,
And sank her in the sea.

Traditional Scottish ballad

By February 1918, when the *Tuscania* was torpedoed, the tide was just beginning to turn against the terror of the U-boats – but only just in time. In April of the previous year Britain and her allies had lost nearly a million tons of shipping to the Kaiser's submarines. The German strategy of strangling Britain seemed to be working. In the darkest period, twelve ships a day were being lost. Historian Basil Liddell Hart claimed that: 'Only the "guts" of her merchant seamen in going to sea after being several times torpedoed lay between Britain's stomach and starvation.' Under such pressure, Britain began to develop effective anti-submarine strategies. As well as the convoy system, in which flotillas of ships could be protected by fast destroyers, aerial reconnaissance, hydrophonic listening devices, underwater mines and depth charges all helped swing the odds against the *unterseeboot*.

Eventually, Britain managed to provide almost every vessel in its merchant fleet with at least one 12-pounder gun, so that they could fight back against submarines on the surface. And then there were the Q-ships. These were former merchant ships that had been heavily armed with well-concealed heavy weapons manned by skilled gunners. They set themselves up as U-boat bait. A German submarine usually surfaced to sink a sitting-duck merchant ship with its gun, rather than waste a precious and expensive torpedo. But when attacked, a Q-ship would throw off its disguise, hidden guns would roar and the U-boat would be blown out of the water. Few on the British side felt squeamish about such tactics. The war had put iron into Scottish souls and Harry Lauder, the well-loved comic songster and war-charity fundraiser, was a relentless hawk. Even before the death of his only son, a captain in the Argyll & Sutherland Highlanders, in 1916, Lauder had proclaimed: 'I know that I am voicing the sentiment of thousands and thousands of people when I say that we must retaliate in every possible way regardless of cost. If these German savages want savagery, let them have it.'

The savage Q-ships were a ruthless answer to a desperate problem. Just how ruthless they could be is illustrated in the notorious action of Q-ship, *Barralong*. A former cargo liner, she'd been armed with three hidden 12 -pound guns. Off southwest Ireland the *Barralong*, which was flying the (then) neutral US flag, encountered German submarine *U-27* on the surface. The U-boat had ordered the crew of merchant ship, *Nicosian*, to abandon ship and had put a boarding party aboard it to scuttle it. The *Barralong* signalled that it would pick up the *Nicosian*'s survivors and closed in. Briefly screened from the U-boat by the bulk of the *Nicosian*, the Q-ship shrugged off its merchant disguise, hauled up the White Ensign and presented its hidden guns. As soon as the *U-27* hove into view, the *Barralong* let fly with its three 12-pounders, heavy machine guns and small arms, mortally injuring the submarine. As the *U-27*'s crew evacuated their ship and swam for the *Nicosian*, they were machine-gunned in the water. Marines from the Q-ship then swarmed aboard the *Nicosian*, killing the German boarding party. The excuse was that the Q-ship couldn't let its identity filter back to Germany, but the truth behind the atrocity may be that the sinking of the *Lusitania*, less than four months earlier, had bred fear and loathing of U-boats and their crews, and that the British sailors and marines sought vengeance. One victim of the Q-ships was Walther Schwieger who, as commander of the *U-20,* had sunk the *Lusitania.* But by the time his U-boat went down with all hands, Schwieger had sunk 49 ships in 34 missions.

While Q-ships destroyed a number of German submarines, they also made the U-boat commanders less likely to surface and order merchant seamen to abandon ship before opening fire. Q-ships only sank 14 U-boats during the war – about a tenth of German submarine losses. But by making U-boat commanders more cautious about fighting on the surface and calling on their victims to abandon ship before sinking them, the Q-ships had put the lives of merchant sailors even more at risk.

By 1918, technology and tactics had finally turned the tables on the U-boats. Their construction was now only keeping pace with their losses, and they were sinking fewer ships. In January that year, 123 British, allied and neutral ships were sunk. But by November the monthly losses had fallen to 15. In the months between the departures of the *Tuscania* from New York Harbour, to the *Otranto*'s, the ocean had become safer – or at least, safer from man. The Atlantic convoys were getting through, with half the troopships being British vessels.

❧

In early 1918 the American involvement in the battlefields of World War One began in earnest. By the end of the year it would have put 2.8 million men into uniform, and sent more than a million of them to fight in France and Belgium. In February 1918 – the month the *Tuscania* was torpedoed – more than 5,000 American servicemen crossed the Atlantic. Month on month the numbers rose – more than 26,000 in March, more than 27,000 in April, until the flow reached its zenith in July with 167,512 men crossing. As many as 20,000 doughboys might cross in a single convoy. Most soldiers made their European landfall in Liverpool, where the American Red Cross had established a 'coffee factory' capable of producing 360 gallons of the piping-hot drink per hour.

Once in Europe the American Army took time to grasp the realities of the static, trench-dominated war that had developed on the Western Front. The 'bibles' of US Army instructors – *Infantry Drill Regulations* (1911) and *Field Service Regulations* (1914) – were the fruits of wars against Native Americans and Mexicans that required rapid movement and accurate rifle fire. Massive artillery barrages, poison gas, tanks, aircraft and machine guns were not what General 'Black Jack' Pershing knew about, and doughboys landing in France were usually sent to camps for final training before being sent 'over the top.'

But despite their lack of experience, the Americans were impressive. Robert Munro, the Secretary for Scotland, had encountered 'lithe, sinewy, purposeful' US troops in London. Just weeks before the *Otranto* sailed for Britain he told a cheering audience that thronged the Rifle Hall in the town of Wick: 'Now the sons of America are streaming month by month across the trackless ocean to join with the Allies. Transport follows transport, in proud defiance of the sudden death which lurks beneath the waves.' Vera Brittain, the writer, feminist, pacifist and mother of the politician Baroness Shirley Williams, was serving as a VAD (Voluntary Aid Detachment) nurse in France when she witnessed the arrival of the fresh young doughboys at the port and rail depot of Étaples in April 1918. 'Then I heard an excited exclamation from a group of Sisters behind me. "Look! Look! Here are the Americans!" I pressed forward with the others to watch the United States physically entering the War, so God-like, so magnificent, so splendidly unimpaired in comparison with the tired, nerve-wracked men of the British Army. So these were our deliverers at last, marching up the road to Camiers in the spring sunshine! There seemed to be hundreds of them, and in the fearless swagger of their proud strength they looked a formidable bulwark against the peril looming from Amiens.'

Nurse Brittain, whose own fiancé had been killed on the front, wept with relief when she saw her country's brave New World allies march to war. British men were now in short supply. In seven months between the burial of the *Tuscania* victims, and the departure of the *Otranto* for Europe, Islay lost fifty more of its own warriors. Four were lost at sea. The others lie buried far from home, some in cemeteries at Arras, the Somme, Ypres, Cambrai, Egypt, Macedonia and Mozambique. But the Islay soil that these men might have eventually lain in, if the world had been at peace, was soon to be enriched once more by the youth of another nation.

∽

Among the Americans serving in France were the survivors of the *Tuscania*. After recovering and being re-equipped, Arthur Siplon of the 100th Aero Squadron had made the final stage of his journey to war in a cattle boat from England to Le Havre. Edward Lauer eventually got to France in mid-March and, after being briefly billeted in tents with a regiment of 'Scotch Highlanders', finally caught up with the 32nd Division. 'Because of our disaster, instead of being the first, we were the last of the Division to arrive in the 10th training area.'

May 1918 saw the Americans' first major offensive action at the Battle of Cantigny. In June, in the Second Battle of the Marne, American troops played an important role in halting a German thrust towards Paris. In July, 1,000 of them joined a British/Australian attack during the Battle of Hamel, and in September General Pershing commanded more than 500,000 men of the American First Army in the Battle of Saint-Mihiel. One participant in that action was Thomas Conway of the 213th Aero Squadron. Despite scarred hands from sliding down a rope into a lifeboat and permanent lung damage from exposure and inhaling fuel oil, he had completed his air training at the Number One School of Aerial Fighting, at Ayr in Scotland, before transferring to France where he flew numerous reconnaissance missions over the German lines. At Saint-Mihiel, he played his part in the American First Army's first major battle and victory in Europe.

∾

And still they came. On 25 September 1918, HMS *Otranto* left New York as the flagship of Convoy HX-50. She had 701 American soldiers aboard, bound for Liverpool and then the Western Front. One of these men was 23-year-old Edgar Sheppard, the only son of a farming family who lived in Augusta, South Georgia. In July that year Edgar was one of 108 local men to receive their draft notices. He recalled that all his family had sombre faces – except himself. When the day came to leave, his family accompanied him to the rail depot. 'The time comes to kiss my family goodby; and the hardest test to endure was to embrace my mother. With tears streaming from her brown eyes, I told her I would come back. A captain, an officer from Camp Handcock, who was a spectator, said to my mother, "Lady, I have never seen such a courageous goodby! Your son expresses confidence of his return."' But Sheppard admits that as soon as the train began to roll out the depot: 'I could not hold out any longer; and did I boo-hoo, yes, to my fill.'

Sheppard was on his way to Fort Screven in Georgia, a training base on the Atlantic coast, 17 miles from Savannah. Also heading there were men from Sylvania, in Screven County, Georgia. Sylvania was rural small-town America, and home to about 1,400 people. Only a few months before, as new recruits, the Sylvania men had paraded through their hometown to the sound of brass bands and the cheers of their fellow townsfolk, and were treated to a barbecue before boarding a train for induction into the army. Jonas Ossian Johnson was one of more than 60 recruits who posed for a photograph on the steps of City Hall, Galesburg, Illinois, before clambering aboard a train for Fort Screven. Johnson had not long emigrated from Sweden and was now taking the first steps of a journey that would take him back to 'old Europe'. His grandparents and uncle waved him off at the station.

By mid-September the young recruits were deemed ready for war. Now dressed in their coarse olive-drab uniforms and the 'MI917' helmets that were a copy of the British 'tin hat', they were ordered to Camp Merritt in New Jersey, just a few miles north of New York Harbour. Each man had been treated to an 'overseas haircut' – a drastic shearing with horse clippers, to help keep him louse-free in cramped quarters below decks. Said one doughboy: 'Bumps, depressions and scars, hitherto hidden by comely locks, now were pitilessly revealed.'

On Monday 23 September, laden with heavy packs and wearing their winter uniforms and unfamiliar hobnailed boots, they marched the hot dusty miles to Alpine Landing on the Hudson River. Blistered and sweating, they boarded a ferry for the downriver journey to New York City. Disembarking at Pier 95, at the foot of 55th Street, Edgar Sheppard welcomed his first food of the day. 'I do not recall eating anything but two doughnuts and a cup of coffee, issued by the Salvation Army on the trip. We were two weeks from pay-day – no money and an empty stomach.' Fuelled by coffee and doughnuts, Sheppard and 700 others tramped, single file, up the gangplank of HMS *Otranto*.

～

The *Otranto* was a graceful passenger ship built in Belfast for the Orient Shipping Line. Her high superstructure caused her to be called 'the Floating Haystack' during her war years, but the space had once allowed her 300 first-class passengers to dine in a luxury oak-panelled restaurant, decorated in the style of Louis

XVI. There was accommodation for a further 140 second-class and 850 third-class passengers. During her trials on the Clyde, the ship's two sets of quadruple-expansion engines drove her along at nearly 19 knots. The new owners were well pleased, and soon the *Otranto* was plying profitably between England and Australia, carrying passengers and mail. On 4 August, 1914 – the day war broke out – that all changed. Her owners received a telegram. 'Urgent and Confidential. *Otranto* is requisitioned under Royal Proclamation for service as an armed merchant cruiser STOP Owners required to supply coal full bunkers engine room and deck stores for four months . . .' At once work began riveting half-inch armour-plating onto the elegant liner and arming her with eight 4.7-inch guns. Within a week the Steam Ship *Otranto* was commissioned as His Majesty's Ship *Otranto*, an Armed Merchant Cruiser. An officer who knew her before the war recalled: 'The bright ship that I had known in peacetime was a drab one now, both externally and internally. The gleaming paint of her mail-running had given place to the dull Atlantic grey of war. All her interior decorations had been ripped out, every unessential piece of woodwork cut away, and no superfluous deck-house was left standing on her. She was a ship brought to her bare bones.'

Now the *Otranto* was to be run under the strict military discipline of the Royal Navy, although many of her officers and men were drawn from the Royal Naval Reserve. As an Armed Merchant Cruiser, HMS *Otranto* had played a minor role in the Battle of Coronel, off Chile, but because she was hopelessly outgunned by German cruisers she was ordered out of the line, and thus survived the first British naval defeat in more than a century. After three years of arduous and dangerous duty, without sustaining serious damage, the *Otranto*'s crew regarded her as 'a favourite of fortune' – a lucky ship. When one officer joined her in Liverpool, the *Otranto* was being given more punch – eight six-inch guns. 'Men were swarming over her night and day to get her re-fitted for sea again. Their main task was to replace with guns of heavier calibre the poor 4.7's that had given her no real chance of acting other than as a target in the action off Coronel.' In the summer of 1918, the *Otranto* arrived in New York, where she was fitted with accommodation for troops, and made her first voyage as a troopship, transporting doughboys to the Port of Liverpool. One of her passengers was Buster Keaton, who served with the 40th US Infantry Division before becoming a silent movie star.

One of the *Otranto*'s officers was Paymaster-Commander Archibald Bruce Campbell, a colourful character who would survive the war to continue his adventurous career. Possessed of an impeccable Scottish name (it would be unremarkable on Islay), he was born in Peckham, London. His autobiography, *With the Corners Off*, includes a vivid account of the last voyage of the *Otranto*. Campbell was a natural storyteller, a raconteur who became a popular public figure as a founding contributor to *The Brains Trust*, a peak-time radio show, launched by the BBC in 1941. He made 200 appearances on the show and – it is claimed – was only dropped from it when he suggested that scientists, not animals, be used in atomic bomb tests on Bikini Atoll.

Campbell recalled huge crowds assembling to cheer the troops marching down New York's 55th Street to the wharves on the Hudson River, from where they would sail in a convoy for Europe. 'And now along the gaily bedecked street, between the flutter of waving flags and streamers, bringing with them a tidal-wave of cheering, came rank after rank of American citizen soldiers, an endless stream of them, marching steadily in their olive drab with a flittering spearhead of colour – the band in gay uniforms and with their sun-reflecting instruments. Here came the passengers for the twelve liners, a contingent of "dough-boys" bound for the Western Front.' The last troops to arrive climbed up the *Otranto*'s gangplank. At least five almost immediately went absent without leave (AWOL), probably by clambering down the ship's hawsers and back onto the pier, but the official records show that in addition to the 380 crew, and two American YMCA officers, there were 701 US servicemen of all ranks aboard the *Otranto* as she prepared to steam past the Statue of Liberty – in all, 1,083 souls.

∽

Before the *Otranto* had even left New York, a number of men showed symptoms of illness, shivering and coughing. Doctors had ordered nine men off the ship and into hospital. The ship had a stowaway aboard – a microscopic virus that would, in time, be more deadly than any U-boat, or even the Kaiser's entire war machine. Second Lieutenant Bernie Coffman, who commanded the 406th Casual Company, and was the son of a real estate agent from Galesburg, Illinois, was among the first to feel unwell. Soon, other men began to cough and run temperatures. Even as she set sail, the *Otranto*'s sickbay was busy.

That year, death – as if not satisfied with the cull that a mechanised, global war inflicted – launched a biological weapon against the human race. The H1N1 influenza virus was pandemic, affecting entire continents, and in just three years would kill what has been estimated to have been between 50 and 100 million people. About a quarter of a million people in Britain died. Nobody knows where it originated, and it was only named 'Spanish Flu' because uncensored newspapers in neutral Spain weren't banned from revealing to the world how serious the outbreak was. While most flu viruses kill the very young, the very old or the very frail, H1N1 was most virulent among fit and healthy young men and women. It killed by provoking a cytokine storm, an intense over-reaction of the immune system. The stronger the immune system – as in vigorous young adults – the worse the victim suffered. Young soldiers in their teens and twenties were highly susceptible. Fever, swelling, fatigue and nausea were the symptoms. Death was often the outcome. The virus flourished where people crowded together – in military barracks, trenches, hospitals, railway carriages and below deck on crammed troopships. And it had crept aboard the *Otranto*. It is certain that two soldiers died of flu, and were buried at sea during the voyage to Liverpool, but, because the ship's captain and his logbook were lost, we may never know how many of the *Otranto*'s passengers had succumbed to the virus before she sank. And we can certainly never know how many men died because they were so debilitated by illness that they didn't have the strength to fight for their lives. Official US sources reveal that in 1918 nearly 1,500 cases of influenza and pneumonia developed at sea during the convoys, and that seven hundred American soldiers died at sea. Furthermore, 3,000 sick men were removed from troopships at Halifax, where seven hundred perished. Several hundred others also died in France after they'd made it ashore. At a conservative estimate, flu on troopships in 1918 cost America 2,000 lives.

❧

On the afternoon of 25 September, the *Otranto* left New York as the flagship of the British fast-liner Convoy HX-50, with her commander, the experienced Captain Ernest Davidson, serving as commodore of the convoy. Davidson, whose family had been the Lairds of Tulloch Castle near Dingwall in Highland Scotland, was born in Rangoon, the son of a colonial police officer. He joined the Royal Navy in 1889 as a 14-year-old cadet and gradually earned his right to command. By 1903 he was a lieutenant serving on the Yangtze River in China, where he met and married Winifred Lamond, the daughter of a Shanghai-based Scottish marine engineer from Dundee. By the time war broke out, the couple had a two-year-old daughter. Davidson took command of the *Otranto* in September 1916, as acting captain, and successfully guided her across the Atlantic many times during the most desperate period of the U-boats' war of attrition. He was a capable and respected skipper.

When Convoy HX-50 left New York, Captain Davidson's *Otranto* was sailing a day late. Although her principal role was to lead and protect the troopships, at the last moment she unexpectedly had to take on board army units that had been delayed on their journey to New York. Most of them were units of what was called the September Automatic Replacement Draft, from Fort Screven, Georgia. Some of them had been trained to fire heavy coastal artillery, but many were poorly trained. Private Harold English had only been in the army for five or six weeks, and said that he and his SARD comrades 'barely knew squad formations, let alone artillery work'. Also aboard were Casual Companies 406 and 410. These were hastily assembled units, comprised mostly of men for whom the lights of New York City had been irresistible, and who had previously gone AWOL from other units. They were commanded by 2nd Lieutenant Bernie Coffman, who was one of the first officers on board to show symptoms of flu. The enlisted men found their berths deep in the cargo holds. Private English's reaction to the conditions was typical. 'Descending the stairs, one met a strong, sickening odor of phenol used in disinfectants; and this odor, reminding one of a hospital, seemed to pervade the whole ship.' Commissioned officers and the YMCA men were allocated cabins, but the rest of the men slept in hammocks, hanging above rows of tables that would be their day quarters when foul weather kept them from being on deck.

Sometime after midday on 25 September, the *Otranto* cast off to join the convoy anchored at the mouth of the Hudson River. By 3 pm HX-50 was underway. As well as the *Otranto*, there were twelve troopships, eleven of them British vessels and one French ship. Thirteen ships in all. 'Perhaps an ominous number,' Commander Campbell later noted. Statistics show that troopship convoys were a relatively safe way of transporting the

American Army across the Atlantic. But every soldier on board knew the fate of the *Tuscania*, less than eight months earlier. The boasts of its British crew that the *Otranto* – the easily spotted 'Floating Haystack' – was a 'lucky ship', didn't quell talk among the American soldiers about their chances of being 'tin-fished'.

There were 20,000 American soldiers on the thirteen ships of Convoy HX-50 and, with so many young lives at stake, the American Navy took no chances. As the convoy left American waters for the open sea, it was escorted by US cruisers *Louisiana* and *St Louis* and the destroyer USS *Dorsey*. The cruisers would only go partway across the Atlantic, but the *Dorsey* would travel all the way to Ireland where it would join forces with an escort of British destroyers. The troopships sailed in six columns, with the *Otranto* the leading ship of the third column. Column four was led by the converted P&O liner *Kashmir*, with more than 2,000 soldiers aboard. The two ships would zigzag across the Atlantic six cables (1,200 yards) apart. Every ship's captain knew his position in the convoy and was expected to adhere strictly to it. If a vessel became separated from the convoy, its captain had sealed orders that would give him a position to head for, off the northern coast of Ireland, where he could re-join the convoy. There the British destroyers would escort them through the U-boat 'danger zone' to Liverpool. At daybreak, three pairs of American minesweepers and the patrol boat, *Tarantula*, had sailed ahead to make sure that the coast was clear. The minesweepers marked, with buoys, a two-mile-wide safe corridor that stretched eighteen miles out to sea, while the *Tarantula* cut her engine at regular intervals to listen out for the sound of churning U-boat propellers with an underwater sonar device. The most effective submarine-detecting equipment remained, however, vigilance and sharp eyes. The US patrol boat, *Xarifa*, had left at noon, three hours ahead of the convoy. Shackled to her deck was a captive observation balloon, from which lookouts with binoculars scanned the sea for periscopes breaking the surface. While U-boat losses were now high, they were still a major threat to a convoy with more than 20,000 men on board.

The convoy steamed out of New York Harbour toward the Atlantic Ocean. For many of the 701 American soldiers on board it would be their first, and last, view of the Statue of Liberty and the Manhattan skyline. Private James Harmon, who was in the same unit as his brother, Clyde, wrote to his mother: 'We boarded the transport that was to take us "over there." As we left our dear old country and bid adieu to the Statue of Liberty in a mist of rain, so our view of land was hidden.' Despite the weather, Edgar Sheppard drank in that last view. 'As we began to cruise out of harbour, the mayor of the city of New York and others waved us goodby. The mournful sound of our ship whistle blows as we are headed out to sea. We pass Ellis Island and wave goodby to the girls standing by the Statue of Liberty.'

The convoy sailed at a speedy 13 knots. The defensive zigzag path was strictly maintained. To avoid radio messages alerting U-boats, orders to the convoy from the commodore on board the *Otranto* were relayed by flags. Everything was going according to plan. The professionalism of the British and American sailors encouraged the soldiers, most of whom – like Edgar Sheppard – had never been at sea before. 'In those days the commanders of our convoys were in the saddle and knew just what to do. This act of courage helped the morale of all men aboard.'

The US Naval Intelligence Department had received disturbing news. The Nantucket Lightship had sighted two German U-boats lurking in the area. Captain Davidson frowned and pondered. He and his first officer pored over the charts. At last, he made his decision: 'Very well. We'll take the northerly course.' The northerly course would take the convoy over the Newfoundland Banks, and into dirty wintry weather, but Davidson decided that fog was less of a hazard to a well-ordered fleet of seaworthy ships than enemy submarines. Edgar Sheppard remembers the first few days of the voyage as being warm and fair, of watching porpoises follow the *Otranto*'s wake and of being rocked to sleep in his hammock by the rhythm of the ship. But no matter how well organised was the convoy, no military authority could control the weather. Autumn in northern waters is challenging and dangerous. For doughboy landlubbers the wide, lonely ocean must soon have seemed a hostile and sinister place. Buffeted by strong north-westerly winds and heavy seas, and hampered by poor visibility, the convoy reduced its speed to ten knots. The ships wallowed in the waves, and seasickness was rife. With doors and hatches closed against bad weather there was no ventilation below decks. The smells of the retch buckets, disinfectant, boiled mutton and confined humanity made men nauseous, even if the rolling of the ship didn't. The vast majority of American farm boys aboard had never been to sea before, but even experienced British Marines were vomiting. Over the days that followed, almost every soldier on board would be physically and mentally weakened by seasickness. Many a miserable doughboy claimed that he 'wouldn't mind if the damned ship sank.' The story was the same throughout the convoy. On every ship doctors were overworked, trying to tell those stricken with flu from the merely seasick. On the *Otranto* almost 100 men were seriously affected, including 2nd Lieutenant Bernie Coffman, who commanded one of the Casual Companies of deserters that had been rounded up and marched aboard. Extra sickbays were created wherever space could be found. Fit soldiers were detailed to become medical orderlies.

The convoy of camouflaged ships sailed through the nights entirely blacked out, relying on the skill of their navigators to keep them in position and from colliding. Even smoking on deck at night was forbidden. But the 701 soldiers on board the *Otranto* were lucky compared to the men on the overcrowded *Kashmir*. She was smaller than the *Otranto*, and on this trip carried more than 2,000 troops, including 1,368 men of the

126th Field Artillery. Among them was Paul Frederickson, who would later write a gripping account of 'the greatest sea disaster to befall American forces in the war'.

On the stormy evening of Tuesday 1 October, came a crash and violent judder that sent men streaming up onto decks, believing that they had been torpedoed. Six days out of New York, off the coast of Newfoundland, the *Otranto* had rammed the French three-masted schooner, *Croisine*, which was part of a fishing fleet returning to Brittany with a hold full of salted cod. As she rasped along the troopship's port side, the fishing boat's mast ripped away many of the *Otranto*'s lifeboats and their launching gear. For fear of submarines, neither the convoy nor the fishing fleet had been showing lights. Unwilling to have the convoy slow down, Captain Davidson ordered the HX-50 to sail on, while the *Otranto* stopped to assist the *Croisine*. Under the command of Lieutenant O'Sullevan, a boat was rowed out from the *Otranto* to the fishing boat. Such was the damage to her it was decided to pick up her crew. It was a risk. Any U-boat for miles around could have homed in on the *Otranto*'s searchlight as she sat motionless, a sitting duck, while her rescue boat picked up 36 fishermen and captain Jules Lehoerff's Newfoundland dog. Private Harold English said there were 'whispered conjectures' among the demoralised soldiers about the danger of being torpedoed. English watched the fishermen come aboard the *Otranto*: 'The captain was in appearance much like the oldtime sailor one reads about in stories of the days of sail: a huge, rather grizzled man wearing a full beard.' *Otranto* officer, Archibald Campbell, described the rescued fishermen.

> The shipwrecked men were huddled together on our deck. They were scared nearly out of their lives. Some fell on their knees and seemed to beg for mercy. None of us could make out what language the castaways were talking. French, German, Spanish were tried on them,

but they shook their heads. 'Excuse me, sir,' said a quartermaster to me. 'Them blokes seem to be slingin' the same lingo as our Jock Ferguson and Bill Mackay use when they're yarning private.'

'Fetch one of these men along – or both!' I said.

Jock Ferguson was available. He was a Royal Fleet Reserve man, in pre-War days a fisherman in the Orkneys. He had little difficulty in making the shipwrecked men understand him, for they were Breton fishermen, and Jock's Gaelic was akin to their speech.

This may be an exaggerated tale. The Orkney Islands have never been Gaelic-speaking, and while it is possible that a Gaelic-speaking Hebridean had been fishing there, he would have to have been a proficient Celtic scholar to have been able to understand much of the Breton strain of the Celtic tongue. But Campbell is accurate in that the *Croisine* was a Breton vessel, and it may well be that the crew were monoglot Breton speakers. But, whatever language they spoke, the *Otranto* now had 36 more men aboard. Then, reports Harold English, because the wallowing wreck was a hazard to other convoys, the *Otranto* sank it with her guns. 'Twenty five shells, in all, were fired. Soon the *Croisine* was burning fiercely, lighting up the whole sky in a dancing glow of dull red. She had a three-inch gun, and when the flames reached her ammunition hold there was a series of explosions that flung skyward burning planks, which showered off sparks fantastically. To the soldiers lining the *Otranto*'s decks it was a sight they would never forget.'

At 2.30 am on 2 October, the *Otranto* went full steam ahead to catch the convoy. That day, flu claimed its first victim. For days now, the beds of the *Otranto*'s sickbay had been filling up. When the main dining room was turned into an emergency hospital, it filled up too. The following morning, Private Lonnie Smith was buried at sea, wrapped in a weighted canvas bag that had been draped in the American flag. From the masthead, the Union Jack was hauled down to fly at half-mast. 'Taps' was sounded on the bugle and three rifle volleys were fired in salute. Private Smith was not the last to succumb to flu on the *Otranto*. Three days later Private Benton Endfield died. No matter how much effort was made to dignify burials at sea, Commander Campbell remembered them as chilling events. 'It was ghastly to see the corpse, unstiffened from being so recently dead, slide off the gratings. They would double as they fell, and, instead of plunging smoothly into the deep, would hit the surface with a resounding thwack.' Spanish flu was a virulent disease. When *The City of York*, another ship of Convoy HX-50, finally reached port, 28 sick men were taken ashore, of whom 17 died shortly afterwards.

Flu was not the only killer. Edgar Sheppard recalled that sailors on lookout fell into the ocean on account of the heavy seas, and that an American soldier became so depressed that he leapt into the sea from an upper deck and that it was too dangerous for the *Otranto* to stop to attempt a rescue. Commander Campbell recalled an incident that resembles something from a horror story.

> I was stopped one morning by a gum-chewing dough-boy. 'Say, Cap,' said he (anyone in uniform was 'Cap' to a dough-boy), 'there's a guy been lyin' on the smoke-room floor for three days, and he's never moved.'
>
> 'Let's go and look,' I said, and led the way.
>
> In the seats around the lounge and on the deck the soldiers in number sprawled in the misery of sea-sickness or the first onset of the epidemic malady. Over by the piano one man lay face downward, his hands stretched out under the instrument. I stopped and caught hold of his legs to pull him clear. At the first grasp of his limbs a faint nausea gripped me, for they were stiff and leaden. I

dragged him out and turned him over. Glazed eyes stared up at me. The dead wrists had been gnawed by rats.

Not a day passed when a ship of the convoy wouldn't request permission to slow down in order to conduct a burial at sea. During daylight hours the men who braved the weather to get fresh air on the *Otranto*'s deck could see that the stern flags of other ships were flying at half-mast. At least twenty men died on the *Kashmir*, and the doctors on that ship were so overwhelmed that they refused to admit anybody to the sickbay with a temperature of less than 104°F. According to an account in the Museum of Islay Life, by an anonymous storekeeper who served on the crowded *Kashmir*: 'Influenza was rife on the *Kashmir*. A lot of GIs died. There were continual burials at sea. Stern flags on all the ships dipped on each funeral. At one time there was a queue of dead soldiers waiting to be buried, in fact the American padre could not leave his position on the gun platform, he was too busy.'

On the *Otranto*, according to Commander Campbell, Captain Davidson had now caught influenza, but despite doctor's orders, stuck to his duties. Two of his officers were 'babbling in sick-bay'. The ship's doctor and the American Army doctor were 'worn to shadows of themselves by fatigue'.

❧

Dawn broke on Sunday 6 October to reveal Convoy HX-50 being battered by a south-westerly hurricane somewhere off the north coast of Ireland. The *Kashmir*'s storekeeper wrote: 'Boiled eggs were on the menu for the troops, and as the ration for an American soldier was 3 eggs, we on that morning would expect to cook 9,000 eggs. As there were many troops down seasick we just passed the word that whatever any mess wanted in the way of eggs could be had for the asking. It was surprising how few had breakfast that morning.'

There was a much more serious problem than lack of appetite dogging the convoy – nobody was quite sure where they were. Because of the weather, none of the ships' officers had been able to take a 'sight' for four days. The storm obscured the sun and stars, and attempts to find their position by radio had failed. In a pre-radar and pre-GPS era, men like Captain Davidson were used to navigating by 'dead reckoning' – estimating a ship's position from previous positions in its log book, and trying to factor in the likely effect of tide and wind on the vessel since that last position was plotted. But sailing in convoy (the *Kashmir* was only half a mile to starboard), with the ship being tossed about among gigantic waves, in a hurricane, off a dangerous coast, required almost superhuman seamanship, and a dash of good luck.

Private David Roberts, a 17-year-old who had enlisted months before reaching draft age, remembered: 'The waves were like mountains . . . and when I went on deck, the sea was grass green – formerly it had been bluish black – just like the Kentucky mountains. We were like a train going down into the valley.' Wind speeds were between eighty and ninety miles per hour – hurricane force. Pounding waves, sixty feet high, battered the ships, sending towers of spume crashing over them and into the faces of masters, navigators and lookouts. Such was the force of the storm that the British destroyers, sent out from Buncrana in Northern Ireland to meet the convoy 200 miles west of the Irish coast and escort it to Liverpool, had been ordered back to port for their own safety. The following day – Saturday 5 October – they were ordered out again to find the convoy. One destroyer, HMS *Mounsey*, developed a technical problem, and finally left Buncrana seven hours late.

Captain Davidson was following a course that would bring the convoy to the entrance of the North Channel the following dawn, but the straggling convoy was taking a pounding, and had probably been blown twenty miles north of where Davidson calculated it should be. One of the ships reported seeing a light, and thought it was Tory Island lighthouse, nine miles northwest off the coast of Donegal, but the *Otranto*'s watch questioned that.

≫

Calum Anderson lives in the storm-beaten village he was born in – Port Wemyss on the far west point of Islay. Due south lies the north coast of Ireland, and the water that lies between Port Wemyss and Ireland is the gateway to the North Channel – the seaway between the west coast of Scotland and the east coast of Ireland. From his traditional white-painted terrace cottage Calum can gaze out on the Rhinns Lighthouse which stands about 300 yards offshore on the tiny island of Orsay. On wild days the sight of the spray-lashed lighthouse is a sobering reminder of the power and malevolence of the sea. Not that Calum needs to be reminded. He is a retired sailor who first went to sea as a 15-year-old apprentice, and ended his career as fleet commodore of the huge China Navigation Company. In retirement he has been involved in the running of the Islay lifeboat, and has a hands-on role in the restoration of *Auld Reekie*, an old Clyde Puffer. Calum's knowledge of the sea, and respect for it, appear to be bottomless. In his lifetime he has witnessed enormous strides in navigation technology, but as a young man he sailed with old salts who well remembered never having things so easy.

Calum is filled with sympathy for Captain Davidson and the other masters and officers of Convoy HX-50 who found themselves in a Force 11, somewhere off the challenging Celtic coasts of Scotland and Ireland. 'It must have been terrible because they would have no reliable navigation equipment, they would have been running on DR (dead reckoning), just estimated positions all the time. An estimated position is all right for a wee while, but it took them ten days to come across the Atlantic, and if they had not been able to make a sighting for four days – crikey!' Calum is certain that even the sharpest-eyed lookouts on the *Otranto* and the *Kashmir* couldn't have spotted the danger of collision before it was too late. In 1970, when an oil tanker foundered in a storm south of Taiwan, Calum's ship steamed to the rescue. 'She split in half and there were thousands of tons of oil. We went to pick up what we could of the crew, and I launched a lifeboat and told the crew, 'Don't lose sight of the ship'. And of course, they did. And I lost sight of them. Now our bridge height was 45 feet, and with the mast there would have been another 30 feet, so that was about 75 feet. They couldn't see us. That just shows you, you're not seeing anything at all. We had monstrous waves, but because of the amount of oil on the surface we didn't have breakers. But they (*Otranto* and *Kashmir*) would have breakers and spray and all that – so you'd hardly see a thing. They were sailing blind. When you think of them out there . . . what was the state of the tide? If the tide was against the prevailing wind, in addition to everything else you get these overfalls [sudden races of water]. It must have been terrible. In bad weather that west coast out there is probably one of the roughest places in the world.'

≈

Around 8 am on the Sunday morning, the rain and cloud lifted briefly to reveal how scattered the convoy had become. From the *Otranto*'s bridge only eight of Convoy HX-50's 12 other vessels could be seen, some of them too far away to identify. The *Kashmir* was half a mile away, but instead of being abreast, it was 'abaft the beam' – slightly trailing on the *Otranto*'s port side. The *Otranto* was steaming at 11 knots, while the *Kashmir*, anxious to regain its correct position in the convoy, was a little faster, perhaps as much as 14 knots. The weather was bad, with high and very broken seas and gale-force winds from the south-west. Captain Davidson and his navigation officer, Lieutenant Harry Woodcock, took the opportunity of the improved visibility to snatch a quick breakfast. They had only just sat down when the officer of the watch (OOW) spotted land. Was it the coast of Ireland he could glimpse, or that of the Inner Hebridean island of Islay? If it was Ireland, the *Otranto* needed to turn north so as to be able sail round it before steering south into the North Channel. If it was Islay, their route lay to the south. On the *Kashmir* the decision – partly based on depth soundings – was made that it was Islay that they could glimpse through the spindrift and biting rain squalls. On the flagship *Otranto* a different conclusion was reached by the OOW. Although he sent a midshipman to fetch the captain, he decided that the convoy should turn to port and head north, and ordered the helmsman to change course. Transfixed by the sight of the dangerous coast, nobody on the bridge kept an eye on the *Kashmir*. A senior English judge would later be highly critical of the *Otranto*'s 'bad look-out'.

According to Commander Campbell: 'The Officer of the Watch had a signal hoisted for the convoy to alter course to port. The wind almost blew the signal bunting to shreds. In the bad light, that silver gloom in which colours are so difficult to distinguish, the signal must have been misread aboard the *Kashmir* . . . she altered course to starboard.' The decision made on board the *Otranto* was the wrong one: the convoy's route lay south down the North Channel between Ireland and Scotland, not north. But if the *Kashmir* had seen the signal and turned north, even though it knew that they were heading on the wrong direction, the ships wouldn't have been on a collision course. The *Otranto* gave two blasts of its siren to indicate that it was turning to port, but Commander Campbell says that the signal failed to alert the *Kashmir* to the change of course. 'The warning was unheeded by the other ship. It was probably lost to her officers' ears in the clamorous force of the storm.' The *Kashmir* kept to her course.

Captain Davidson, now back on the bridge, ordered 'hard-a-port' and rang 'full-speed-astern' on both engines, while giving three blasts on the ship's siren. The *Kashmir* too desperately tried to manoeuvre out of danger, but the two captains' frantic efforts cancelled each other out. The *Kashmir* – 9,000 tons of Clyde-wrought steel – was now bearing down on the *Otranto* at a speed of up to 14 knots. *Otranto*'s navigation officer, Lieutenant Woodcock, recalled: 'The OOW had altered course to Port and the *Kashmir* had apparently altered course to Starboard for both ships were rapidly closing on each other and steering about very badly owing to the tremendous seas. No whistle signals had been given by either ships up to this time, as far as I am aware. The Captain who got on the Bridge almost simultaneously with myself, then took charge, but it was obvious that collision was absolutely inevitable.'

On board the *Kashmir*, artilleryman Paul Frederickson saw the tragedy inexorably unfold. 'Towards the end neither commander could do more than reverse engines and blow whistles and hope. At 8.43 the two steel ships were close together at right angles, the *Otranto*'s port side exposed to the other vessel. From the *Kashmir*'s hurricane deck a few of us saw the thing happen. The *Otranto* was in a deep trough. A tremendous wave lifted the *Kashmir* and flung her forward. Looking ahead and down, we could see a score of *Otranto* soldiers – lined up at the canteen amidships – break and run wildly.'

On board the *Otranto*, Archibald Campbell was oblivious to the danger until the siren sounded.

I heard the siren warnings while down below. They told me something was wrong, and I ran up on deck to walk forward on the starboard side. An American soldier came to me camera in hand. Many of the troops had cameras, but the rule was that permission had to be asked before photographing ships and so forth. 'Say, Cap,' he said. 'Will it be alright for me to snap that big ship?'

'What ship?'

'The one that's coming so close – on the other side now.' I rushed across the alley-way of one of the rooms, followed by the soldier. As I stepped from the alley-way door to port, my heart, I do believe, stood still. On the crest of a huge wave, not twenty feet from the ship's side, was poised the axe-like bow of the *Kashmir*. Within a second or two she would strike down upon the *Otranto* and cut into her side like a knife into cheese. Not even a miracle could now avert a dreadful disaster. I grabbed the soldier by the arm and hauled him into the alley-way. At that moment the blow fell. The whole ship shuddered as if in the throes of death. With the grinding and crashing of steel plates as they were rent apart, the wrenching of the fittings inside the stricken ship, that dreadful clamour, were mingled the shrieks of crushed and tortured men below.

Paul Frederickson recalled: 'With a grinding, tearing noise, more felt by us than heard, the *Kashmir*'s stem cut into the *Otranto*'s port side almost at midships. It first struck near the hurricane deck and as the *Otranto* rose from the trough it plunged down, smashing some of the running men and not stopping until it had knifed through below the *Otranto*'s water line. Then, as the *Otranto* rolled into a trough again, the *Kashmir*'s prow came up through the same gaping wound. It slit as high as the boat deck, flinging splintered lifeboats aside as a final gesture. The *Otranto* answered with a heavenward puff of steam.' It was 8.45 in the morning. Below decks, only seconds before, soldiers were having breakfast. Private Joseph Hewell had just finished eating. 'All of a sudden there was a terrific jar and the ship trembled all over, so everybody who had been very quiet and who had shown no uneasiness now gave a big rush to go up on deck, but all of us were told to be quiet as there was nothing the matter so everybody sat down again and in about 15 to 20 minutes word came down to us to get up on deck immediately. Everybody went up leaving behind all their equipment and personal belongings. When we came out on deck the wind was blowing at the rate of 70 to 75 miles an hour, probably more or less, but a fellow would have to hold to ropes or something to keep from being blown overboard. Nobody I think knew what condition the ship was in for if they had known I am sure there would have been more excitement or panic among the men.' The *Otranto* was mortally wounded, and in the grip of a storm.

❧

A judge of the Admiralty Division of the High Court of Justice later placed the blame for the collision equally on both ships. It was a judgement that seems to be both fair and harsh. The bleary-eyed and exhausted officers of both ships had strained every nerve to bring their vessels safely to Liverpool through a ferociously stormy and U-boat-infested ocean. Heartachingly close to their final destination and safety, they had failed. But the odds had been stacked against them, and it was a miracle that there were not more fatal collisions among the tightly knit convoys that zigzagged across the perilous waste that is the Atlantic. Perhaps a better judgement might have been expressed in a phrase that Nicholas Monsarrat wrote on page one of his World War Two classic, *The Cruel Sea*: 'the only villain the cruel sea itself'.

For those on board the holed and storm-battered *Otranto* that Sunday morning, it was not the need to blame, but the attempt to survive that would possess them.

❧

Flung forward by an enormous wave, the *Kashmir* had axed a huge gash – 15 or 16 feet deep, according to Lieutenant Woodcock – into the *Otranto*'s port side between its two funnels, crushing men to death in an amidships canteen. A second wave drove the axe further in, breaching the boiler rooms, flooding the stoke holds and drowning crewmen who manned them. The *Kashmir*'s bow had gouged its way into the main sick bay, killing many patients outright. US army doctor Captain Charles Dixon, recalled: 'One of our soldiers had his right foot mashed clear off at the ankle, and three non-commissioned officers in a state room were killed.' Dixon gave the injured soldier 'a hypodermic and a first dressing'. In areas away from the impact many soldiers believed that their ship had been torpedoed, like the *Tuscania*. Those who were fit enough rushed for the upper decks. James Harmon's letter to his mother describes the conditions on the storm-battered decks. 'When we got on deck we found a very strong wind and high waves. One had to hold to something to keep from being swept overboard. The waves seemed like huge mountains. You can never know what it was like until you have been upon a storming sea. We were told that our ship had been rammed by another large ship, which was carrying troops also, the name of this ship was _____ [erased by censor].'

The *Kashmir* reversed her engines, pulling herself free of the *Otranto* and revealing the terrible damage. The storekeeper on the *Kashmir* wrote: 'I felt our engines going astern and we slowly backed away leaving a large hole in the shape of the letter V, from under the waterline up to her top decks. As she rolled away I could see men hanging on for dear life and then having to give up and being washed out to sea. We could do nothing to help them. Our bow was certainly lower in the water than it should be, and the sea in huge waves was crashing down upon us.'

Captain Davidson attempted to turn the *Otranto*'s damaged side alee, so that the gash would not lie face-on to the storm and waves, but the ship had lost steerage. She was dead in the water. Commander Campbell recalled: 'It was then that the Engineer-Commander mounted the bridge to report that no more than a hundred pounds' pressure remained in the boilers, and that even this was decreasing steadily. The stokeholds were full of water, but the engine room was so far only awash. If the bulkheads held the ship might possibly float long enough to allow her to be beached. He had barely finished speaking when the sound of vast rending and tearing rose from the ship's bowels. Men and officers came rushing on deck from below. The vessel gave a great lurch to starboard, and to many it seemed as if she was taking her last plunge. "There go the bulkheads!" said the engineer. With that all the lights went out. Escaping steam shrieked deafeningly. The presence of mind and the personal bravery of one of the engineers below had saved the ship, beyond doubt, from immediate destruction. He had crawled and swum about the engines, opening and shutting the essential cocks to allow free escape of the steam. But for this the inrush of water to the boilers must have brought an explosion.' Such an explosion would have sent the *Otranto* to the bottom immediately. But, in the meantime, she was afloat. While she was afloat, there was hope.

As far as the *Otranto*'s navigation officer Harry Woodcock could see, the destroyers accompanying the convoy hadn't seen the collision through the mist and squalls, and couldn't be contacted by the ship's radios. 'Our wireless was carried away by the impact and the Aux. set was apparently not in working order . . . the Destroyer that picked us up reported that they heard nothing. Our distress signal was hoisted, but there was far too much sea for any ship to attempt to stand by close enough to be of any material assistance, and it was decided to try and beach the ship if possible, when sufficient steam was raised. Unfortunately at this time it was reported that the water was flowing from the stokeholds over the Bulkhead into Engine Room, so that idea had to be abandoned and every effort made to save the troops.'

Captain Davidson ordered soldiers and crew to their 'abandon ship' stations. Edgar Sheppard was at the bow of the *Otranto*. Fit, and with a strong religious faith, he confronted the situation with a confidence that was not shared by all the troops. 'As a boy, I learned to swim in the big rivers in South Georgia, and I came near drowning several times. I also loved to fish; but swimming was my greatest sport, and I dearly loved the water. I felt so sorry for the troops who were much older than I as they were running up and down the deck crying and wringing their hands.' The *Otranto* was now so close to Islay that Sheppard could see cattle and sheep grazing on its pasture. The ship was being driven inexorably toward the rocky coast.

On board the *Kashmir*, the 2,000 American doughboys were ordered to huddle in the stern of the ship. They were shaken, and terrified. Many were seasick or ill with influenza, but they were still useful. Their combined weight in the stern would force the ship's damaged bow up, and keep the jagged hole in it at least partly out of the water. The *Kashmir*'s master – Captain Edmund Burton Bartlett, who had already made two transatlantic trips carrying troops – turned his ship for Glasgow, leaving the *Otranto* wallowing helplessly. The mutual protection of the convoy was now forgotten, as Commander Campbell describes. 'Whether or not her people realized how deadly a wound the blow had dealt it is hard to say. But, acting strictly in accordance with Admiralty regulations, they wheeled their ship away and drove her on her course as if without a thought for the sinking ship they were leaving. A hard rule, it may seem, that bade seamen leave stricken comrades to their fate, but so many good ships had been sacrificed to the enemy while standing by to rescue drowning crews that firm adherence to the principle of no attempt at life-saving was insisted upon. A sanely cruel rule.' Captain Bartlett nursed the holed *Kashmir* to the shelter of the Clyde Estuary, where he dropped anchor for the night. In the morning, the vessel slowly made her way upriver to Glasgow where a fleet of ambulances waited to take her flu victims to hospital. The fit soldiers disembarked, but before marching off gave Captain Bartlett and the *Kashmir*'s crew three rousing cheers.

As the *Kashmir* had retreated into the storm, many of the soldiers on board the *Otranto* had reached the open decks and saw her go. Already their own ship was listing heavily to star-board, but they were assured that they were safe because enough bulkheads held to keep the *Otranto* afloat, although the ship's boiler rooms were flooded and she had no power. The storm was too violent for men to take to the surviving lifeboats. All that could be done was to let the *Otranto* drift, and hope that she came ashore on one of Islay's sandy beaches. Meanwhile the gale was relentlessly driving it north-east – not towards a beach, but onto Islay's rocky coast.

The *Otranto* was now alone. Apart from the *Kashmir*, no other ship in the convoy knew of her plight. Soldiers on deck were told by the crew to lash themselves to something solid to prevent being swept overboard. Many of the troops were hor-rified to find that lifeboats on the port side had been destroyed in the collision, but there was little panic – at least to begin with. Commander Campbell admired the soldiers' calmness, but suspected that this was born of 'ignorance of the gravity of the situation'. One witness claimed he heard shots being fired, and Campbell recalls one young US officer being in great distress. 'I myself had just left him with an encouraging word when a revolver shot rang out. I turned to see the American running round in circles, screaming, with one side of his head blown off. He had tried to blow out his brains, but had managed only to take off a portion of his skull without making himself un-conscious. His screams were awful. Word of the tragedy went along the line of patient soldiery like an electric wave. For a moment or two they wavered; then panic broke among them. Their ranks dissolved, and they swarmed up the companions to take themselves as far away as possible from the encroaching seas.' Others aboard the *Otranto* told of hearing gunshots, but Commander Campbell's account of a suicide is uncorroborated.

Almost 100 men lay in the sickbays deep in the hold. Some were at death's door, others delirious. Second Lieutenant Bernie Coffman had been seriously ill, but had now passed the crisis.

Illness would not now kill him, but were men like him strong enough to do anything to save themselves if the ship foundered? The ship's doctor, American medics and volunteers from among the ranks wrapped them in blankets and carried them through blacked-out corridors and up stairwells to decks where they might have a chance of surviving if the ship went down.

As the men flocked to the higher decks, their weight destabilised the ship. At the stern of the *Otranto*, the crowded boat-deck collapsed, throwing men into the sea and crushing others on the aft well-deck. It nearly killed Captain Davidson, who was on deck inspecting damage. The ship was now listing heavily to starboard. The wind howled through the rigging, unnerving even the stoutest heart. One of the crew told a soldier that the situation 'looks pretty damned rotten'. Even the farm-boy landlubbers among the American soldiers knew that their plight was desperate. 'We had no hopes – to jump into the sea meant death, for one could not live long in such a mad sea. The lifeboats were useless, as they had been crushed to pieces. We could see, over to the right, a great high cliff of rocks, not more than a half-mile away, but no hope there, as we knew we would be dashed to death against the rocks. You could see the waves break upon them.' James Harmon and the other soldiers on deck could clearly see Islay, but then something else was spotted on the *Otranto*'s starboard side. A glimmer of hope triggered a spontaneous cheer from many of the thousand men aboard. 'To our great joy a British destroyer greeted our eyes, for here lay our only hopes.'

7

And There Was a Seaman!

Sea of stretch'd ground-swells,
Sea breathing broad and convulsive breaths,
Sea of the brine of life and of unshovell'd yet always-ready graves . . .

Walt Whitman, *Song of Myself*

Through the storm and spindrift a small vessel could be seen approaching the wallowing *Otranto*. She was the British destroyer HMS *Mounsey*, a 'Yarrow Special' – a successful Glasgow-built adaptation of the 'M' class destroyer, with just two rather than the usual three funnels. Under a previous commander, the *Mounsey* had been at the Battle of Jutland – but now she was heading for an even more desperate action. On her bridge as master was Lieutenant Francis W. Craven. He had spent just over half his 29 years in the Navy, had served in the Dardanelles campaign, and was highly regarded. Seldom has a man had such an inappropriate surname. According to the *Mounsey*'s third officer, Craven was a lean, swarthy and round-shouldered man – but his thrust-out jaw gave him an air of authority that none of his crew of 73 cared to question.

The *Mounsey* was one of the 'reception committee' of destroyers based at Lough Swilly, on the north coast of Ireland, that were detailed to escort transatlantic convoys on the last stage of their journey to Britain. Delayed by a technical problem, she was now cruising alone in search of convoy HX-50. At about five or six o'clock in the morning of Sunday, 6 October, Petty Officer Fred Robinson, the *Mounsey*'s chief gunner, sighted some of the straggling ships of the convoy. The ships he saw were already being escorted by destroyers, so the

146

Mounsey continued to look for unprotected strays. Robinson recalled: 'The Captain remarked to me, "The weather can't get much worse than it is Gunner," and I hardly think I have seen it worse, in my twenty-six years' experience of the sea, and I have been in seven of them. Except in the Australian Bight I don't think I have seen worse, as I logged the force of the wind at 11, which is a hurricane, and the state of the sea at 10, which is waves forty feet high. After cruising around for about an hour, I sighted the *Otranto* flying H8 which is "destroyer close me". I also took in semaphore, "stand by me". This was about 9.30 am. We were about a mile away, doing ten knots, which was as much as we could stick. The Captain apparently made up his mind quickly.'

Robinson recalled that Craven had said either 'Neck or nothing' or 'Nothing ventured nothing gained.' Despite 40-foot waves, 70-mile-an-hour winds, and the 12,000-ton *Otranto*'s serious list, Craven would manoeuvre his little 896-ton destroyer alongside and try to save the troopship's passengers and crew. He was taking a calculated risk with his vessel and the lives of the 73 men who served under him.

Otranto's navigation officer Lieutenant Harry Woodcock, an experienced Royal Naval Reserve officer who had seen action on the *Otranto* at the Battle of Coronel, thought Craven's seamanship 'brilliant and daring'. Craven's cool heroism also won the lifelong admiration of Commander Campbell. 'And there, by the living God, was a seaman! The commander of the *Mounsey* was prepared to risk bringing the thousand tons of his little ship alongside the crushing bulk of a ship ten times its size . . . with incomparable skill and daring the little vessel was brought near to the waterlogged *Otranto*. The first boat gave with a rending crash, and the destroyer was swept alongside by an oncoming wave.'

A memoir by Private Edgar Sheppard, of Augusta, Georgia, is lodged in the Museum of Islay Life. 'Now we got a close up view of the commander of the destroyer. A trim athletic looking officer who began waving two flags. Knowing the semaphore code, I read the message to the commander of the *Otranto*: "I am coming alongside to take off the American troops." The reply to the destroyer *Mounsey* from the captain of the *Otranto* was: "Steer clear or you will lose your crew and your ship." The reply to the Captain of the *Otranto*: "I am coming alongside. If we go down, we shall go down together." What a brave decision.'

Craven, the lieutenant, was defying the instructions of an experienced and highly regarded captain. Lieutenant Wilfred Warner, the *Mounsey*'s third officer, commented: 'This may be construed as disobedience of orders, but Craven knew his capabilities and those of his ship's to a hair's breadth. Disobedience of orders was a secondary consideration with Craven when the saving of life or the destruction of the enemy was involved.'

Craven signalled the *Otranto* to lower its lifeboats. While it would have been suicidal for men to try and abandon ship in them in such a storm, they would serve as fenders to soften the impact of steel hulls pounding against each other. The lifeboats were crushed to smithereens as the hull of the *Mounsey* ground into the side of the *Otranto*. An unidentified *Otranto* crewman later told a newspaper reporter: 'Her commander deserves a double Victoria Cross as I have spent my life at sea, but I have never seen such a magnificent piece of manoeuvring and ship handling in all my life. The destroyer was in danger of being dashed to pieces time and time again . . . it was a miracle how she got alongside.'

Private Joseph Hewell recalled: 'The sea was so rough that the little boat was tossed about like a feather. One wave would take it some 15 to 20 feet or probably more away and then another would bring it back with a slam against the large ship.' The crew of the *Mounsey* were also in extreme danger as their ship ground against the *Otranto*'s hull. Gunner Fred Robinson narrowly missed being crushed to death as a damaged lifeboat swinging from the *Otranto* crashed into the destroyer as he struggled to clear a rope caught on the *Mounsey*'s rail. 'I won't forget that first crash in a hurry. It was a rather nasty sensation, the grinding tearing sounds, which cleared the portside from masthead, bringing down wireless and foreyards of the *Mounsey*, smashing the port side of the bridge, breaking all the stanchions along the deck and making a lot of wreckage, and some of the men had very narrow shaves. I saw the head of our boat's davit catch in the head of the *Otranto*'s boats' davits. I thought there would be a nasty tear in our deck but by some miracle it cleared.'

As the ships came alongside, their hulls briefly crashed and ground together, and then were swept apart again. As they reared and plunged in the mountainous waves, the vessels' decks were sometimes fleetingly level and then, within seconds, the *Mounsey*'s had lurched 40 feet below. Ropes were thrown between the ships, but the men who tried to haul themselves along them were swept into the sea. Craven could be seen on the *Mounsey*, waving and using a megaphone, urging the soldiers to jump for their lives onto his deck. On the *Otranto*, Captain Davidson, realising that this was the men's best chance of survival, gave the order – 'Abandon ship!' Private Harold English recalled: 'The young ship's bugler, who kept at his [the Captain's] side, drew himself to his full height and blew the notes of 'abandon ship' clearly. This done, he flung the bugle into the water saying, "I'm through with this old bugle. Maybe I'll get me a new one."' English believes that the bugler stayed with Captain Davidson during the evacuation, and perished with him. Others say they saw him hurl himself over the side, in an attempt to land on the *Mounsey*'s deck.

Every man on the *Otranto*'s deck was faced with a choice. A mistimed jump could see a man cut in half by the two ships' wire rope rails, pulverised between the heaving hulls, or crashing 40 feet onto a hard steel deck. Even if a man reached the

Mounsey uninjured, a breaking wave could sweep him into the sea. Some soldiers jumped still wearing their heavy boots and greatcoats. Nothing in their training had prepared Georgia farm boys for this challenge. Commander Campbell noted: '"Jump, men – jump!" yelled the destroyer men. Our seamen, used to the motion of ships, could exercise judgement in their jumping. At times the deck of the destroyer would rise to within eight or ten feet of *Otranto*'s, but within a second would have sunk to forty feet below. But the soldiers, panicky and unused to the ways of ships, could neither hear orders nor grasp the importance of waiting for the word to jump. Some crashed on the destroyer's deck when it was in the trough, breaking arms and legs. Some struck with such force on the rise that they were bounced off the deck into the sea. In a sudden low roll of the destroyer a man even threw himself down one of her funnels. The fate of those unfortunates who fell between the two ships was usually awful, for while a lucky few managed to climb aboard ere the gap closed, the majority were crushed as the waves forced the vessels together.'

To jump, or not to jump? Soldiers, like 17-year-old Private David Roberts, brothers Arthur and Clyde Harmon, and artillery sergeant Charles McDonald, knew nothing of the sea. None of their military training at Fort Screven, or anywhere else, had prepared them for this ordeal. Fear rooted some men to the *Otranto*'s decks. Desperation forced others to make the leap onto the pitching and rolling *Mounsey*. Private Harville Marsh, of Georgia, was among the young Americans confronted with the awful choice. 'The men started leaping across the yawning chasm between the ships. Some I saw reach their mark, but others missed and were drowned. I saw them down there drowning before my eyes.' Private Edgar Sheppard recalled: 'The troops were in a panic and some jumped off with heavy marching order packs and guns held in hand, and they fell between the boats and were crushed to pieces.'

Private Joseph Hewell's journal reveals how he watched men leap to their deaths before making his own choice. 'I then began to notice men jumping onto it, some landing safe and others, mistiming their jump, went down between to be crushed when the ships would crash together again. I stood there watching the fellows jump when a fellow (Henry Delaney from Nashville, Georgia) who was sitting there by me said, "Let's go and jump too."' It was the right choice. Both men survived. Jules Lehoerff, the skipper of the French fishing boat that had been rammed by the *Otranto*, made his leap, followed by his Newfoundland dog. They fell short, plunged into the sea, and were lost. Harville Marsh, fully aware of the danger, made his decision to leap across the 'yawning chasm'. 'I jumped fully 15 feet. It was a horrible moment. My feet touched the edge of the deck of the destroyer. I thought I was going down, and I should have done so if I hadn't had my socks on. They gave me a moment's foothold and time to grasp a wire around the destroyer.' Joseph Hewell, who'd watched his friend, Henry Delaney, make the desperate leap, now jumped himself. 'Seconds after he jumped, I jumped, landing safe on the deck and immediately caught hold of a gun that was mounted on the bow of the destroyer. I was clinging on to this when a large wave washed over the deck and changed ends of the gun but I still held on . . . the sea was rolling in waves 30 to 40 feet high and the destroyer was headed right in the direction, one of the waves came over the bow and tore me loose from the gun and when I found myself and got to my feet again, I was 50 or 60 feet from the gun. Came very near going overboard, but stopped right on the edge of the boat. I made cover as soon as I could and was soon down in the hole with several other fellows, mostly sailors.'

Men lined the decks of the *Otranto*, desperately trying to make up their minds if and when to make the leap of faith. It took a lifetime's ration of good luck to jump, land on the *Mounsey*'s deck, grab hold of something to stop your being swept off, and then be dragged to safety by the ship's crew. Often the jumping men plummeted onto men who'd already landed on deck, injuring not a few. As men landed on his deck, Craven pointed them towards a hatchway while shouting to those already below decks: 'Make way lads, make room for more!' Lieutenant Warner recalled: 'During the whole of this operation he never showed the slightest excitement, and during the worst of the business he was laughing. To use an Americanism, he "scared the pants off me".'

According to the *Mounsey*'s second-in command, Lieutenant R. S. Stewart, Craven managed to manoeuvre his ship 'at least eight times' close enough to the *Otranto* for men to jump onto her. Victor Perrin, a 22-year-old from Atlanta, Georgia, jumped from the top deck when he judged that the *Mounsey* would be at its wave peak. But the destroyer had plunged into a wave valley, and by the time Perrin hit its deck he'd spun in the air, and landed painfully on his shoulder. He wrapped himself around some railings and grimly held on. Edgar Sheppard waited until the *Mounsey* made its fourth contact with the troopship before he jumped. He'd seen men plunge to their deaths because they were wearing their packs, and now made his leap in his shirt sleeves. 'I jumped with all my might and speed and just did make it. A sailor grabbed me by the belt and pulled me onto the ship.'

Private Donald Cooper was a black soldier from a share-cropping family in Screven County, a cotton-growing area of Georgia. The US Army was strictly segregated in these days, but although Cooper served with an all-black labour battalion he was on deck with a white friend as the *Mounsey* made its 'next-to-last' attempt to take men off. His white friend told him to 'move out the way', to let him jump. He would never forget the sight of his friend being smashed between the two ships.

James Harmon, searching for his brother, waited till the last moment to jump onto the *Mounsey*. 'I waited until she came alongside for the last time. I had looked for my brother but was unable to find him. An impulse seemed to tell me to jump, so I jumped and landed safely on the bow of the ship. The waves were so high and the destroyer so heavily loaded until she turned almost over. When I jumped I fell between the two anchor chains, which were stretched along the deck floor, and held on. Just then a great wave rushed over the top and I was completely under water that was icy cold. Somehow the waves carried my left leg underneath one of the chains and the weight of the anchor chain held me in a straining position until another wave loosened me. I was under water for the third time. I think I held to this chain for nearly an hour; but I wasn't lonesome, as two other soldiers were holding to the same chain. One of them was brother Clyde's top sergeant. Others were on deck, but their hold wasn't very good and they were swept overboard. We finally managed to get below to safety but it was a trying hour, believe me.'

Otranto officer Commander Campbell had been on deck helping soldiers to time their jumps. By the time he decided to jump himself, it was clear that the *Mounsey* was not coming alongside again. He decided to swim for it and plunged into the water. 'My word, that water was cold! It took my breath away. When I did come to the surface the bow of the destroyer was only about fifty yards distant. It was useless to try and make any progress by swimming, but I had my lifebelt on and this kept me well above water. Then along came another "purler" of a wave. It picked me up like a piece of wood and hurled me clean on to the fo'c'sle of the destroyer. So sudden was the impact that for a second or two I was stunned, then the water began to slide across the open deck and I felt myself being carried with it. In another moment I should have been in the sea the other side. Just then my head came into violent contact with something solid. I flung my arms round it and hung on. It seemed ages before the bow cleared of water, but when it did

I saw that I was hanging on for dear life to an anti-aircraft gun. In this perilous position I was seen by the men on the bridge. With the seas that were running, the destroyer was "taking it green", and her captain brought the ship about to make as much lee as possible forward. A rope was thrown to me then. I caught it and fastened it under my arms, and was hauled to safety round the break of the bridge.'

Not every man had a choice to jump or to stay. There was no question of the 100 or so seriously ill flu victims on board the troopship leaping for their lives. Nor was it thought possible to lower them or even throw them bodily onto the *Mounsey's* deck. They would have to take their chances on the *Otranto*.

At each contact with the *Otranto*, the *Mounsey* had sustained more damage and had become more and more crammed with rescued men. Lieutenant Warner describes them as, 'dumb with shock, cold and the frightful noise of the storm'. The *Mounsey* was now top-heavy with the weight of survivors, and its officers were desperate to get them below deck. Many had lashed themselves to anything they could on the *Mounsey's* decks. The ones on the fo'c'sle were being half drowned by the heavy seas breaking over the ship, and the destroyer's crew had to struggle with clumsily tied water-swollen knots to free the men before they could drag them below. Gunner Robinson recalled: 'The seas were pouring down the engine room and stokehole hatches, several men being washed or carried down by weight of water. Every space below was filled with men, and we took in so much water that things were becoming dangerous. The Engineer had to shut off sea suction and pump the water from the bilges, through the main circulators and condenser, to keep the water under, and this acted very well. Also in the stokehold – which was badly damaged, the bulkhead being cracked and boiler slightly shifted – an oil lead pipe from a tank broke and water got into the fuel and caused the steam to drop. We had no steam to get away earlier. But due to the presence of mind of two stoker petty officers, in changing over the oil lead to the other side of the ship, we were able to get sufficient steam in a few moments to go slow astern.'

Lieutenant Stewart thought it impossible for the *Mounsey* to remain afloat. 'The water was up to the floor plates of the Engine Room and it was all the pumps could do to keep the water under. The port side was like a concertina. It was extraordinary that the ship could take such a hammering. She was so overladen was she that she was in danger of turning turtle.' Craven ordered the Americans below deck to give the ship more stability, but they were terrified of being trapped beneath the waterline. Commander Campbell recalled: 'For the safety of all, of themselves, the troops had to be compelled to go below, and it was even done at the point of revolvers.'

The *Mounsey* was heavily overladen with nearly 600 survivors. Her deck was constantly awash and she was in serious danger of capsizing. Down below, rescued men stood shoulder to shoulder, knee-high in sloshing seawater. At about 11.00 am, Commander Craven made the bitter decision to disengage and turn his ship for a safe port. As the *Mounsey*'s helmsman put the ship about, Craven turned to Lieutenant Warner and told him: 'I wish to God this ship were ten, then I could get the whole lot off.' Harold English states that as the *Mounsey* pulled away from the *Otranto*, Captain Davidson could be seen on the deck of the stricken troopship, waving farewell. If there was one man on the *Otranto* who would never have jumped, it was Ernest George William Davidson. He would do all in his limited power to get every man safely off the ship before giving a thought for his own life. It must have been a heartrending sight for Francis Craven. The *Otranto* flashed a final signal on an Aldis lamp from her bridge – 'Thanks. Good luck.' And then Commander Campbell witnessed a chilling sight. 'On the after end of the *Otranto* a man could be seen sitting on a pile of life rafts slapping his thighs and laughing as though he were enjoying a huge joke; he had cracked under the strain.' Campbell watched his old ship disappear into the distance with a heavy heart. 'She was sinking fast, but drifting towards the land. Our hope was that she would beach in such a way as would let our comrades still aboard get ashore safely. We now knew that the land we saw was the Hebridean island of Islay.'

Craven set course for Belfast, the nearest port. Lieutenant Stewart described the ship's condition: 'The bridge had been smashed, all oil fuel tanks except one punctured, two out of the three boiler rooms flooded, boats, davits and upper deck gear smashed to bits, spare depth charges rolling about the upper deck, both masts carried away with the wireless and all signalling gear, the pumps only just able to keep pace with the water pouring in through the holes, cracked seams and wrecked ventilators; and deck full of debris, ropes and survivors being washed about by the tremendous seas in the worst shambles I have ever seen.'

Battened-down below decks for more than ten hours were 313 American officers and men, one YMCA official, 239 of the *Otranto*'s crew, and 30 fishermen from the *Croisine*. Many were ill or injured; all were frozen, exhausted and traumatised. The *Mounsey*'s third officer, Lieutenant Warner, described their condition: 'It was quite impossible to get any provisions for the survivors, and they must have suffered all the tortures of the Black Hole of Calcutta; crammed below; wet, sick, cold and beaten by nature into a numb horror, wondering if they had gone from the frying pan into the fire, chucked about like corks and half stifled. I was glad to be on deck with work to do, my job as navigator kept me on the bridge, or in the remains of the chart-house.' In an outstanding feat of seamanship, Craven nursed the *Mounsey* to safety. One of his crew, Engineer Brown, stated: 'I think our Captain's best work was done going to Belfast. He gradually worked the ship across the North Channel under the lee of the Irish coast, and the manner in which it was done kept the water (in the engine room) down to a minimum and relieved me of a good deal of anxiety in the engine room department.'

The *Mounsey*'s radio had been destroyed by the storm, but, using either flags or a signal lamp, Craven managed to signal the destroyer HMS *Mindful* to radio the Royal Navy authorities in Belfast that he was arriving with hundreds of *Otranto* survivors. About 7.30 pm the blacked-out *Mounsey* entered Belfast Lough as fast as she dared, flashing her code number to the coastal defence lookouts. Just over an hour later she tied up in Spencer Basin where a fleet of ambulances waited to rush the injured to the Royal Victoria Hospital. Those waiting on the dock could see a huddle of men shivering on the *Mounsey*'s deck. Some had been lashed to the ship's deck gear for nearly twelve hours. A medical officer shouted from the shore through cupped hands, 'How many have you aboard?' 'Between five and six hundred, I think, Sir,' was Lieutenant Craven's astonishing reply.

Scores of the men had broken arms and legs when they jumped from the *Otranto*. Many were so frozen and exhausted that they had to be carried off the *Mounsey*. Victor Perrin, who'd been clinging onto railings on the destroyer's deck since he jumped, was so cold that he had to be prised loose before he could be taken for treatment. Others blazed with fever, the symptom of flu or pneumonia. About fifty-five men were sent immediately to hospital, but a dozen would succumb to illness or injury, and be buried in Belfast with full military honours.

The fittest American soldiers lined up and trudged to the Queen Victoria Barracks to be fed and rested. Many of the survivors were only half-dressed and without boots. Commander Campbell, who had kicked off his shoes before abandoning ship, found himself being painfully marched through cobbled streets in his socks to a Seamen's Mission where he and surviving *Otranto* crewmen were fed hot coffee and fried eggs and potatoes. Nobody had eaten since eight o'clock the previous morning. The food 'disappeared as if by magic'. After making sure the crew of the *Mounsey* had a hot meal and a change of dry clothes, the exhausted Lieutenant Craven fell asleep on a chair in his ship's wrecked wardroom with a half-eaten sandwich in one hand and a mug of cocoa in the other.

≈

The pitiful state of the young Americans, and their unexpected numbers, had prompted a swift emergency call to the American Red Cross station in Belfast and its headquarters at 52 Grosvenor Gardens in London. The loss of the *Tuscania* only eight months previously had blooded the Red Cross. It had spent the intervening period carefully planning for another such disaster and had established a network of bases throughout the British Isles. It had also set up a 'Flying Squadron' that could descend anywhere in the UK to aid distressed American servicemen. The Flying Squadron's office was manned 24/7 and its duty crew would sleep there with their clothes arranged 'fireman fashion' for instant donning. The ethos was to 'get things done', without the necessity of permission from higher up the command chain. This small but highly motivated team was commanded by 1st Lieutenant James Jeffers. Fate would decree that Jeffers would form a close bond with the island of Islay and her people.

Hunter Sharp, the American Consul in Belfast, was the first American to witness the condition of the *Mounsey*'s rescued souls. According to the official history of the American Red Cross's World War One operations in Britain, Sharp found the organisation's presence a surprise as well as a relief to the shivering soldiers.

> He found the American soldiers gathered in the large military gymnasium, a bedraggled, woe-begone lot. They

were rigged out in whatever odds and ends of clothing the men of the destroyer and the barracks troops had been able to furnish them. Some were half naked and wrapped in blankets while others were shivering in their still wet uniforms. Miserable as they were, their faces brightened as they thronged up to shake hands with Mr Sharp when he told them who he was. 'And I've also come to tell you,' he added, 'that the American Red Cross is here in Belfast and will be here in the barracks in a very few minutes to do everything for you and bring you everything you need.' The men who crowded around him were frankly incredulous. It wasn't so strange to find the American Consul, because there had to be one everywhere, but the American Red Cross in this out of the way place – ! 'Sure it's the *American* Red Cross?' Yes, Mr. Sharp was quite sure. Very quickly, Fred Cleaver, the Red Cross representative in Belfast, arrived with car loads of underwear, socks, shirts, blankets, biscuits, chocolate and American cigarettes that had been stored for such an event at an American Red Cross warehouse. 'Did you know we were coming?' asked a soldier. 'No, we didn't, and we're sorry it was you,' replied Cleaver, 'but we felt that, perhaps, something of this kind might happen someday through storms or submarines, or mines, so we made ready for it, that's all.'

In the morning light of 7 October, the battered *Mounsey* was a grim sight. As well as the living, she'd brought home to port the mangled remains of men who'd mistimed their jumps and been crushed between the hulls of the destroyer and the *Otranto*. Commander Campbell helped identify the remains. 'We had the dreadful task of ferreting through the mass of indistinguishably mingled flesh clinging to the ship's side for identity disks of what had once been separate living beings.' According to Lieutenant Warner, the body of a young American soldier was found on deck, under a pile of wreckage. But that morning nearly 600 men woke up in Belfast lucky to be alive, thanks to Francis Craven and the crew of the *Mounsey*.

For Private James Harmon it was a bitter-sweet experience. He'd last seen his brother, Clyde, as they prepared to jump from the deck of the *Otranto*. A week later, from hospital in Belfast he had to write to their mother in Inman, South Carolina, to tell her that he had no news of Clyde's fate.

Dear Mother, the saddest thing that I have to write is that I haven't heard a word of brother Clyde, but I am living in hopes that he was among the number saved. It is awful to think of Clyde as going down in that terrible water. My search for him that Sunday morning one week ago today was in vain. I cannot learn anything about him here, and I cannot get out of the hospital yet to search for him. I am sure if he was lost you will hear it from Washington before you get this letter. My hopes and prayers are that he may yet survive. Mother, it is with a sad heart that I write of Clyde, but we have hopes yet . . . I pray for brother's and my chums' safety. I cannot write any more. Give my love to dear Mary and tell her there are hopes yet. Give my love to all the others and love and kisses to you, the dearest of mothers!

A handful of the men rescued by the *Mounsey* would die of influenza, but the great majority survived. *Otranto* crewmen were sent home, while the doughboys travelled to a rest camp in England before being sent to France. Most of them arrived there almost a week after the war had ended. As for HMS *Mounsey*, she had to be extensively rebuilt, with new plating along her port side, and new frames for two-thirds of her length. But she never saw active service again. Lieutenant Wilfrid Warner paid tribute to her and her Clydeside builders: 'There is no doubt that we all of us owe our lives to the workmanship of Sir Alfred Yarrow and his men.'

~~~

When Lieutenant Craven reluctantly had to abandon his rescue mission, nearly 500 men remained on board the stricken *Otranto*. By 11.00 am the ship had been inexorably driven for two hours by storm and sea toward the coast of Islay, a little to the north of Rhinns Point. Captain Davidson dropped anchors in an attempt to stop the *Otranto* drifting toward the rocks, but to no avail. From the decks men could see cows in the field, and waves crashing onto the ragged, rocky shoreline of the Rhinns. The Rhinns (or 'promontory') of Islay is the island's westerly bastion against the anger of the Atlantic. Its geology includes some of the oldest rocks on the planet, and its coastline bears witness to the eternal battle between these two forces. The four-mile hike from Kilchiaran, north to Coull Point, takes you along a wild, serrated coastline deeply indented with steep gullies into which the hydraulic force of the ocean funnels with fearsome power. But in the midst of this inhospitable and treacherous coastline lies one of Islay's must beautiful golden sand beaches. The broad sweep of Machair Bay (sometimes called Kilchoman Bay) and the church and community of Kilchoman could clearly be seen by the anxious watchers on the *Otranto*, and there was a chance that the vessel might successfully beach on the sand there. Only the previous year the Admiralty rescue tug, *Flying Falcon*, had been driven into the bay after a tow rope fouled her propeller. Three of the crew drowned trying to launch a lifeboat, but the others waited till the vessel hit the sandy beach and were able to wade safely ashore. The *Flying Falcon* was later re-floated and returned to service.

But to the south of the bay, about three-quarters of a mile offshore, lies a submerged reef, the *Botha na Cailleach* – the Old Woman's Reef. As well as meaning 'old woman' in the Gaelic language, *Cailleach* can also mean 'hag', or even 'witch'. From his home at Coull Farm, volunteer Coastguard Donald Jones looks down on the beautiful and popular sandy beach of Kilchoman Bay, and out to the waters that cover the reef. He reflects on what might have been. 'Fate seems to have conspired against the men on the *Otranto*. If the wind and been in a different direction and the collision had been further north, then the ship would have missed the reef and would probably have come ashore onto the sand. While they wouldn't exactly have been able to walk ashore, hundreds of men could have been saved.' But that was not to be HMS *Otranto*'s fate.

At about 11.55 am, a huge wave raised the great ship up, and then crashed her down onto *Botha na Cailleach*. Repeatedly the massive rollers pounded thousands of tons of steel against unyielding rock. Her back was broken and her hull was ripped asunder. Men lying ill with flu were doomed instantly. Those on deck jumped – or were thrown – into the freezing sea. Captain Davidson is reported to have shouted: 'Boys, we've got to swim for it after all!'

Sergeant Charles McDonald – described by the *Indianapolis News* as 'a husky Illinois boy' – lived to tell his story: 'About five other fellows, including the mate, and myself stood with our backs to the cabin walls staring out at the water when a tremendous wave wrenched loose the rail we were holding to and washed us to the other side of the deck. I now decided to leave the ship. Looking around I found a rope dangling from one of the smokestacks. Grasping this, I climbed on the ship's rail. I stood and watched until a huge wave surged round the *Otranto*. I slipped over the side, let go of the rope and rode away on the wave.'

Among the jumpers was 17-year-old David Roberts. His lifeboat station was so high on the *Otranto*'s bow that the leap onto the *Mounsey*'s deck would have been suicidal. But when the ship hit the reef, he had no choice. 'We had no one to command us, it was every man for himself. When I saw the boat was beginning to break up, I waited until it leaned almost over to the water, then jumped over. I had on a good life belt, one that slipped on like a vest. The waves carried me away from the ship, then a wave about as high as a house came over me and whirled me around like paper in a whirlwind.'

Sergeant McDonald couldn't swim. He was wearing his cork lifejacket, but grabbed a floating life-ring and grimly held onto it. Another man in the water clung onto it as well, and, each putting an arm through it, they tried to paddle toward the breakers on the shore. Looking back at the wreck, McDonald could see Captain Davidson on the top deck. Blood was streaming down his face as if he'd been struck.

Donald Jones knows the west coast of Islay like he knows the boundaries and contours of his farm, and, with more than forty years' experience in the Coastguard, is still in awe of the power of its weather. He remains amazed that anyone got ashore alive. 'There was a Force 11 wind and these enormous waves crashing onto the shore. If a wave had picked you up and battered you down on the rock, the force with which you hit it would probably have killed you outright.'

But there was another danger. When the ship broke in two she disintegrated in the seething water. The bow half of the vessel plunged to the bottom, while the stern was still impaled on the reef, being pounded to pieces by the sea. Floating wreckage now sliced and crushed the men who'd been cast into the water. Lifeboats had been shattered to shards. The ship's cabins and corridors had been lined with timber which now – torn and splintered – was being hurled around in the waves and surf. Far from being saved by clutching onto a floating plank or spar, a man was more likely to be speared or crushed by the wreckage. It is probable that more men died from wreckage trauma than by drowning.

One of the men in the water was in the same company as Joseph Hewell, who had earlier made the desperate leap onto the deck of the *Mounsey*. This unnamed soldier later told Hewell his story: 'He said that everybody stuck to the ship as long as they could and then they began jumping overboard and tried to make it ashore which was only one-and-a-half to two miles off. He said that the last he saw of the ship was when she broke in two, in the middle, half going one way and half going the other. There were numerous pieces of wreckage floating about and everybody who could was trying to grasp something that would help him. This fellow said that he saw something white not very far from him and he made for it. On reaching it he clasped his arms around it and it happened to be a tub of lard which was floating around. The tub had been bursted off and when he caught on to it his arms mashed right into the lard and he said he was nothing but grease from head to foot. After some one-and-a-half or two hours of struggling he finally made it ashore frozen and in a semi-conscious condition.'

Sergeant McDonald, still holding on to the life-ring with another man, saw what he thought to be the timber side of the *Otranto*'s stateroom floating close to him, with two men on it. They now clambered onto it, with McDonald still clutching the life-ring. 'It was very hard to hold onto the raft; the waves would almost tear the arms out the sockets. We would wash off, and we found it very hard to get back on again. The air was so cold that we were compelled, at intervals, to drop into the water, which although ice-cold, still seemed warmer.' Eventually, McDonald was torn from the raft by a tremendous wave that drove him toward rocks, where he expected to be dashed to pieces. He'd hung onto the life-ring, and had managed to get it round him. He now found that it acted as a buffer that protected him from the wreckage that was being tossed around. Another wave dragged him under – and then threw him up in a gully. McDonald managed to scramble over the raft of wreckage that had been driven against the coastline, and found a spot where he could drag himself ashore. His feet were so cramped and frozen that he collapsed whenever he tried to walk, but he was alive.

The odds against survival were stacked against the men in the freezing water, but miracles – or, at least random good fortune – did happen that day. David Roberts was another of the few lucky ones who wasn't drowned or pounded to death by the waves. 'I went under about three of them, but I then got hold of a raft and drifted close to the shore. Another big wave came and swept me off the raft. I got hold of a rock and hung on.'

～

Ileachs habitually keep their eyes on the sea and the weather. Even today, islanders whose families have not farmed or fished for a generation or more still take an obsessive interest in the capricious climate under whose spell they live. In the terrible weather of 6 October all eyes on the west coast of the island would have been cast seawards. The *Oban Times* described the storm: '. . . one of the wildest gales of west wind that can be recalled prevailing around the island, blowing with great intensity on the western shore.' Islay's most senior policeman, Sergeant Malcolm MacNeill, recalled: 'The wind was blowing with terrific force from the south-west and a tremendous sea running on the shores. The oldest inhabitants in the neighbourhood of the wreck say that they never saw a heavier sea on the Machrie sands and very seldom a higher tide.' To MacNeill it was: 'a marvel how any at all escaped being dashed to pieces on the rocks.'

The stricken ship could clearly be seen from the shore, and the few islanders living on this remote corner of Islay rushed to the coast to see what they could do. So great was the storm that a car carrying four would-be rescuers was blown off the road into a ditch on its way to the coast. According to a painstaking account of the disaster written shortly after it by Sergeant MacNeill, the foundering of the *Otranto* was first witnessed by Donald McLachlan, a ploughman who lived at Machrie, less than half a mile from the pounding surf. McLachlan ran four or five miles to Kilchiaran to call out the island's volunteer lifesaving crew. McLachlan then ran back to the shore to see what he could do. First on the scene was probably David McTaggart, the farmer at Kilchiaran, a mile or so to the southeast of where the *Otranto* struck the reef. Seeing what was unfolding, McTaggart had sent a horse and van, or carriage, to collect life-saving equipment. McTaggart was joined on the shore by Donald McLachlan, who had raised the alarm. When he spotted a struggling, drowning man, McTaggart plunged into the maelstrom as far as he dared with McLachlan holding on to the tail of his jacket. Together – and at considerable risk of being swept out to sea by a giant wave – the pair pulled three men out of the furious surf with just a broom handle.

An American report into the disaster names the Reverend Grant, Mrs Isabella McIntyre, and Duncan McPhee and his two young sons, Donald and John, being among the first on the beach. Donald Ferguson, a Kilchiaran shepherd, joined the desperate rescue mission, and he and David McTaggart pulled another half-drowned soul to safety, after securing themselves with a rope against being swept away.

According to the *Oban Times* of 19 October, a lifesaving crew from Lochindaal Distillery in Port Charlotte hurried to the coast in the distillery lorry with 'rocket apparatus' – to fire a breeches-buoy to the *Otranto*. The equipment turned up, but proved to be useless under the circumstances. The distance to the ship – about a mile – would have been too great for the rocket, according to modern Coastguard Duncan Jones, who worked with the equipment in the 1970s. The horse and van, however, was a blessing for the exhausted and hypothermic survivors, who were taken back to McTaggart's farm at Kilchiaran in it, where they were tended by Mrs McTaggart and the farm servants.

Donald McPhee, an 18-year-old shepherd from Kilchoman, and his brother John, who was a year younger, also risked their lives to help exhausted men ashore. They used a walking stick, or possibly a shepherd's crook, to reach out to men desperately clinging onto rocks for their lives, and hauled three to safety. According to a report from Lieutenant James Jeffers of the American Red Cross: 'It was simply a miracle that the two lads were not carried away. Seven times they rushed into the sea, and each time brought out an American soldier.' One of the men they saved was Private David Roberts, who had been clinging to a rock. He was almost ages with the McPhee boys who rescued him, just seventeen. Roberts later told of being helped to safety by 'a Scotch lad', who took him, and an *Otranto* sailor, to his mother's cottage.

Private William Richards somehow made it through the pounding wreckage and was swept alive onto the rocks beneath a cliff. There he was spotted by an islander who threw him a rope with which he climbed to safety. Richards survived, but was haunted by the noise of the wreckage grinding on the rocks, and the sight of dead comrades floating around him, their faces blue.

When Sergeant McDonald crawled ashore he sat on the rocks wriggling his toes to get the circulation back. When at last he could stand, he began to look for shelter, and found a young Cincinnati, Ohio private, Earl Garver, lying on the ground exhausted. He helped Garver to his feet and dragged him along. After half a mile they met Donald and John McPhee, who were helping David Roberts and an *Otranto* crewman back to their mother's house. The McPhees pointed McDonald and Garver to the little hamlet of Kilchoman where they and several other survivors were taken in and cared for by Isabella McIntyre, the local teacher.

John McPhee left David Roberts and two other survivors in the care of his mother and sister, Margaret, at the family home in Kilchoman, and then returned to the eye of the storm. There, he and Andrew Stevenson, a sailor home on leave at Machrie, spotted another man, trapped in a deep but narrow gully amid a raft of churning driftwood that was pounding against the rock. Only Private Thomas Kelly's head was showing. McPhee and Stevenson managed to lower a rope to him, but a badly broken arm made it impossible for Kelly to struggle free from the wreckage. Eventually a boy was lowered down perpendicular walls into the gully. He managed to haul away enough wreckage from around Kelly for him to be pulled to safety.

Donald and John McPhee's parents and sister, Margaret, were on the beach, and helped carry and drag survivors to their home. According to Lieutenant Jeffers: 'Mr McPhee, although 68 years of age, with his wife carried the men up the rough road to the little cottage over a mile away. They accomplished the journey with the men on their backs, and having taken them to the humble cottage did all they could to make our men comfortable, even turning out of their rooms and sleeping ten nights in a barn near their home.' David Roberts gratefully remembered: 'When we got to the cottage they gave us dry clothing and put us to bed. It sure was fine, two pairs of woollen blankets. The people there could not have treated us any better.'

Gilbert Clark, of Port Charlotte, who would make a reputation as a fine boatbuilder as an adult, was 14 when the *Otranto* was wrecked. He and his father walked the five miles to the coast off which the *Otranto* lay, 'one of the worst places on the west coast', and he never forgot what he saw. In a letter to Neil McCart, the author of *Passenger Ships of the Orient Line*, Gilbert recalled the terrible sights he had witnessed. 'It was such a stormy day that the vessel was torn to pieces in a short time. In these days these liners were all done up in wood paneling, so the shore and the sea had so much wood and wreckage floating. We could see so many people swimming or being swept by the heavy seas along the shore to a large gully that was full of wreckage, where the poor soldiers and crew had no chance of being rescued. They must have been killed within moments, and all the local people waiting on the shore had to look on helpless as it was impossible for anyone to reach them owing to every gully and all the shore being covered with floating wood. No wonder so few survivors got ashore.'

Two Port Charlotte men, home on leave from the army, could see an American desperately clinging to a rock which was separated from the coast by a 'broad chasm' six or seven feet wide, through which the waves pounded. Archibald Torrie of the South Staffordshire Regiment, and Argyll & Sutherland Highlander, Donald McIndeor, risked their lives to leap to the American's aid. A slip, or sudden strong gust as they jumped, would almost certainly have meant them falling to their deaths. As they got hold of the exhausted and frozen man, other rescuers found some timber to create a makeshift bridge over the torrent. Torrie and McIndeor pulled their man across it to safety.

Sergeant MacNeill noted that 75-year-old Peter Ferguson of Machrie and 70-year-old Duncan McRae of Kilchoman also did 'brave work' on the shore. MacNeill's account shows clearly that Ileachs of all ages played their part in the aftermath of the *Otranto* disaster, just as they had done when the *Tuscania* was torpedoed. 'One girl, Katie McLellan, of Coulerarach, in my opinion deserves special mention. She happened to be on the rocks when the McPhee boys rescued the first three survivors, one of who was scantily clad. This girl at once in the midst of hail and sleet stripped off her own overcoat and wrapped it round the rescued soldier, and at once set off to Kilchoman Manse, the residence of the Rev M. D. Grant and informed

Mrs Grant of what was happening. Mrs Grant made coffee and tea and this girl along with Mrs McIntyre, Kilchoman school teacher, started on their errand of mercy to the shore. They met some of the survivors on the way and the coffee etc they got from these two women greatly revived them.'

David Roberts may well have been the 'scantily clad' survivor that Katie McLellan had wrapped her coat around. He had been careful to follow the *Otranto* crew's advice to strip off before he had plunged into the sea. 'All I had left on was my underwear, pants and shirt and one sock. I had taken off the other clothing before I left the ship.' That night the McPhee boys, Donald and John, slept in a shed so that David Roberts and the *Otranto* crewman they had saved could sleep in their warm and comfortable beds.

At 9.45 that evening, the British Admiralty received a terse telegram from the Portnahaven Signal Station announcing the worst convoy tragedy of World War One.

> HMS *Otranto* carrying 900 USA troops . . . in collision. A destroyer took 300 men off heavy loss of life. 20 washed ashore alive. Bodies still coming ashore Kilchoman Bay Islay. Coastwatcher and inhabitants attending scene of wreck recovering bodies.

Of the likely 489 doughboys, British crew and Breton fishermen left aboard the *Otranto* when it struck the reef, just 21 made it to the shore alive, to be dragged from the surf, and enveloped in warm blankets and the common humanity of ordinary folk. Seventeen of the survivors were Americans, the others British crewmen. One of the sailors and one soldier were too far gone. The sailor died within hours, and the soldier nine days later, of pneumonia.

The people of Islay lavished care and attention on the *Otranto*'s shipwrecked souls, and, in an official report, Sergeant

MacNeill was at pains to praise not only the men who battled to drag survivors from the waves, but also the women who cared for them on land. In particular, he paid tribute to the selflessness of Mrs McPhee and her daughter Margaret, the teacher Isabella McIntyre, and Elizabeth Grant, wife of the local Kilchoman minister. It is beyond doubt that some of the men hauled from the sea by Islay's menfolk owed their recovery to the island's women. The American Red Cross reported: 'Mrs Grant, the preacher's wife, worked for hours endeavoring to restore three men. Two of them recovered, but unhappily the third died from the severe buffeting he had suffered.'

Whatever dreams survivors like David Roberts had, as they lay wrapped in warm woollen blankets in the McPhee house, they could not have been as terrible as the waking nightmare the searchers on the shore experienced in the deep and dangerous gullies of Islay's coast. As darkness fell on that awful day, the rescuers on the shore were only pulling lifeless bodies from the sea.

There was a Force 6 – a strong breeze – blowing down the Sound of Islay when I climbed the stairs leading to the crew room of the Royal National Lifeboat Institution station at Port Askaig. From the enormous picture window I could see the wind whipping up foamy crests on dark muscular waves that now undulated over the half-mile wide channel that separates Islay from its near neighbour, the island of Jura.

Islay's lifeboat station is modern and comfortably warm, tea and biscuits were generously supplied, and the easygoing good nature of the crewmen I met all belied the reason for the Islay lifeboat's existence. But its existence is, literally, a matter of life and death. Not long before my visit, Coxswain David MacLellan had earned a Royal National Lifeboat Institution medal for gallantry. In a severe gale he and a four-man crew had rushed to the aid of a lone Russian yachtsman who had struck a rock and was helplessly drifting toward the Skerryvore Reef, 46 miles north-west of Islay. If he had been driven onto the reef, the seventy–mile-an-hour wind and eight-metre swell would have dashed him and his yacht to pieces. The pitching and rolling of the two vessels made it impossible to take the yachtsman aboard the lifeboat but, in the nick of time, MacLellan and his crew were able to get a line to the yacht and tow it clear of the reef to relative safety, from where the Russian was eventually rescued by helicopter.

'It was a team effort,' said David MacLellan rather testily when I offered my congratulations, 'the medal belongs to all of us, the whole crew.' David McArthur, the lifeboat's mechanic, rolled his eyes and waved the compliment aside. I quickly turned to the purpose of my visit – my need to understand the ferocity of the storm encountered by the *Otranto*, and the chances of survival of men thrown into an icy sea and cast onto a rocky shore. Slowly and thoughtfully David MacLellan answered my questions. There was no need for oratorical flourishes, as the plain facts he related spoke for themselves. 'The weather can be ferocious in the winter months. You get all that cold water coming in from the north Atlantic and it starts to funnel in between Islay and the north of Ireland. It's a small channel there, so on the west of Islay you can get some horrendous seas at times. Our chief, Lord Boyce (Chairman of the RNLI), was in the Navy. He's been all round the world as a commander in submarines and he says the worst seas he's ever seen are between the north of Ireland and Islay. And he's an admiral!'

I asked about what it would it have been like on the *Otranto* in the Force 11 storm, and found that, as a new member of the Islay lifeboat crew, Coxswain MacLellan had been in such a storm in 1991 when Russian factory ship, the *Kartli*, was caught in a violent Force 11 storm with wave heights of about forty feet. This was the same ferocity of storm that the *Otranto* encountered off Islay. David recalled: 'She was hit by a huge wave which smashed the wheelhouse, killed two of the crew and broke the skipper's leg. As the night went on they were taking the crew off by helicopter, which transferred them onto a big merchant ship that arrived on the scene. There were four or five helicopters working through the night to get all the crew off. We were tasked to go and look for life-rafts. They were quite hard to see with the big swell. Another two crew died of exposure. The *Kartli* ended up being driven ashore on Gigha.'

Based on experiences like that, David MacLellan doesn't believe that many of the men thrown into the sea from the *Otranto* would have been saved by their lifebelts, as the sea was so rough that the spray would have drowned them as they gasped for air in the icy water, inhaling salt water and sand. And then there was the danger of being crushed by the wreckage. Even today, wreckage is a major hazard for lifeboat crews, he told me. 'You have to watch what you're doing when you're standing by a vessel, especially when it starts to go down. Buoyant flotsam comes to the surface with such force that it flies into the air and can knock you out. If you came ashore onto rocks among all this heavy stuff from the wreck, your chances of survival are very small. In that weather it would be like being in a meat-grinder.'

When I left the lifeboat station I stopped to watch the waves. Port Askaig is in a beautiful spot, with views of the majestic conical hills called the Paps of Jura, which are separated from Islay by a narrow but powerful tidal rip. The scene was awe-inspiring and dramatic as Force 6 winds whipped up powerful waves with white foaming crests. But wrecked on a pitiless coast in a Force 11? I still couldn't imagine it, but David MacLellan's words haunted me: 'Like being in a meat-grinder'.

8

A Gloom over the Whole of Islay

~~~

On chosen ground on Islay's shore those gallant lads are laid
And by the kindly Highland folk their lonely graves were made.
When tales are told of other days and sorrows that have been
May we then tell theirs and keep their memory green.

Anonymous poem donated to the Museum of Islay Life

Overnight, the western coastline of Islay became a morgue. Prevailing winds, tides and currents ordained that the great majority of the dead would be cast up on the island. Of the *Otranto*, there was no sign – except for the tangled mass of wreckage grinding against the rocks of the Rhinns. She had broken her back on the *Botha na Cailleach*, split asunder and plunged beneath the surface of the sea in two separate pieces. Men and wreckage were driven in a churning mass into the narrow gullies of Islay's ragged west coast, where the men were crushed or drowned. Every incoming tide brought another mass of entangled bodies and flotsam. Just eight months after they had recovered and buried nearly 200 victims of the *Tuscania*, the people of Islay set to work again, only this time it was much worse. Among the men scouring the coastline was Donald Grant, the Kilchoman minister whose wife had been among the first to care for the survivors. It was a very local affair. The McPhees of Kilchoman, the Clarks of Rockside Farm, the Clarks of Sunderland, the McEacherns of Smaull – people with Islay names from Islay farms – devoted themselves to finding bodies, pulling them from the tangled wreckage, and carrying them to Kilchoman Church on stretchers and carts.

The weight of the task hung heavily on the shoulders of the most senior civic official on the island – a lowly police sergeant.

Once again, Malcolm MacNeill rose to the occasion, cycling the long miles from Bowmore to Kilchoman to take charge. Nothing in the training or experience of a rural 'bobby' had prepared MacNeill for the horrors of the *Tuscania* disaster. Now he was to be tested again. It was a lonely business. Islay had no telephones, nor did it have an airstrip. Help was days away, and he was left to cope, or organise, to record and to lead.

Even though the storm continued for two days, the island-ers systematically searched every inch of coastline where the tide could have driven a corpse. Many of the volunteers were sharp-eyed fishermen who knew the moods of the sea. In some gullies and crevices the wreckage was piled more than fifteen feet high, and men were lowered by rope to drag bodies from the tangle. It was a gruesome and heart-breaking job. The sea is cruel to the dead, and the bodies were often battered and torn beyond recognition. Often it was body-parts, not bodies, that were being found.

Within a day or two the searchers were joined by staff of the American Red Cross' Emergency Relief Department from the mainland and Ireland, and then, a few days later, by detachments of British and American soldiers. As soon as the storm-ravaged telegraph system had allowed the news of the *Otranto*'s final destruction to reach Ireland, two trawlers loaded with Ameri-can Red Cross supplies had been dispatched from Buncrana for Islay, quickly followed by a torpedo boat carrying the members of the organisation's emergency 'Flying Squadron'. They had been assured that the storm was abating, but the torpedo boat found the trawlers anchored off Port Charlotte in Lochindaal, unable to put ashore. *The Passing Legions*, the American Red Cross history of the time, states:

> However, at one o'clock, as the wind held up a bit, those
> on the torpedo boat decided to risk a landing. But when
> the pinnace, bearing five of the party and an emergency

outfit, drew near the narrow beach, it was found impossible to take her in. The wind and the sea were high and "blowing right on" and the approach to the beach, save in one place, perilous with rocks. Still determined, the party got aboard a fishing boat moored about a quarter mile off-shore in the hope that she could be used in landing, but this, too, was out of the question. By this time a number of the inhabitants, who had been gathering to watch the fortunes of the party, began waving signals and soon a plucky small boat put off from the beach and by making several exciting trips succeeded in landing everyone wet and safe in Port Charlotte.

Hearing that there were six American survivors at Kilchoman, the medics among the Red Cross team borrowed a motor car and raced there, while the others struggled to land stores. At Kilchoman the Americans were deeply touched at what they found.

Although Kilchoman's resources were few – the entire settlement consists of a church, three dwellings and a school-house – everything possible in that remote and primitive region had been done for the survivors. They had been attended by the British Medical Officer on the island, two were in the manse of the Reverend Donald Grant, Padre of Islay, and four in cottages close to his weather-beaten church. Slender of means as they were, the people of this small community had made unhesitating sacrifice, not only in taking in and nursing the sick but providing as many of the survivors as they could with clothing which demanded not a little unselfishness to spare. It is quite impossible to say too much of the humanity of all these peasant people, of their readiness to accept any hardship in the name of mercy, of the gentle, steadfast nursing they gave the soldiers, virtually bringing them back to life.

A report by the Argyllshire Constabulary, written on 19 October noted:

The names of the survivors at Kilchoman School and Kilchearan [sic] are as follows:–

(1) <u>Kilchoman School</u>

719078   Pte. Charles Smithson, Fort Screven, Georgia, September Replacement Draft, I002, R. Coast Artillery.

3372669	Pte. David Roberts	do.	do.	do.
720309	George S. Taylor	do.	do.	do.
2902652	Noah E. Taylor	do.	do.	do.
3239972	Earl Garvar	do.	do.	do.
2595863	Steward Early	do.	do.	do.
813640	Sergt. Chas. M'Donald	do.	do.	do.
3372671	Pte. Robt. F. Shand	do.	do.	do.
2595465	Wm. J. R. Cooney	do.	do.	do.
2595479	Thomas A. Kelly	do.	do.	do.

1278382   John E. Wean, 406 Casual Co.
Lieut, W.B. Grandion, R.N.R.

(2)   <u>Kilchearan Farm House</u>

A.E. Tilbrook, Junior Engineer, H.M.S. "Otranto"

W. Holmes, Stoker, M.M.R.		do.	do.
2595522	Pte. Ben Smith	U.S.A	
2595461	Robert Brown	do.	

718854	Joseph Richards	do.
813672	Emil Petersen	do.
2595488	Joseph Tullock	do.

As soon as the news of the *Otranto* sinking had broken, a group of American officers, including Captain R. H. Puffer, of the US Army, and Lieutenant James Jeffers, of the American Red Cross, had been hastily sent to Ireland from London to do what they could for the survivors rescued by the *Mounsey*. At Dublin station they met four American officers and 200 enlisted men who were deemed fit enough to travel on to England. With heroic fortitude the survivors told Puffer that they were 'alright'. The Americans were being fed coffee and sandwiches, and Lieutenant Jeffers doled out cigarettes and chocolate.

US 2nd Lieutenant R. E. Condon had arrived in Lochindaal from Belfast two days after the *Otranto* foundered. With him he'd brought 36 gallons of precious petrol. He went straight to Kilchoman Bay, and found 11 of the 17 American survivors being cared for in the homes of Isabel McIntyre and the Reverend and Mrs Grant. Six others, billeted in Port Charlotte, left the island for Belfast by destroyer later that afternoon. Five others deemed fit enough to travel were sent to Glasgow the following day. US Sergeant Charles McDonald, although physically fit, was left on Islay to look after the five remaining soldiers who were too unwell to travel. One of them, Private William Cooney, died of pneumonia at Kilchoman manse nine days after the shipwreck, despite determined efforts to save him. Mrs Grant and an American Red Cross officer were at his bedside when he passed away.

While the survivors were cared for, the search for the dead went on. Seventy local men were spending all daylight hours recovering bodies from the shore, before they were dragged out by the tide again, and carting them to the temporary morgue in Kilchoman Church. Despite the perseverance and determination shown by the islanders and local police, Lieutenant Condon realised that the scale of the tragedy was too great for the locals to handle alone. He reported: 'In some places bodies were piled up 10 to 15 feet deep in crevices of the rocks. By the night of October 10th, 200 bodies had been recovered and transported to Kilchoman Church. It was evident that a larger force of labour was immediately badly needed to remove the wreckage where it was known that there were a good many bodies, and to assist in removing bodies; local labour already being utilised.' A telegram from a Royal Navy Officer to the Admiralty sent five days after the wreck ended: 'Many bodies under wreckage and kelp which are piled ashore in very large quantities and need more labour than available locally to clear.'

On the evening of Friday the 11th, a tug docked at Port Askaig with 30 soldiers from a British labour battalion and a hold full of timber. Thanks to the kindness of Mrs William Harvey, the wife of the owner of Bruichladdich Distillery, the men were billeted in a distillery house and given a workshop. Mrs Harvey had already been touched by the war – her own son, Douglas, had been killed in action the previous year, fighting in Mesopotamia. In a workshop where coopers had once assembled whisky barrels, soldiers now made coffins. Army carpenters, detailed to lead the work, had failed to catch the boat at Liverpool, but three local men stepped forward to do the job. Islay carpenter James MacTaggart – whom we last encountered making coffins for the victims of the torpedoed *Tuscania* – was one of the three. His pencil-written diary tells us:

Sat: Dressed wood for cart

Mon. Oct. 7. At Kilchoman recovering the bodies of American Soldiers off *SS Otranto* on Sunday Oct. 6.

Tues. At Kilchoman.

Wed.   "   "

Thurs. Making coffins for officers

Frid. At funeral of   "

Sat. Started making coffins for the soldiers at Bruichladdich Distillery

Mon. 14	"	"	"	"	"
Tues.	"	"	"	"	"
Wed.	"	"	"	"	"
Thurs.	"	"	"	"	"

A lorry owned by Port Charlotte man, Alex McMillan, was used to transport men and lumber. The 36 gallons of petrol that Lieutenant Condon had brought with him from Belfast were a blessing in these times of scarcity. Command of the American relief effort on Islay had now been taken over by Captain Puffer of the US Army, who had arrived in Port Charlotte from Belfast by trawler and established his headquarters at the Bridgend Hotel. Puffer was impressed by the 'very good work' that Lieutenant Condon had already done on Islay.

The bodies piled up. They were carried to Kilchoman Church and laid on the pews, but so many were washed ashore that there wasn't room for them all. A contemporary photograph shows bodies lying in the churchyard amid the gravestones. Every possible effort was made to identify them. One hundred and sixty bodies were quickly identified, including that of Captain Davidson, but often the identification tags that the soldiers wore round their necks had been torn from the bodies by the force of the waves. Captain Puffer paid tribute to the efforts of Sergeant MacNeill and his constables to identify each corpse, and collect and list effects. Each body – identified or not – was given a number with a list of possessions and a note of any distinguishing marks. 'The constables were extremely careful, and I cannot say too much for the efficient manner in which they carried on this work.' Captain Puffer also reported that where bodies could not be identified a US medical officer took fingerprints.

As late as two months after the wreck, the identity discs of Privates Robert Simmons and George House were washed ashore at Kilchoman. A practical but bathetic note was struck in the report of one American officer, who observed: 'It was noticed that the longer the bodies stayed in the water, the fewer the identification disks remaining upon them. This I believe is largely due to the poor string that was used in securing the identification tag around the neck. Inspections are frequently made as to whether or not a man has the identification disk, but the string is seldom noticed. A good string or chain should be supplied by the Government at the same time as the identifications disk, and the serviceability of the string or chain should be frequently inspected.'

The notebook used by the dedicated and efficient Sergeant Malcolm MacNeill as he worked to identify the body of each victim is now one of the most treasured possessions of the Museum of Islay Life. It was gifted by Islay-born Lord George Robertson of Port Ellen, a former British Cabinet Minister and Secretary General of NATO, who is a grandson of Sergeant MacNeill and is the energetic patron, and dedicated supporter, of the Museum. The notebook makes heartbreaking reading, and it is hard to imagine how MacNeill managed to function so professionally when confronted with the sheer horror of what he witnessed. In his notebook he faithfully recorded details of height, hair colour, birthmarks, tattoos, and the contents of pockets. These pitiful possessions he tied in bags to be returned to their next-of-kin. Here are just a few examples:

2595720, F. Deal Carswell, USA. Property nill

2595948, Wade L. Usher, USA. Property – 38 Dollars, gold watch, shaving kit

2595809, Carlton N. Hooks, USA. Property – purse and 3 cents

718816, Wylie C. Harmon, USA. Property – 12½ dollars 10 cents and testament

Private James Harmon had last glimpsed his brother, Wylie 'Clyde' Harmon, as he himself jumped for his life onto the deck of the *Mounsey*. In his letter to his mother from the Royal Victoria Hospital in Belfast, James had dearly hoped that Clyde too had jumped. But Clyde had stayed on board the stricken *Otranto*, had finally leapt or been swept into the sea when it broke its back on the *Botha na Cailleach* and had drowned or been crushed in the wreckage. Clyde Harmon's body was the 38th to be discovered by the searchers on the shore. He was buried at Kilchoman on Friday 11 October. Other grieving families in both America and Britain were even more unlucky than the Harmons, for they had no known graves as a focus for their grief, although Sergeant MacNeill did all he could to give each lifeless body the dignity of a name. His notebook runs to eighty-one pages.

Unidentified (no disc). Description, 5 feet 10½ inches, between 20 and 25 years of age, light brown hair, ordinary build, fresh complexion, mess ticket in pocket with rank Private, Sec A, Mess 2. Property – 27 dollars and knife.

Unidentified, evidently member of ship's crew. Description, 5 feet 7½ inches, 25 to 30 years, dark brown hair, clean shaved, ordinary build, strong features, no teeth, tattoo marks – On right forearm, boomerang at bottom of design, shield with cross and kangaroo in centre, flags at sides, five spears on top; 'Advance Australia' on sides of shield. Dress, navy blue suit, cross anchors with crown on left sleeve of jacket (in red), black buttons with crown and anchor thereon. Property – waist belt and 2½d.

Unidentified soldier, USA. 5 feet 11 inches, 20 years, dark hair, ordinary build. Property – trench mirror

(No disc) USA soldier. Description, 5 feet 8 inches, 25 to 30 years, ordinary build, dark hair, clean shaven, broken upper and lower mouth, some teeth gold filled, tattoo marks, on right forearm (1) design with 'Love' thereon (2) design, cross and heart with spear through. No property.

(No disc) USA soldier, 5 feet 10½ inches, 30 to 35 years, stout, 1 upper front tooth encased in gold, others good, tattoo nude lady on right forearm. No property.

Unidentified nude body. Head, and legs from knees downwards gone. Description for identity impossible.

(No disc) USA soldier. Head and part of feet gone. Description impossible. Looks like a man of 5 feet 8 or 9 inches, ordinary build, wearing USA trousers. No property.

Sergeant MacNeill's catalogue of nearly 383 bodies – some mangled, decayed and headless – is desperately hard to read. As the days went by, the bodies became more distressing to recover. The last entry in the sergeant's book – more than two months after the *Otranto* was wrecked – reads:

Apparently a seaman. Nude body of a seaman. No identification possible. No property. Found at Machrie Bay on 9/12/1918.

One simply cannot comprehend the horror that this dedicated and humane man went through in his attempt to identify victims. For some families, the identification of a body was a comfort, and their loved one's sacrifice a source of pride, as in the case of a young midshipman.

> Midshipman Benjamin Cresswell Gibbons, RNR, HMS Otranto
>
> Property – letters and 10/- notes
>
> Body so decayed that it is crumbling to pieces
>
> Found in first gully 26-10-18

Midshipman Gibbons' 'dead man's penny' – a plaque given to the families of British war victims – has been donated to the Museum of Islay life by his nephew. Beside it is displayed a photograph of Gibbons. From under the Royal Navy cap a fresh-faced teenager stares out, a little anxiously. It is a photograph that would have brought patriotic pride to the family who placed it on their mantelpiece, and would have remained there to bring them heartbreak after his death. The broken body of the boy was buried at Kilchoman, where he still lies.

Correspondence from Argyllshire Constabulary tells of the discovery of Captain Davidson's body.

> Received from Sergeant Malcolm MacNeill, Bowmore, Islay, the aforementioned property found on the body of Captain GW Davidson of HM Troopship "Otranto" washed ashore at Machrie Bay, Kilchoman, Islay: 1 Pair Binoculars Glasses; 1 wrist watch; 1 gold ring; 1 silver cigarette case; 1 tobacco pipe.

The *Otranto* is said to have hit the reef and broken her back at 10.45 am. Captain Davidson's dented watch had stopped at

11.05. Ernest Davidson's daughter, Jean, was just six years old when her father died. Her memories of him remained strong until her dying day, in 2009. Numerous family photographs testify to the deep bond of affection between father and daughter. Jean's son, Nick Hide, believes that his mother never really got over her father's death.

≈

Day-to-day island life ground to a halt as resources – human and material – were dedicated to the *Otranto*'s drowned and saved. The log-book of Rockside School, which usually recorded absences and prizes, reads: 'Owing to premises being occupied in connection with shipwrecked crew of *Otranto* no openings have been made from Oct 7th until October 14th. *Otranto* was shipwrecked Sunday 6th October.' Lieutenant Jeffers reported: 'The little schoolhouse was turned into a hospital, and the school mistress, Mrs M'Intyre, the wife of a soldier in France, with her father, nursed the injured men for over a week until help arrived.'

Time and decay wait for no man. The islanders urgently needed to arrange the hygienic disposal of the dead, but they did so with respect and compassion, even though these burials would be temporary ones until enough coffins were made. Local men and soldiers from the British Labour Battalion, under the direction of Colonel Heaton-Ellis, the most senior British officer that the disaster had brought to Islay, dug mass graves, sixty feet long, seven wide, and four deep. Below the cemetery, ten men continued to patrol the beach, looking for more bodies even as the graves were dug.

On Friday, 11 October, five days after the sinking of the *Otranto*, a mass funeral was held in a newly created cemetery close to Kilchoman churchyard, on high flat ground that overlooks the place where the vessel foundered. Kilchoman was appropriate, for there is an ancient burial site there. The prefix 'Kil' is from the Gaelic, meaning 'church' or 'chapel', and it is likely that Kilchoman Kirk was originally dedicated to Commán, a seventh-century saint associated with St Columba. One of Islay's most famous Celtic crosses, a fourteenth-century carved masterpiece of the Iona School, stands more than eight feet high in the churchyard. On a fine day, Kilchoman is a beautiful place, but Islay photographer Archibald Cameron's sombre black-and-white images of the burial reveal the mood of that heartrending and solemn ceremony. From Kilchoman Kirk two pipers led the funeral procession. An American account says the pipers played 'Flowers of the North', but, if such a tune exists, it is little known, and it is much more likely that the nerve-tingling lament, 'Flowers of the Forest,' was what they played. One American source simply calls the tune 'a Highland dirge'. A firing party marched behind, with arms reversed in respect. Three coffins – the only three to be found on the island – followed, borne on a simple cart. The island's churchmen followed, along with British and American officers, Red Cross officials, standard bearers, an honour guard and a host of Islay men, women and children. Many of them had helped care for the survivors, or had recovered the bodies of the dead.

Captain Davidson and two American officers were given the honour of being buried in coffins. But as the mourners approached the new burial ground there lay before them two long mass graves, dug by local Islay men and soldiers of the British Labour Battalion. In them – lying shoulder to shoulder – were the bodies of 120 American soldiers, and 46 British sailors and Breton fishermen. They were not entirely uncovered. Blankets, and flowers gathered by local people, had been laid over the corpses. Fifty-two of the bodies were nameless.

Donald Grant, the Kilchoman minister who had done much to recover the bodies of the dead, and whose wife had cared for the survivors, led the service. At the end, the British and

American flags were lowered, and the honour guard fired a six-volley salute. Archibald Cameron's photograph shows the Stars and Stripes, blowing bravely in the breeze, carried by Sergeant Charles McDonald of Galesburg, Illinois, one of the seventeen American survivors washed ashore. Captain Griscom Bettle, an American artillery officer who was part of the relief party sent from Belfast, was deeply moved when the bareheaded mourners sang *The Star-Spangled Banner*. 'The service was most impressive and most dignified, the prayers of the ministers containing most complimentary sentiments for America and what she was doing to help the Allies. The services were ended with *God Save the King*, followed by our National Anthem, which was an unprecedented compliment.'

The bodies in the mass graves lay covered with just a light layer of soil as the local carpenters and soldiers of the labour battalion hammered away night and day making a coffin for every victim. Five days later the men lying in the Kilchoman earth were reburied in coffins there. In the meantime, eleven more bodies had been found, and were laid to rest at the same ceremony. Captain Puffer recorded that a stock of 43 coffins was kept at Kilchoman, 'to take care of bodies which may be recovered from time to time'. In the days that followed, the 280 graves at Kilchoman became 315. The body of Corporal Jonas Ossian Johnson, the young Swede who had emigrated to Galesburg, Illinois, was washed up on the strand along with several other bodies almost a month after the sinking, and just six days before the war ended. The Reverend Donald Grant wrote a letter of condolence to his aunt in Galesburg, and told her that her nephew was one of 381 men he had buried. A further soldier, US Sergeant Tom Davis, was washed ashore on the little island of Muck, to the north of Islay, and buried there.

The body of Signalman James Brennan, one of the *Otranto*'s crew, did not come ashore on Islay until five weeks after his ship was lost. The war in which he served had been over for two days. The lower half of a body, wearing US Army trousers, was found in 'Big Gully', Machrie Bay, on 6 December. And a few days later the identification disc – but not the body – of soldier Samuel Bennet was washed up at the same spot. The remains of Frank Dinsmore, an American soldier, were discovered among wreckage at Kilchoman in early March of 1919.

≫

Of all the Americans to descend on Islay following the tragedy, it was Lieutenant James Jeffers, of the American Red Cross, who was to develop the most profound relationship with the islanders. Jeffers recalled: 'When I reached Islay the good folk there had given all their food and clothing to the survivors. The American Red Cross has done something to show its gratitude to the splendid people, but I can tell you that the last has not been heard of this, for Americans will be thrilled when the full story is told of the noble self-sacrificing efforts of the humble people in the tiny island far away from the mainland.' Jeffers began by helping out local people who sacrificed their time, energy and possessions with gifts of food and clothing, and he presented money to the Reverend Grant 'to put the church in usable shape'. Its floor was covered in bloodstains.

James Jeffers had a clear affinity for the people of Islay, and his records at the American Red Cross reveal why. Jeffers was an Irishman. A naturalised US citizen, he had been born in 1882 in Lurgan, County Armagh, and so, to the Ileachs, he was almost a neighbour or a distant cousin. Jeffers' wife, Lydia, was also born in Ireland, and in 1917 he visited the land of his birth to buy linen for his handkerchief importing and manufacturing business. Although an officer, a 'Yank' and a New York busi-nessman, James Jeffers would have absolutely understood the hard, rural and Celtic lifestyle of the majority of Islay people, and would have appreciated the value of the sacrifices they made to help the American survivors and to bury the dead. Captain

Puffer singled Jeffers out for his outstanding humanitarian work: 'Lieutenant Jeffers seemed to be everywhere, doing his work in a tactful manner. I recommend that some official note of our appreciation be sent to American Red Cross Headquarters.' Even after the war, when he had returned to civilian life, James Jeffers continued to correspond with the families of victims, and to work with Sergeant MacNeill on Islay in an attempt to identify their dead. His letters to the Sergeant recall fond memories of enjoying Mrs MacNeill's home baking.

Before Captain Puffer left Islay, he paid personal visits to the local people who had assisted in the care of America's drowned and saved. His final visit before leaving the island forever was to the graves of the men who had been lost when the *Tuscania* was torpedoed, eight months previously.

Among the post-war tasks carried out by the American Red Cross was the photographing of the graves of American servicemen who had been buried on British soil. Copies were sent to families, and not a single one was missed, not even that of Sergeant Tom Davis who had been lost on the *Otranto*, and whose body had been buried in a homemade coffin by the inhabitants of the Inner Hebridean island of Muck. Only days after the *Otranto* was lost, Major General John Biddle, who commanded the American forces in Britain, paid tribute to the American Red Cross in a speech in London. 'The emblem of the Red Cross is two small pieces of red tape, laid neatly across each other. But, so far as I know, this is the only bit of tape they've got. They can do things unhampered by rules and regulations. When our men are sick or wounded we need quick action unhampered and free. Disasters like the *Otranto* show how valuable is its work – all that has been taken care of by the Red Cross.'

Islay's senior policeman too received praise for his devotion to duty. Just five weeks after the war ended, he received a postcard from Great Falls, Montana.

Kind friend,

This is a thank you for your able administration of the work of rescuing our shipwrecked men of the *Tuscania* and the *Otranto* and for your kindness and care of them. May happiness abide, always, with you and yours.

Very sincerely,
Mr & Mrs D. A. Willis,
Great Falls,
Montana, USA.

The tragic loss of young lives, and the horror of what was being found on their shores, deeply affected Ileachs like Malcolm MacNeill. Not that they were strangers to the hurt of war. About 180 Islay men had already been killed, on land and on the sea, by the time the *Otranto* sank, and everyone in the closely knit communities of the island would have lost a friend, relative or loved one. But the scale of the disaster, and how it must have brought home the violence of the deaths of their own sons, brothers and husbands, was profoundly distressing for the people. The *Oban Times* of 19 October noted:

> The wreck of the transport ship *Otranto* with the loss of life involved, has cast a gloom over the whole of Islay. Distress and sorrow in Port Ellen district over the calamity are witnessed on every hand, and there is no meetings of individuals without an expression of grief at the sacrifice of so much valuable life on an exposed coast in a tempestuous sea, when human aid was impossible. Pulpit witnesses voiced the sympathy and condolences of the community with the bereaved relatives of the brave American soldiers and British seamen lost on this lamentable occasion.

The sinking of the *Otranto* was the worst convoy disaster of the war. In America, the sense of shock was palpable. *The New York Times* broke the story in page after page of horrific detail. Up and down the land, in cities, small towns and remote farmhouses, casualty lists printed in America's network of local newspapers shocked readers. Nowhere was the blow more profoundly felt than around Berrien County in Georgia. A disproportionate number of *Otranto* victims came from the area, and of the 60 names carved on the war memorial in Nashville, Georgia, 25 are those of men lost in the terrible tragedy off Islay.

The mother of Private Edgar Sheppard read in her Augusta newspaper that her son was one of 26 local men who had been lost. Her religious faith prevented her from believing that her son was dead. Shortly afterwards, an Army telegram notified her that Edgar was alive and well. The telegram from Washington to Mrs Sarah Roberts, mother of one of the very few who'd been washed up alive on the coast of Islay, says simply:

HAPPY TO INFORM YOU THAT PRIVATE DAVID ROBERTS COAST ARTILLERY CORPS WAS SAVED IN SINKING OF OTRANTO OCTOB SIXTH
HARRIS THE ADJUTANT GENERAL

The telegram is dated 27 October, a full three weeks after the sinking.

For years after the loss of the *Otranto*, grieving families of victims whose bodies were never identified corresponded with Sergeant MacNeill in the hope that a detailed description of their loved ones might let them rest in graves with names, rather than just plots with numbers. Many of the letters had first gone to the former American Red Cross officer, James Jeffers. The brother of Private Jesse Johnson – Paul Johnson, of Atlanta, Georgia – wrote: 'Practically all that we have been able to learn is; the fact that he sailed on the *Otranto* and was lost when it went down. My mother and I would be very thankful for any information you might be able to give. Whether his body was recovered; whether he was drowned or crushed in trying to get aboard the destroyer, or anything concerning his last.'

A grieving mother from Ray City in Georgia wrote to Jeffers:

May 26, 1920

Kind Sir:

We lost a dear Boy on the ship *Ortranto* [sic], Shellie L. Webb, and your name has been given to me as one who was there at the time and I am writing to you to see if I can get any information as to my dear Boy. We can't find where he was ever picked up. There are fifty-one unidentified buried there and my boy could be identified very well as his big toe on his left foot was off; also he had a scar on his left hand caused from a burn also he had a good watch that I would be so glad to get. It would be some relief to the heart-broken family to know that he was buried. Now Kind Sir if you can help me in any way I assure you it will be appreciated.

Hoping to hear from you real soon I still remain a heart-broken mother,

Mrs J. T. Webb.

Jeffers had returned to his civilian occupation of handkerchief manufacturer and importer, but, despite the preoccupations of running a business and the illness of his wife, continued to do all he could for the likes of Mrs Webb. His respect and affection for Sergeant MacNeill is clear from the letter he wrote to the policeman at his Bowmore home.

My dear Sergeant,

I received a letter this morning of which I am sending you a copy and I would ask you to look over your records of the disaster . . . and see what you can do in identifying this boy and where the grave lies. Send all mail addressed to my place of business, 42 White Street, New York City. I hope to see you and your good people sometime in the latter part of this year. I hope to see your good wife and family and I hope to enjoy a good cup of tea and one of those scones which still I will not forget.

With kindest regards to you and your family, I am

Yours very sincerely,
James Jeffers.

Sergeant MacNeill was never able to identify a body as Shellie Webb's. The boy was officially listed among the 'missing', and his heartbroken family had no grave for him. Then, several years after the war had ended, his mother finally received word that Shellie's grave had been located in Ireland. In the confusion following the disaster, Shellie's body had been discovered, identified and buried – all without being officially recorded. In 1928 Shellie Webb, after ten years and a journey of 6,000 miles, was finally laid to rest at home, near Ray City, Georgia. In October 1928, *The Adel News* reported:

The funeral services for Mr. Webb were largely attended and were deeply impressive. Mr. Webb was a perfect specimen of manhood being nearly six and a half feet high and weighing close to two hundred pounds. He was a gallant young man and had many friends who were grieved when he died. Indeed, Berrien county felt the pang of anguish in almost every home when so many of her brave young men met death at one time while on their way across the mighty deep to meet a foreign foe. Mr. Webb is survived by his devoted mother and ten brothers.

9

The Bivouac of the Dead

I saw the debris and debris of all the slain soldiers of the war,
But I saw they were not as was thought,
They themselves were fully at rest, they suffer'd not,
The living remain'd and suffer'd, the mother suffer'd,
And the wife and child and the musing comrade suffer'd,
And the armies that remain'd suffer'd.

Walt Whitman, *Drum-Taps*

The saga of the *Otranto* and the *Kashmir*'s fatal collision didn't end on the wild shores of Islay. It finished in a rancorous legal dispute in the British courts. While the families of American soldiers, British merchant seamen and Breton fishermen were desperate to understand why their loved ones had perished, there were far more mercenary motives driving the demand for an inquiry – the cash-driven forces of culpability and compensation. At the outbreak of war, the *Otranto* had been requisitioned from its owners by the Admiralty, to be converted into a Royal Navy armed merchant cruiser. But, now that the war was over, the Admiralty had no *Otranto* to hand back to the Orient Shipping Line. The cost of a replacement vessel would be enormous, so the Lord Commissioners of the Admiralty decided to sue the Peninsular & Oriental Shipping Line, the owners of the *Kashmir*, for damages. To do this they had to prove that the *Kashmir* was entirely to blame for the disastrous collision.

Ernest Davidson, the *Otranto*'s captain, had died shortly after his ship's back was broken on *Botha na Cailleach* – the Old Woman's Reef. His log-book had gone down with him. Meanwhile, the log-book of the *Kashmir* – whose captain had nursed her into Glasgow despite the gaping hole in her bow – revealed only the bare facts from the perspective of the *Kashmir*'s commander.

> 6th October 1918. 8.45 am, Latitude 55° 47½ N, Longitude 6.34 W.
>
> . . . land was sighted right ahead and about two points on Port Bow by the Officer of the watch, which land was taken to be the high land Islay Island. The helm was immediately put to port, and the starboard engine stopped to enable ship to turn quicker owing to the force and direction of the wind (S.W. 10 to 11) and heavy sea running at the time. The barometer at the time was 28.89. HMS *Otranto*, who was one point forward of our starboard beam, suddenly went hard to starboard and it was evident that a collision was about to occur. On seeing this we stopped both engines, and tried to alter our course to port, but owing to the force of the sea and heavy sea running at the time, the Ship would not answer her helm, and we consequently put the engines full astern so as to avoid collision but without effect, and at 8.45 am struck the HMS *Otranto* amidships on the port side. There was no loss of life aboard.

At Yorkhill Warf, and then at Govan Dry Dock, the *Kashmir* was meticulously examined, and the damage to her – from a plate-to-plate description of the serious structural mutilation of her bow, to the loss of her carpenter's hammer – duly listed over eleven pages of closely typed foolscap. The total cost of repairs and loss of equipment was nearly £13,000. The carpenter's hammer – a heavyweight 14-pound job – accounted for 12 shillings and three pence of that. In terms of cost, the total loss of the *Otranto* was a much more serious business. With the owners of neither ship admitting to liability, the business of apportioning blame was left to a judge of the Admiralty Division of High Court of Justice.

~~~

No seaman alive today has more knowledge of the hazardous waters of the west of Scotland's seaboard than Isle of Lewis-born Eric Smith, a Northern Lighthouse Board skipper with more than 30 years' experience. The NLB has, for more than two centuries, been responsible for building and servicing the lighthouses, lesser lights and navigation buoys that ring Scotland and the Isle of Man. The Board's two ships, the *Pole Star* and the *Pharos*, vigilantly ply the seas maintaining, repairing and generally troubleshooting in order to give other vessels the greatest possible chance of a safe arrival at port. As a documentary filmmaker, I've been fortunate enough to have sailed with Eric on both vessels. On a trip from Oban, to carry out work on the Flannan Isles Lighthouse, I used the opportunity to tap into his encyclopaedic knowledge and experience in an attempt to understand what went on during the last frantic moments on the bridges of the *Otranto* and the *Kashmir* before the two vessels collided.

Our course to the Flannan Isles Lighthouse – infamous because of the mysterious loss of its three keepers in 1900 – took us through the Sound of Harris. It is a dangerous skerry-strewn channel that separates Harris from its Outer Hebridean island neighbour, North Uist. Over many years the NLB has marked the safe passage through the Sound with navigation buoys, and the *Pharos* has a sophisticated autopilot system that will keep it to a precise course, leaving the ship's officers to act as lookouts. But for all the navigational aids and gizmos aboard this modern vessel, Eric always prefers to take her through the Sound with his hands firmly on the controls, making each change to the ship's zigzag course himself. As I watched him manipulate the twin levers, eyes flickering between the electronic chart and the sea ahead of us, I could see that navigating these waters even in good weather still demands skill, experience and intense concentration. Once the *Pharos* was safely through the Sound, we turned north to drop anchor in Loch Roag on the west coast of Lewis to spend the night. During this downtime – with the aid of British Admiralty chart 2635 (Scotland West) and two stubby pencils to represent the *Otranto* and the *Kashmir* – Eric analysed for me what happened during that terrible storm of 6 October, 1918.

They had some really rough weather crossing the Atlantic and they couldn't find their correct position. There was no sun or stars and they couldn't take any 'sights'. All they could do was use what they call DR, Dead Reckoning – using your last sight and taking your speed, currents and wind into consideration to guess where you were as best as you could. They had no radar, no GPS, they had no idea where they were. I remember, when I first went to sea at the start of the Seventies, I was crossing the Indian Ocean up to the Persian Gulf, and although we had radar we had nothing in terms of 'sights', and we weren't 100% sure where we were. In World War One they were just using the stars and the moon and the sextant to work out their position, but in the winter on the Atlantic Ocean you can go a whole week without seeing the sun or the stars. And they couldn't stop out in the ocean to wait for a 'sight'. They had to keep on going because of the U-boats. What happened on the morning of the disaster was that the *Otranto* believed that the land they sighted was Ireland. The *Kashmir* was sure that it was Islay. Now if the *Kashmir* was correct they would have taken the southerly journey, so that was the direction they took. If the *Otranto* was correct they would have had to go northerly, so it did. So the two ships were going in opposite directions. They used flags to communicate. But if you have really rough weather, a hard gale, the flags are difficult to see. The *Otranto* put up a signal, turn to north, turn to port. He thought the *Kashmir* would then do that, but that's not what happened. Maybe he didn't see it, who knows, and before they knew it there was no time to do anything. They were using the engines and the rudders, but they thought: 'If I go this way the other ship will go that way' – but they were both thinking the same thing and they turned in on each other, and that's how it happened. They couldn't do anything about it because the two ships were so close. And they were going at quite a speed – probably 10 to 12 miles per hour, and that's a fairly fast speed for ships to hit each other.

The Admiralty's claim was that the collision was entirely due to negligent navigation by the officers of the *Kashmir*, while the owners of the *Kashmir* argued that the collision was inevitable or, alternately, that both vessels were equally to blame. The case was heard at the Admiralty Division of the High Court in London. Alongside the judge sat two ships' captains, in their capacity as Elder Brethren of Trinity House, the body responsible for England's lighthouses and pilot vessels. The Brethren are mostly experienced Royal and Merchant Navy men, and Captains O. P. Marshall and Owen Jones were present on the bench to give expert maritime advice to the judge.

Judge Mr Justice Hill sifted and weighed the evidence, and tried to make sense of the confusion that reigned on the bridges of both vessels, and the orders and counter-orders that fated the two ships to a collision course. On 21 May, 1920, the judge reached his conclusion. In his summing up, Mr Justice Hill used the expressions, 'hard-a-starboarded' and 'hard-a-ported'. It is important to understand that these expressions came from a time when to order the tiller to be turned hard-a-starboard turned the rudder (and therefore the vessel) to port, and that an order to turn the tiller 'hard-a-port' was an instruction to steer the ship to the starboard, or right. Mr Justice Hill concluded:

Each sighted land and took helm action to avoid it. The *Otranto* first sighted land on the starboard bow. The *Kashmir* first sighted land ahead on the port bow. Various estimates of the distance of the land were formed and given in evidence; but it was common ground that land was so near that it was a matter of urgency to take action for it. Neither side complains that the action taken by the other to avoid the land was, in the circumstances, wrong. The *Otranto* hard-a-starboarded and stopped the port engine to assist the helm. The *Kashmir* hard-a-ported and stopped the starboard engine with the like object. The other ships of the convoy, so far as observed – they were not in sight – did as the *Kashmir* did and turned to starboard. The effect of wind and sea upon the ships was such that the swing under port helm was more rapid than the swing under starboard helm. The effect of starboard helm upon the *Otranto* was all the slower because she was already carrying starboard helm. Whether the two ships took action precisely at the same moment is a matter which cannot be determined. But there came a time when the *Kashmir*, turning to starboard, was heading for the *Otranto*, turning more slowly to port. When they were in that position, most unfortunately, each began a change of manoeuvre. I say began, because, so far as the *Kashmir* was concerned, the change was quickly countermanded. It came about in this way: the *Otranto*, at a late stage, observed the *Kashmir* heading for her, and sounded two short blasts, and almost at the same time hard-a-ported and put the port engine full ahead. The two short blasts were heard aboard the *Kashmir* and her helm was ordered hard-a-starboard and was actually put over, but immediately the order was changed to hard-a-port again and both engines were reversed. The collision followed soon afterwards. I am advised that but for these changes of manoeuvre it is almost certain that the two ships would have swung clear of one another.

Mr Justice Hill's analysis is as clear an explanation for the disaster as we can ever hope to have. But its precise prose can never convey what must have been a frantic struggle for the masters and helmsmen of both the *Otranto* and the *Kashmir* as – amid a terrible storm – they desperately tried to second-guess and outmanoeuvre each other. The judge concluded that the *Otranto* had mistaken the coast of Islay for Ireland, and turned north. The *Kashmir* had correctly identified Islay, and turned south. But it was the fatal last-minute orders to attempt to avoid collision that finally drove the ships together. The judge ruled that the *Kashmir* could not be acquitted of blame and 'ought to have avoided the *Otranto*'. But neither could he acquit the *Otranto*. He outlined the confusion which reigned on the *Otranto*'s bridge when she altered course on sighting land, just as her flu-struck captain and his navigation officer were down below snatching a quick breakfast:

> The watch keeping officer of the *Otranto* says that when he ordered hard-a-starboard, he looked and saw that the *Kashmir* was apparently in station. He then fixed his attention upon the land and not upon the *Kashmir*, and no one called his attention to the *Kashmir* until he himself saw the *Kashmir* heading almost straight for the *Otranto*. This he saw just at the time when the Master and the Navigator reached the bridge. A messenger had been sent to summon them at the time the helm was

hard-a-starboarded. The period which elapsed while the messenger went to them and they came to the bridge can, upon the evidence, have been hardly less than two minutes. During these two minutes the *Otranto* had been under hard-a-starboard helm, with port engine stopped, and no one had paid any attention to what the *Kashmir* was doing.

The judge summed up:

The above are the conclusions at which, with the great benefit of the advice of the Elder Brethren, I have arrived. Upon these conclusions I pronounce both to blame.

Mr R. H. Balloch, one of the Admiralty's legal team, was quickly on his feet, saying: 'Your Lordship did not say anything with regard to the degrees of fault; I assume your Lordship means both equally to blame.' Mr Justice Hill replied, simply, 'Yes.'

In December that year both sides in the case went to the Court of Appeal to contest the judgement. Lord Sterndale, Master of the Rolls – and the second most senior judge in the English High Court – sitting alongside two other High Court Judges, carefully examined Judge Hill's decision. Lord Sterndale pointed out that neither ship had made effective use of the manoeuvrability that having twin screws gave them. He noted that the *Kashmir* had only stopped – not reversed – her starboard engine when she ported, and that the *Otranto* had failed to reverse her starboard engine when she ported. He added: 'I think the Judge is quite right in finding that there was a bad look-out in the *Otranto* and that she continued to turn under starboard helm until she got very near the *Kashmir*, or the *Kashmir* got near to her, because she had a bad look-out.' The Master of the Rolls and his two fellow judges dismissed the appeal. Both ships were to blame.

The American authorities also launched an investigation. Major William B. Davis of the US Army, described as a 'Special Inspector', reported that the *Otranto*'s boat-drill during the stormy voyage had been 'somewhat perfunctory'. But what the American Army really wanted to know was not how the ships had come to grief, but how its 'boys' had reacted to the crisis. Major Davis found that while the men had efficiently made for their designated lifeboat stations, it was almost impossible to convey further orders to them. 'As one witness testified, an order could only be heard a few feet from where it was given owing to the roaring of the wind and sea. The engine room was flooded and the fires put out, leaving the ship without fires or lights and no headway, and she began to drift on the rocks at the Island of Islay, which at this point presents a rocky and forbidding coast . . .'

In contrast to the evidence given about the conduct of the officers and crew of the *Tuscania*, it seems that the *Otranto* officers were actively trying to help the inexperienced American doughboys. 'Orders had been given and obeyed to remove overcoats, shoes and leggings. It is difficult to ascertain who gave orders, but all orders seemed to emanate from the ship's officers.' Davis' investigation confirmed that pistol shots were heard following the collision. He does not, however, substantiate Commander Campbell's story that a panicking young American officer had attempted to blown his own brains out. 'There was some testimony about pistol shots being fired after the collision took place, but the source of this, if such shots were actually fired, could not be accurately traced. That they were not fired to quell disorder is certain.' While one witness, who testified from a hospital bed in Belfast, claimed that he had seen Lieutenant Levy, the most senior Army officer on board, leap onto the *Mounsey* well before many of his men, the report found that this was not the view of Lieutenant Levy himself – or that of other enlisted men who had made the leap. Davis concludes: 'It does not appear in the exhaustive testimony taken that there was an instance of an Officer depriving a soldier of his turn.'

The fate of nearly 100 men seriously ill with influenza, and too feeble to look after themselves, was carefully investigated. Major Davis came to the conclusion: 'There was no method by which they could be lowered, nor was it thought they could have been bodily thrown aboard the rescuing vessel, and those unable to assist themselves had to be left to their fate. That includes Lieut Coffman.' Bernie Coffman, of Galesburg, Illinois, who commanded the 406th Casual Company, had been among the first men on board the *Otranto* to be stricken with flu.

Of nearly 400 Americans left aboard after the departure of the *Mounsey*, only seventeen survived. The testimony of four of these survivors, including that of Private David Roberts, allowed Major Davis to come to some conclusion about the behaviour of the *Otranto*'s doughboys. 'Their account of what happened after the *Mounsey* left and the details of their remarkable escape is more than interesting. This escape from what seemed like certain death was accompanied by acts of gallantry and heroism. In fact the entire conduct of the enlisted men, their courage and coolness in the face of such imminent danger; and the many acts of bravery and devotion shown makes a splendid addition to the heroic traditions of our armed forces.'

While Major Davis was investigating the conduct of the Americans, he was generous in his praise of their British allies. He applauded the 'daring and masterly seamanship' of Francis Craven, the nobility of Captain Davidson and the other *Otranto* officers who went down with their ship, and the Laird and people of Islay for the relief work they did.

The people of Islay had buried and mourned the young Americans as if they were their own sons. But America wasn't prepared to let its young men go. Of the nearly 560 American *Tuscania* and *Otranto* victims, only Private Roy Muncaster of the 20th Engineers still lies in Islay soil, at Kilnaughton Cemetery, close to where he lost his life beneath the sea-lashed cliffs of the Oa. This was his family's wish. Except in such circumstances, the American government fulfilled its promise to repatriate every American body back to the United States, or to the officially recognised American Cemetery in England, where the lost men could lie among their own.

In late June 1920, it was announced in the American press that the exhumations on Islay would begin on 1 July. The local newspaper in New Richmond, Wisconsin, which had lost one young citizen on the *Tuscania*, reported the repatriation of the bodies in a highly romanticised way.

> The Scottish clan which inhabits the lonely spot has taken tender care of the graves and the chief has given a pledge that the clan would look after the graves as if they were its own until the end of time. The chief pleaded that the bodies be left on the island, but the relatives in many cases wished the return of the bodies and it was decided by the graves registration service to remove them all. The coast of Islay is so steep and rocky that the coffins will have to be carried down steep trails cut in the rocks or lowered by ropes and tackles to a waiting barge, which will convey them to a transport standing off shore.

The grisly job of digging up the bodies began. As a boy, James McFarlane, a Port Ellen fisherman of many years and a significant Islay tradition-bearer, knew Archie Livingstone (Erchie Dubh, or 'Black Archie'), an old fishermen who helped with the exhumation. 'Erchie Dubh always told that it was a pretty grim task. Some of the bodies weren't in coffins, they were just wrapped in canvas, and he said that the only thing that kept them going was that there was a distillery manager, or managers there, who supplied them with "strong drink" – he didn't call it whisky – just "strong drink", and kept them plied with it. Without that they could never have faced it – it was horrendous. They say that the ship that came in to take the bodies away carried lead-lined coffins.'

The hastily created cemeteries at Port Charlotte and Port nan Gallan disappeared faster than they had been created. Many of the bodies were returned to the American towns and cities that had been home to the young soldiers. Others were finally laid to rest in Arlington National Cemetery, in Virginia, across the Potomac River from Washington DC. More lie at Brookwood in Surrey, where part of the vast cemetery that lies there was officially handed over to America.

Washington Post June 24 1924
London, June 23rd. Brookwood military cemetery in the London district, was officially turned over today to the United States Government by the British owners. Four hundred and twenty-eight American soldiers and sailors are buried there, including 60 unidentified men mostly from the wreck of the *Tuscania*. General Pershing visited the cemetery on Saturday and also inspected the marble memorial about to be erected there.

At Kilchoman, on Islay, the carefully tended military cemetery lies perched on a low hill, close to the sea. Far to the west lies the land from where the *Otranto* left on her final voyage, and just below is Machair Bay, where the vessel and so many of her soldiers and sailors met their end. Once, more than 300 American dead had shared that plot. Today there are just 74 graves there, all of British sailors. All but three of the men who lie there were lost from the *Otranto* – 31 of whom, including Captain Ernest Davidson, are identified. The gravestones of the other 43 crewmen buried there bear the words, 'Known unto God'. One member of the *Tuscania*'s crew also lies there. The body of Breton fishing-boat skipper, Jules Lehoerff, was repatriated to France in 1924. The views west from the graveyard, over cliff and golden beach, are spectacular. One recent visitor to Kilchoman Cemetery, a Royal Navy officer, remarked that he 'couldn't think of a better place on land' for a seaman's final resting place.

~~~

Efforts were made to honour the living as well as the dead, most notably HMS *Mounsey*'s heroic skipper, Lieutenant Francis Craven. He was promoted to Lieutenant Commander, and given a new ship. America awarded him the Navy Cross and the Distinguished Service Medal – a rare decoration for a non-American citizen – while Britain pinned the Distinguished Service Order on him, a 'gong' just short of the Victoria Cross. When it announced the award of the DSO, the *London Gazette* printed a detailed account of Craven's actions, but Lieutenant Woodcock, navigation officer of the *Otranto*, summed up Craven's achievement more succinctly: 'Thanks to his skill nearly 600 lives were saved, which would have been lost because no lifeboat would have lived five minutes in the sea running and I venture to say not one man in a thousand would have had acted as he did in coming alongside a ship in such a mountainous sea. I wish I could emphasise more strongly the fine way he worked.'

Sadly, Craven's story does not have a happy ending. He was just one of many thousands of young officers who had had a 'good war', but who now struggled to find rewarding roles in peacetime. Craven resigned his Royal Navy commission and joined the Auxiliary Division of the Royal Irish Constabulary, a paramilitary unit comprised mostly of British former World War One officers recruited to put down the Irish Republican Army. In February 1921, Craven was in command of 17 men who were travelling in two lorries when they were ambushed by a much larger force of the IRA in the village of Clonfin, County Longford, now in the Irish Republic. District Inspector Craven and three other RIC men were killed in the two-hour firefight that followed.

Islay's steadfast police sergeant, Malcolm MacNeill, was made a Member of the Most Excellent Order of the British Empire (MBE) in recognition of his work in recovering and identifying the dead of the *Tuscania* and the *Otranto* and 'other equally important police duties during the period of the Great War'. The award had come out of the blue, and MacNeill was at a loss for whom to thank. His suspicion fell on his chief constable, to whom he wrote: 'I have no knowledge as to the source of the information laid before the Home Office Authorities to warrant them to recommend me for this high honour, but I feel that I must, most respectfully, thank you for this mark of appreciation of my service.'

<hr />

The Armistice that brought the war to an end was signed 36 days after the *Otranto* sank, but it took many months to bring the more than a million-strong army of doughboys back to America. Many were needed to serve in the Army of Occupation in Germany, but at least the fighting and dying had ended. Some of the men – like 17-year-old David Roberts – knew they were lucky to be alive. Roberts was a boy with limited schooling, but grew up to be thoughtful, inquisitive, an avid reader and an accomplished carpenter and pattern-maker. His grandson, Dr Mark Jabbusch, believes that the teenage soldier's life was profoundly marked by his experience of being washed ashore on storm-bound Islay as so many of his comrades died.

David Roberts wrote only one letter home to his mother after his rescue. Reserved and reassuring, and without a hint of bravado, it was an indication of how he would deal with his extraordinary adventure in later life. His grandson, Mark, wrote to me saying: 'Disappointing to me is the reluctance on David's part to share his story in any expansive or recorded way, but my mother has no memory of him elaborating on the original events. He was always a quiet man, not one to show any bravado or much emotion. I can add that my grandfather had a great zest for life, and knowledge of world events that may well have had its spark in his rescue. I consider my grandfather's story a small miracle and a linchpin to my own story.'

Mark Jabbusch says that David sometimes teased his wife, Maude, with stories of 'Margaret', the 'other woman' in his life. 'Margaret' was Margaret McPhee, the sister of Donald and James McPhee, the teenagers who had dragged him from the surf and to their home. She would help nurse the young soldier back to health, and although the two never met again, or corresponded, Margaret had won at least a small corner of his heart. David Roberts returned twice to Islay. In 1978 he walked into James MacAulay's long-established shop on the seafront in Port Ellen. James recalls: 'An elderly but fit American walked in. He introduced himself as Dave Roberts and asked if I could take him to the American Monument. He'd been to see Gilbert Clark in Port Charlotte, who had taken him to the wreck site and then passed him on to me. We jumped into the car and drove to the road end. He was with his daughter, but I seem to remember that it was just the pair of us who walked to the monument. He chatted as we walked. He told me that from where he was on the *Otranto* he could never make the leap onto the *Mounsey*, so just jumped into the sea and swam for it. When we got there we sat and had some quiet minutes of reflection.' David Roberts also visited the McPhee family, who had rescued and cared for him, and given him a second chance to live a full and precious life. The *Ileach*, Islay's community newspaper, reported:

> Visitors to Islay during September included Mr and Mrs David Roberts, from Orville, Ohio. Mr Roberts was one of the survivors from the ill-fated troopship *Otranto*, which perished on the Kilchoman shore under the shadow of *Creag Bhealach-na-Caillaich* (Rock of the Old Woman's Pass) with the loss of hundreds of lives in October 1918. Mr Roberts looked fit and well, though it is almost 60 years since the tragedy. He and Mrs Roberts were accompanied by their daughter whose husband is in business in Italy. Mr Roberts made the pilgrimage six years ago to the spot where he came ashore, almost dead so many years ago.

His grandson tells me that on one of his visits his grandfather did visit Margaret McPhee's grave. David Roberts died in 1983 at the age of 81.

In my research for this book I closely studied the Xeroxed copy of Paul Frederickson's 1938 article for the *New York Times Magazine* that is held in the archives of the Museum of Islay Life. One afternoon I happened to turn over the five stapled pages to find on the back a handwritten note to a former curator of the museum. It had been penned by David Roberts on the second of his 'pilgrimages' to Islay. Never one to dramatise his own part in the story, he'd simply written: 'We think it is a very good and complete description of the trip across the Atlantic and the disaster at the end. I hope you enjoy reading it.' I had thought Frederickson's article to have been a very vivid account, but for me, the instant I saw David Roberts' signature on that old Xeroxed copy, it became a precious manuscript.

In the same archive is a copy of *Sinking of the HMS Otranto in Collision with the HMS Kashmir Off the Northeast Coast of Ireland*

October 6, 1918. It is a privately printed little book of just 30 pages, published in 1941. The book is dedicated to Commander Francis Craven and those who lost their lives on the *Otranto*. After all these years, I expect that it is a fairly rare text now. But what makes the Museum's copy unique, and beyond price, is that it is also inscribed by David Roberts: 'In appreciation to the people of Islay especially the McPhee family of Kilchoman who took me into their home after being helped from the wreckage by one of their sons.'

The Museum of Islay Life has other such treasures. It has, for instance, a lengthy descriptive poem by an unknown hand which includes the lines:

> On chosen ground on Islay's shore those gallant lads
>   are laid
> And by the kindly Highland folk their lonely graves
>   were made.
> When tales are told of other days and sorrows that
>   have been
> May we then tell theirs and keep their memory green.

The poem had lain unread for years in the attic of an Islay woman living on the mainland. When it was rediscovered its value was recognised and it was handed in to the Museum. Even after the victims fade from living memory, Islay still keeps their memory green.

Occasionally, the passing of survivors made news stories – or at least interesting angles of news stories – as when Harry Randall Truman refused to leave his mountain home when the active volcano, Mount St Helens in Washington State, began to rumble in 1980. A private in the 100th Aero Squadron who had survived the *UB-77*'s torpedo, he died – along with his 16 cats – when his lodge was buried by the eruption under 150 feet of volcanic ash. The last-known survivor of the *Otranto* was

Private Donald Cooper, an African-American from the town of Sylvania, Georgia. Born in 1896, he passed away in 2001 just short of his 104th birthday, having lived his life in three centuries. Cooper had volunteered in April 1918 and served in an all-black Labour Battalion. He'd leapt from the troop-ship onto the deck of the *Mounsey* and been dragged to safety by its crew. Once in France, he was shot in the stomach and hadn't been expected to survive. In fact, he lived for another 82 years. Shortly before his death a Consul General of the French government made him a Chevalier of the Legion of Honour, saying: 'Eighty years ago you came for us, and today I come for you.' This remarkable old soldier was interviewed, around the same time, by R. Neil Scott for his book on the *Otranto* tragedy, *Many Were Held by the Sea*. Professor Scott believed that even then, Donald 'seemed still to be haunted by the memories of his friends from back home who were killed in the loss of the *Otranto.*'

James Jeffers, the Irish-born American Red Cross power-house, died – probably of appendicitis and pneumonia – in 1938 at the age of 48. His wife had predeceased him two years earlier, but he had married again, to Clara May Jeffers. He seems to have been successful in business and had moved to Los Angeles where he owned a factory.

Kapitän Wilhelm Meyer had gone on from sinking the *Tuscania* to torpedoing and severely damaging the 21,000 ton-liner *Celtic*, south of the Isle of Man, less than two months later. The *UB-77* survived the war unscathed. Meyer thought it 'a tragedy' that she was surrendered, and finally broken up at Swansea. He had become a POW when the Armistice was signed and was not released until February 1920. The battleship he was serving as torpedo officer on, SMS *Kronprinz Wilhelm*, was scuttled in Scapa Flow in June 1919, to prevent it falling into British hands. In the years that followed, Meyer wrote a number of letters to the National Tuscania Survivors Association, describing his actions on the day of the ship's sinking, and was invited to attend a reunion in Chicago in February 1933. The former U–boat commander accepted the invitation, and was quoted in American newspapers as having written that it 'stresses the fact that there are no thoughts of bitterness or revenge lingering in the hearts of the survivors', and that they understood, 'that I and members of the crew of the *U-77* merely did our duty as duty was understood at the time.'

But Meyer did not attend. On 30 January, shortly after Meyer had accepted the invitation, Adolf Hitler became Chancellor of Germany. This may have prompted Meyer to harden his attitude to former enemies of the Fatherland. Letters sent by Meyer, to a submarine veterans' association in California, had condemned the Treaty of Versailles – the surrender document Germany had been forced to sign at the end of the war – as 'disgraceful' and 'insults done to the German People'. American newspapers of 5 February reported that the German Embassy had confirmed that Meyer was not joining the 400 survivors that evening for a banquet in Chicago's Great Northern Hotel. During World War Two Kapitän Meyer served the Nazi Germany regime in navy intelligence and propaganda roles. He died in 1950.

≈

The end of the Great War – as the 1914–18 conflict had begun to be called – saw a frenzy of War Memorial construction in Britain. The litany of names on many of these monuments testifies to the tradition of recruiting soldiers from distinct localities into specific regiments – the Argyll & Sutherland Highlanders being the most common unit for Islay men to join. While these soldiers enjoyed the camaraderie of enlisting with and fighting alongside pals, in an instant a single enemy shell or machine gun could wipe out the young men of an entire community. American communities suffered in the same way. In 1919 'The Spirit of the American Doughboy', a seven-foot-high bronze

sculpture of an American soldier going into combat, was commissioned to stand in the little town of Nashville, in Georgia's
Berrien County, and paid for by public subscription. As already
mentioned, twenty-five of the sixty men commemorated on its
plinth were lost on the *Otranto*. In nearby Screven County, the
small town of Sylvania – from where local men had paraded to
the sound of brass bands and the cheers of their neighbours – has
a monument to 17 local men lost on the *Otranto*.

The urge to commemorate the American war dead of Islay
came even before the end of the conflict. The *Tuscania* had put
Islay firmly on the American Red Cross's map of Britain, and
many months before the *Otranto* was lost plans were underway for an American monument on Islay. In March 1918 the
American Red Cross sent one of its officers, Captain Henry
Pearce Jnr, to find a suitable location. Captain Iain Ramsay
of Kildalton, one of the island's chief landowners, had already
donated plots on the Mull of Oa where more than a hundred
bodies were buried. The Red Cross plan was that the proposed
monument would stand, 'overlooking the various small cemeteries in which the American soldiers are buried'. Captain
Pearce wrote to Ramsay: 'Can we once more impose on your
generosity by asking you if you will give us permission to erect
the monument there?' The American Red Cross had thought
long and hard about erecting a *Tuscania* monument, as *The
Passing Legions* – a history of the American Red Cross during
World War One, written in 1920, reveals:

> The matter of designating thus only one particular group
> of Americans and erecting a monument to them and
> not to others was, of course, duly considered, but it was
> decided that such a question did not fairly arise. The
> reasons were: first, that the *Tuscania*'s dead represented,
> in a way, the first American casualties in the war; second,
> that their graves were remote from the general theatre of

war and were likely to be neglected unless some especial action of this sort were taken; and third, that the sinking of the *Tuscania* was, as one might say, a special occasion, like a particular battle.

Designs were drawn up for a simple shaft of granite that was to be erected on the Mull of Oa. But events overtook the planners. When the *Otranto* was lost it was decided that the projected memorial would commemorate the American dead of both tragedies. George Buchanan Fife, author of *The Passing Legions*, noted:

> Islay folk were accustomed to mark their important graves or sites with cairns, or towers, built of rough-hewn native stone. In view of this, the American Red Cross adopted the design of a watch tower sixty feet in height and twenty feet in diameter at the base, to be constructed of stone gathered in the neighboring fields or from the cliffs. After this plan had been approved, President Wilson volunteered to give a bronze wreath to be placed upon the monument which, from its rocky headland five hundred feet above the sea, also overlooks the spot at which the *Otranto* was struck by the *Kashmir*.

From a distance, the American Monument looks like a lighthouse, or perhaps one of the high towers the ancient Picts built, like the one in Abernethy in Fife. The Pictish tower description isn't entirely fanciful. The monument's designer, painter and architect Robert Walker was raised in Fife and had a lifelong interest in Scottish vernacular architecture. On clear days there are spectacular views from the monument of Ireland to the southwest and mainland Scotland to the east. To the west there lies nothing but the wide North Atlantic, and nearly three thousand miles beyond the horizon, North

America and the homeland of those the monument honours. The base of the monument bears the plaque, gifted by President Woodrow Wilson, with an inscription which ends with lines by an American warrior poet:

> On Fame's eternal camping-ground
> Their silent tents are spread,
> And Glory guards, with solemn round,
> The bivouac of the dead.

The same lines appear above the gates of the Arlington National Cemetery, close to Washington DC, where some of the *Tuscania* and *Otranto* victims now lie. As in many American war memorials – especially in northern states – the poet is uncredited at Arlington and on Islay. The fact that the poet, Theodore O'Hara, was a Kentucky man who fought as a Confederate colonel in the American Civil War, probably accounts for that.

Islay has a reputation for producing poetry, much of it in the Gaelic-language Bardic tradition. Kilchoman – off which the *Otranto* finally sank – was the home of two bachelor brothers who were bards, Charles and Duncan MacNiven (born in 1874 and 1880). Most of their lives they worked as farmhands at Rockside, although Duncan served in the Navy during World War One. Both men were highly accomplished Gaelic poets, and are known on Islay today as 'the Kilchoman Bards'. Charles was so moved by the loss of the *Otranto*, as to compose a lament for it.

> Òran mar Chuimhneachan air Call na h-Otranto
>
> Air mios deireannach am fhoghair –
> Am seathamh latha ma's maith mo chuimhne,
> Nuair a thainig an "Otranto"
> 'S iomadh gaisgeach a bha innte,
> Dhol a sheasamh saors' an t-saoghail,

Chan e mhàin air raoin na Frainge,
Air gach uile chearn 'ga sgaoileadh,
Bratach shaors' o dhaors' a naimhdean.

Bu bheag a shaoil' nuair rinn iad fàgail,
Seadh, gu'm b'ann air tràigh an Ile
A thachradh Righ Fuar a' bhàis orr',
Chum am fàgail ann 'nan sineadh;
Is ged nach d' fhuair iad cùis air Nàmhaid,
Fhuair iad bàs a cheart cho dileas:
Fhuair gach aon dhiubh bàs mar ghaisgeach,
Fad o dhachaidhean a shinnsear.

Thiodhlaic sinne iad leis gach urram,
A b'urrainn sinn a chur air saighdear;
Chaidh am pasgadh mar bu mhiann leo,
Anns a' Bhrataich Stiallaich Reultaich;
Is am beagan a bha beo dhiubh,
Nochdadh coibhneas mòr is bàigh dhoibh;
Fhuair iad dion is blàthas is fasgadh,
'S tric a thaisbeanaich na Gàidheal.

'S iomadh màthair 's maith glé aosds,
Chaill a h-aon mhac mùirneach gràdhach,
'S iomadh nighneag bhòidheach bhanail
A chaill a leannan air an tràigh ud;
Is O! cha till, cha till a h-aon dhiubh,
Dh'ionns' na dùthcha 'rinn iad fhàgail;
Tha iad tosdach fuar, 'nan cadal,
Fad o dhachaidhean an àirdean.

A chaoidh bidh blàthas gus 'n latha mu dheireadh
Aig America ri Ile,
Oir tha còrr is ceithir cheud dhiubh,

Air an tiodhlacadh ann gu dilinn,
Fo thulachean gorma Chille-Chomain
Tha na h-òganaich 'nan sineadh,
'S los gu'n dùisgear o na mairbh iad,
Ghiulan arm do dh'Iosa Criosda.

Song in Memory of the Loss of the Otranto

'Twas the latest month of Autumn –
The sixth day as I recall –
When we hailed the ship "Otranto"
With full freight, and heroes all:
They left home to fight for justice,
Liberty had heard the call;
And the Stripes were now unfurling,
On the war-torn fields of Gaul.

Little thought they when they parted,
From their friends beyond the main,
That upon the shores of Islay,
Soon that Death would make his claim;
Though they fought not in the battle,
Nor did to the strife descend,
Far from dear ones, home and kindred,
Still they met a hero's end.

On the peaceful sward full daisied,
Where the winds of ocean blow,
Shrouded in their own loved banner,
Tenderly we laid them low;
And the few that Death had spared us,
To the utmost love can know
They were tended well and bravely,
As our Gaels were wont to show.

218

Many are the loving mothers,
That now mourn the sons they bore;
Many are the winsome maidens,
Lost their loved ones on yon shore.
Never more with hearty greetings,
Will they meet them on the Strand,
For, alas, they now lie sleeping,
'Neath the flowers in distant land.

Till the last dread trump be sounded,
Never will Columba's Land,
Cease to think with pride, but sadly,
Of green Islay's distant land.
There full more than four hundred
Brave ones sleep beneath its sod,
Till they waken on yon morning,
In the skies to meet their God.

The men and women who experienced the tragedies that occurred off the coast of Islay in 1918 have faded into history, but the solitary tower they raised to commemorate the American victims still dominates the southwesterly headland of Islay's Mull of Oa. Close by, two unseen monuments also endure.

The *Tuscania* lies at 55°36'30"N, 006°26'24"W.

HMS *Otranto* lies at 55°45'46"N, 006°28'40"W.

Acknowledgements

When asked what I have been 'up to' over the past eighteen months, I've usually answered, 'My book'. A more generous, and accurate, answer would have been, 'Our book' – for *The Drowned and the Saved* could not have been written without the help and support of many people and organisations.

Most of all – Jenni Minto, dedicated chairperson of Islay's WW100 Commemoration Committee, stalwart of the Museum of Islay Life, comrade, best friend, and my loving and supportive wife.

The Museum of Islay Life. It is the Q-Ship of local museums – at first glance homely, but packing a big punch! As well as curating a wealth of Islay social history material, the staff and trustees maintain a rich *Tuscania/Otranto* archive, are helpful and cheerful, and still find the time to keep the brass ship's bell from the *Tuscania* well-polished.

American Red Cross Archive, Washington DC.

US National Archives at College Park, Maryland.

US National Archives at Kansas City, with special thanks to archivist Pamela J. Anderson.

The Mitchell Library, Glasgow.

The National Maritime Museum, Greenwich, London.

The members of Islay's World War One – 100 Committee, whose enthusiasm and commitment have been an inspiration.

Captain Calum Anderson of Portnahaven – for his friendship, shared enthusiasm for the Clyde Puffer, *Auld Reekie*, and for his generosity with his experience and knowledge of the sea in its many moods.

Marilyn Gahm, of Spooner, Wisconsin, USA, for giving me an exclusive preview of her meticulously researched *The Sinking of the Tuscania: Spooner's Historic Part in the Great War,* setting me straight about Captain Meyer's non-appearance at the National Tuscania Survivors Association reunion, and reminding me of how email has shrunk the world.

Stuart Graham, fellow traveller in the wake of the *Tuscania* and *Otranto*, and author of the painstaking researched *These Men Are Worth Your Tears* – a worthy tribute to the men of Islay and Jura who lost their lives in World War One.

Nick Hide, grandson of Captain Ernest George William Davidson, captain of the *Otranto*. Nick generously shared his family history and photograph album with me, and proved to be a true Highland gentleman, at least by descent.

Chris Howland of Galesburg, Illinois, for coming to Islay and sharing the story (and photographs) of her mother's cousin, Corporal Jonas Ossian Johnson.

Iain Hunter, for his dogged efforts in unearthing and untangling for me the details of the 1920 *Otranto-Kashmir* legal case.

Dr Mark Jabbusch of Washington State, USA, grandson of *Otranto* survivor, David Roberts, for sharing his thoughts on how being dragged ashore alive at Kilchoman Bay marked his grandfather's life.

Donald Jones, who generously imparted to me his knowledge of Islay's weather, learned from farming at Coull on the wild west coast of the island, and from 40 years' service as a Coastguard.

James MacAulay of Port Ellen, whose treasure-chest of stories includes accounts of meeting *Otranto* survivor David Roberts on his pilgrimages to Islay.

Dougie MacDougall, for sharing with me the story of his grandfather's part in guiding a *Tuscania* lifeboat safely into Port Ellen bay at night.

James McFarlane, veteran Port Ellen fisherman – and significant tradition-bearer in both Gaelic and English – for sharing his lore over many years and projects.

Faye MacLean, my colleague at Caledonia TV, for her help on various voyages on the *Pole Star* and the *Pharos*, for her advice on Gaelic words and meanings, and for being the long-suffering producer of the BBC ALBA documentary I directed about the *Tuscania* and *Otranto*.

Port Charlotte builder Alasdair MacLellan and his merry men – Malcolm (Malky) Jackson and Duncan (Duck) Shaw – for converting the hayloft of the old byre behind our house into a warm, quiet and comfortable study where I could research, think, and, finally, write this book.

David MacLellan, coxswain of the Islay lifeboat, and engineer David 'Beastie' McArthur – for their courage, wisdom, tea and biscuits, and for recounting their experiences of Islay's vilest weather.

Donald James McPhee, a grand-nephew of the McPhee boys of Kilchoman who pulled David Roberts from the sea, and a devoted Ileach.

The Right Honourable Lord George Robertson of Port Ellen, grandson of Sergeant Malcolm MacNeill, inheritor of his grandfather's police notebooks, former UK Cabinet Minister and Secretary General of NATO, dedicated patron of the Museum of Islay Life and keeper of the *Tuscania* and *Otranto* flames.

Seona Robertson and Domhnall Alasdair Campbell – my co-conspirators in a hard-fought campaign to make a high-end international drama-documentary about the *Otranto*. We never raised the budget, but we unearthed a wealth of information.

Christie Simpson, of New York, for coming to Islay and sharing tales of her grandfather, *Tuscania* survivor Thomas Conway.

Captain Eric Smith of the Northern Lighthouse Board – who probably knows more about the hazards of navigating the West Coast of Scotland than any man alive. Eric shared his knowledge on our voyages together on the *Pole Star* and the *Pharos*.

Acknowledgements

And last, but not least, Nell, our nine-year-old Border collie who was (mostly) content to lie at my feet while I worked, but instinctively knew when I needed to leave my desk, pull on my boots, and spend time with her on the beaches and rocky shores that were the background to many of the dramatic, heartrending and inspiring stories revealed in this book.

Thank you, shipmates.

Bibliography

A. C. Bell, *History of the Blockade on Germany*, Historical Section, Committee of Imperial Defence, 1938 (but not released for general circulation until 1961).

Vera Brittain, *Testament of Youth*, Victor Gollancz, 1933

Dr David Caldwell, *Islay, The Land of the Lordship*, Birlinn, 2008

Commander A. B. Campbell, *With the Corners Off*, George Harrap & Company Ltd., 1937

Commander A. B. Campbell, *Yarns of the Seven Seas*, Sir Isaac Pitman & Sons, Ltd.

Winston S. Churchill, *The World Crisis, Volume III, 1916–1918*; Odhams Press, 1950

Benedict Crowell and Robert Forrest Wilson, *How American Went To War, An Account from Official Sources of the Nation's War Activities, The Road to France, Volumes 1 and 2*, Yale University Press, 1921

Peggy Earl, *Tales of Islay*, The Celtic House, Bowmore, Islay, 1980

Professor T. M. Devine, *Scotland's Empire 1600–1815*, Allen Lane, 2003

Harold F. English, *The Sinking of the "HMS Otranto"*, privately published, copy from the Museum of Islay Life.

George Buchanan Fife, *The Passing Legions, How the American Red Cross Met the American Army in Great Britain the Gateway to France*, Macmillan, 1920

Paul Frederickson, 'HMS Otranto: The AEF's Great Sea Tragedy', *New York Times Magazine*, 2 October 1938

Stuart Graham, *These Men Are Worth Your Tears, Islay and Jura in World War I*, Ailsapress, 2015

B. H. Liddell Hart, *History of the First World War*, 1930

Thomas A. Hoff, *US Doughboy 1916–19*, Osprey Publishing, 2005

The Ileach, Islay's community newspaper

Neil McCart, *Passenger Ships of the Orient Line*, Patrick Stevens Ltd, 1987

William MacDonald, *Sketches of Islay*, George Gallie, 1850

Peter Moir and Ian Crawford, *Argyll Shipwrecks*, Moir Crawford, 1994

Trevor Royle, *The Flowers of the Forest*, Birlinn, 2006

Professor R. Neil Scott, *Many Were Held by the Sea*, Rowman & Littlefield Publishers Inc., 2012

Dr Margaret Storrie, *Islay: Biography of an Island*, The Oa Press, 2011

Derek Tait, *Glasgow in the Great War*, Pen and Sword, 2016

National Tuscania Survivors Association website: *https://en-gb.facebook.com/Tuscania-Survivors-Association-220503601482123/*

Gordon Williamson, *U-boats of the Kaiser's Navy*, Osprey Publishing, 2002